Reclaiming the Artistry of Teaching

ALSO AVAILABLE FROM BLOOMSBURY

Teacher Education in Crisis, edited by Viv Ellis
Teacher Agency, Mark Priestley and Gert Biesta with Sarah Robinson
Transforming Teacher Education, Viv Ellis and Jane McNicholl

Reclaiming the Artistry of Teaching

EDITED BY GERT BIESTA
AND RAMSEY AFFIFI

BLOOMSBURY ACADEMIC
LONDON · NEW YORK · OXFORD · NEW DELHI · SYDNEY

BLOOMSBURY ACADEMIC
Bloomsbury Publishing Plc, 50 Bedford Square, London, WC1B 3DP, UK
Bloomsbury Publishing Inc, 1359 Broadway, New York, NY 10018, USA
Bloomsbury Publishing Ireland, 29 Earlsfort Terrace, Dublin 2, D02 AY28, Ireland

BLOOMSBURY, BLOOMSBURY ACADEMIC and the Diana logo are trademarks of
Bloomsbury Publishing Plc

First published in Great Britain 2026
Copyright © Gert Biesta, Ramsey Affifi and contributors, 2026

Gert Biesta, Ramsey Affifi and contributors have asserted their right under the Copyright,
Designs and Patents Act, 1988, to be identified as Authors of this work.

Cover design: Grace Ridge
Cover image Warchi via Getty Images

Bloomsbury Publishing Plc does not have any control over, or responsibility for,
any third-party websites referred to or in this book. All internet addresses given in
this book were correct at the time of going to press. The author and publisher
regret any inconvenience caused if addresses have changed or sites have ceased
to exist, but can accept no responsibility for any such changes.

A catalogue record for this book is available from the British Library.

A catalog record for this book is available from the Library of Congress.

ISBN: HB: 978-1-350-50658-9
          PB: 978-1-350-50657-2
          ePDF: 978-1-350-50660-2
          eBook: 978-1-350-50659-6

Typeset by Integra Software Services Pvt. Ltd.
Printed and bound in Great Britain

For product safety related questions contact productsafety@bloomsbury.com.

To find out more about our authors and books visit www.bloomsbury.com
and sign up for our newsletters.

CONTENTS

FIGURES

CONTRIBUTORS

Ramsey Affifi teaches and writes at the University of Edinburgh.

Gert Biesta has been Professor of Educational Theory and Pedagogy at the University of Edinburgh, and is currently Emeritus Professor of Public Education at Maynooth University and Visiting Professor at Western Norway University of Applied Sciences. Since 2023 he is an appointed member of the Education Council of the Netherlands, the advisory body of the Dutch government and parliament. His work focuses on the theory of education and the philosophy of educational research, with a particular interest in teaching, teacher education, citizenship education, arts education, religious education and education policy.

Laura Colucci-Gray is Professor in Science and Sustainability Education at Moray House School of Education and Sport, University of Edinburgh (UK) and she is Professor II at Høgskulen på Vestlandet – HVL (Norway). Laura has a long-standing career of teaching and research in science education with a particular focus on the theorization and design of transdisciplinary and participatory approaches in sustainability education. She has led and has been co-investigator on several international projects and has published extensively with a research portfolio spanning contributions across teacher education, ethnographic research in school gardens and interdisciplinary collaborations in citizen science. In 2018, Laura led the first Research Commission on STEAM education, funded by the British Educational Research Association; she is currently involved in multi-partner projects 'Feeling the untouchable: Haptic touch experiences for naturalistic learning' (UKRI funded, 2024–6) and SENSE.STEAM, funded by the Horizon Europe Programme 'A Roadmap to STEAM' (2022–5).

Lorna Hamilton is Senior Lecturer in Education Research at the University of Edinburgh. She draws on considerable teaching experience both in primary school and as an English language teacher and has researched various aspects of ITE and early professional development. Her key research areas are professional/personal identity and agency, inclusion and new/early career teacher education and development.

Mike Jess is Senior Lecturer and Teacher Educator at the University of Edinburgh. Mike's academic, research and professional interests focus on the relationship between complexity thinking, curriculum development and practice. He is particularly interested in complex adaptive practice, boundary crossing, transdiscipliniarity, lesson study and self-study. Over the last twenty years, Mike has worked on many international projects across the UK, Europe, Japan, Vietnam and Myanmar. Early in his career Mike spent twelve years as a physical education teacher in primary and secondary schools in Scotland and Kuwait. He has also worked as a visiting professor in the United States. Mike has presented at many international conferences and has written extensively on complexity thinking, physical education and professional practice.

Chang Liu is a PhD candidate at the Moray House School of Education and Sport, University of Edinburgh, UK. Her research interests include philosophical inquiries into how to live, the purpose of education, pedagogy, Confucianism and Taoism. Formerly supervised by Prof. Gert Biesta, and currently supervised by Dr Ramsey Affifi and Dr Aline Nardo, her thesis, *Education for a Meaningful Living*, explores the role of education in addressing the question of leading a meaningful life, primarily through the lens of Confucius. Her research interests began with questioning the aims of the current educational system and her personal encounters with ancient Chinese philosophy. Engaging with classic Confucian wisdom, she developed a deeper, more holistic understanding of education. Inspired by Biesta's work, she also approaches Confucius from an existential perspective. She is increasingly interested in the comparative study of Eastern and Western philosophy and its implications for meaningful living education, which she hopes to explore further in future research.

James MacAllister was Senior Lecturer in the philosophy of education at Edinburgh University until he died in service in July 2025. His recent research focused on the relationship between art (especially film), ethics and education. He has an edited Bloomsbury volume in press, Artful Education and the Downward Journey: Facing Finitude and Death, with Dr Ramsey Affifi and Dr Anne Pirrie. He has published widely in a range of philosophy of education and education journals on topics, including the purpose of educational institutions, the curriculum and epistemology, tragic films and educational possibilities in them, environmental tragedy in film and the ethics of adventure education. He also has a monograph about discipline in schools in philosophy, policy and practice (2016).

Paul McMillan is Lecturer at the Moray House School of Education and Sport, University of Edinburgh. His research explores the complex and dynamic nature of teaching and teacher professional learning, with a particular focus on how complexity can be understood and engaged with in everyday practice. Paul's work draws on concepts such as teacher vision, adaptive teaching, and teacher–student relationships, and is often underpinned by complexity thinking, self-study and lesson study. He is particularly interested in the interplay between professional development and practice. Paul has presented his research at a range of international conferences and has a growing portfolio of publications in leading education journals.

Shari Sabeti is Reader in Arts and Humanities Education at the University of Edinburgh, UK. Her research focuses on the relationship between the arts (particularly literature and visual art), pedagogy and curriculum. Taking ethnographic and arts-based approaches, she pays detailed attention to the creative practice of artists, writers, art-educators and their students. She has conducted research in a variety of contexts including schools and museums, as well as community and commercial settings. Most recently, she has been engaged in several projects focused on art education, indigenous creative practice and the decolonization of curricula in the Pacific region, notably Hawai ʻi, the Marshall Islands and Sāmoa.

Sonia Sjollema is a clinical and organizational psychologist with extensive experience in HRM and organizational development within the public and non-profit sectors. As the managing director of NSvP and the Knowledge Centre for Innovation in Work, she leads research and pilot projects that explore the future of work, aiming to enhance fair and meaningful employment opportunities for all. Additionally, she served as the chair of the steering committee for 50 WON-schools, a network of secondary schools committed to inquiry-based learning. In 2025, she completed her doctoral studies at the University of Edinburgh, Moray House School of Education and Sport. Her PhD research examined the evolving educational and public roles of libraries, focusing on non-formal education and public pedagogy. Conducted at the Amsterdam Public Library, this work critically explores how libraries navigate increasing pressures of accountability while maintaining their emancipatory and democratic mission as institutions in the public sphere.

Stephen Sowa is Teaching Fellow working in the Education School at the University of Southampton. He is Associate Programme Lead for the BSc Education & Psychology programme. Stephen teaches across a range of undergraduate and postgraduate modules, and he is the creator of a year three philosophy of education module for undergraduates. His research activities and interests span various topics within the philosophy of education, as well as carrying out some empirical research projects. At present, Stephen is concerned with undertaking a comprehensive analysis of rule-governed approaches to teaching and reconceptualizing teaching as an art form. He is also studying the notion of thick concepts in educational research. This includes how researchers might collaboratively set ethical boundaries with stakeholders when measuring and drawing inferences from thick concepts (i.e. concepts which are simultaneously descriptive and evaluative).

Introduction

We Need to Talk about Teaching

Gert Biesta and Ramsey Affifi

The Teacher as Technician?

There is an ongoing tendency in contemporary research, policy and practice to see the teacher as a technician who, with guidance or instruction from scientific evidence about 'what works', will become increasingly more effective in generating the measurable learning outcomes that count in international comparisons of the performance of national education systems. While the idea of the teacher as technician, as the one who ultimately will have everything 'under control', may sound attractive – which is a key reason why it keeps resurfacing and is being pursued with much vigour in many places – it rests on an enormous simplification of what teaching is, how teaching happens and what it requires from teachers.

For one thing, the idea of the teacher as technician reduces the teacher to someone who should only be interested in the effectiveness of their 'interventions' and not in complex normative and practical questions about what good education entails and what education should be good for. Also, in the suggestion that the professionalism of the teacher is purely technical in nature, it is (conveniently?) forgotten that students are not the objects of teachers' interventions, but human beings who can think, judge and act, and thus can make up their own mind. Rather than seeing this as a problem that in some way needs to be 'solved', education, unlike indoctrination, is actually always aimed at enhancing students' capacity for thoughtful action.

An Impossible Profession?

Although the idea of the teacher as technician keeps raising its head and is put forward again and again as an attractive perspective, the idea that education would all be fine if teachers would just do what the scientific evidence says they should be doing, is actually naïve. It is just as naïve as the idea that students will be fine if they just do what their teachers say; that society will be fine if all citizens just do what the government says, and that psychotherapy will all be fine if the client would just do what the therapist says. However, the fact that Sigmund Freud names education, politics and psychotherapy as three 'impossible professions' (see Freud 1937) is not because there is nothing to do or achieve, but because what is at stake in each of these domains is the freedom of the student, the citizen and the client – which always entails the challenge for students, citizens and clients to use their freedom well.

The chapters brought together in this book are not just intended to show why a technical understanding of teaching is problematic. They also explore in detail what can be gained from understanding teaching as a situated art which requires the purposeful combination of craft – teachers' 'know how' – and wisdom – the ability to make educationally meaningful judgements about what needs to be done in the always concrete and unique situation of the classroom. The suggestion that teaching is a situated art which requires teacherly artistry also brings into view the aesthetic qualities and dynamics of teaching, and thus opens up different ways for understanding and 'doing' teaching, and for approaching teacher formation and teacher professional development.

In this book we therefore ask what the artistry of teaching is, how it matters for teaching, what it looks like and feels like for both teachers and students, how the arts can help in deepening our understanding of teaching, who may benefit from the artistry of teaching, and what this means for becoming and being a teacher, individually and collectively.

Reclaiming the Artistry of Teaching

The ambition of the book is not to invent an entirely new account of teaching, but rather to reclaim an understanding of teaching that has become marginalized as a result of attempts to turn teaching into a 'delivery system', as Lawrence Stenhouse, one of the early advocates of the artistry of teaching, has called it (see Stenhouse 1988: 50). Reclaiming the artistry of teaching partly requires an understanding of why such an account of teaching has become marginalized over time, which is one theme of this book. Reclaiming the artistry of teaching also requires exploring what artistry in teaching entails, why and how it matters, for both teachers and students, and what it requires from teachers to take their artistry seriously, individually and collectively. This is the second major theme of this book.

The suggestion that teaching is a practical art that requires artistry is not just meant to highlight that teaching needs to be understood as a craft and not a technique or technology, but also allows for an exploration of the relationships between education and the arts and, more specifically, of the aesthetic dimensions of teaching. The insight that teaching has aesthetic qualities and ought to have aesthetic qualities in order to be educationally significant is the third major theme of the book. The chapters in the book therefore contain a combination of historical and political reconstruction, theoretical and conceptual exploration, and the study of teacherly practices.

It is perhaps important to mention that most of the authors of the chapters in this book are teachers, working in a range of educational settings, also including teacher education and adult education. Moreover, this book is the result of a series of 'slow conversations' amongst the authors about teaching, about their own teaching, about research on teaching, about teacher education and professional development, and about the contemporary educational policy landscape. It is not, therefore, that the authors of the chapters in this book only look at education from the outside and only write *about* teachers and teaching. Much of what is to be found in this book is connected to the authors' own teaching practices and their own ongoing attempts, sometimes in rather hostile policy environments, at taking the artistry of their own teaching seriously. So what is there to be found in this book?

An Overview

In Chapter 1, 'Reclaiming the Artistry of Teaching', Gert Biesta sets out the case for why teaching needs to be understood as an art and why the artistry of teaching and the artistry of teachers matters. He provides a reconstruction of recent trends in educational policy, research and practice, and highlights the importance of engaging with the point and purpose of education in order to make clear that teaching is not a matter of implementing prescribed interventions but always needs to engage with the multiple purposes that education must serve. Based on Aristotle's distinction between *poiesis* and *praxis* – in English sometimes translates as 'making action' and 'doing action' – he argues that teaching is a 'double art' that requires both craft and judgement. He discusses ideas from Lawrence Stenhouse, who has been an important advocate for the artistry of teaching and an important reference point and source of inspiration for the book. He concludes that the turn towards artistry should not be seen as a step backwards but rather as an urgent antidote against the ongoing reduction of teaching and the work of teachers to mere technical matters and concerns.

In Chapter 2, 'Teaching under the Spectre of a New Industrial Revolution', Stephen Sowa delves into the wider historical socio-political context of the discussion about artistry and teaching. He makes the case that arguments for and against conceptions of teaching as a science rather than an art have largely omitted an analysis informed by the historic and institutional conditions in which mass schooling and teaching have been and continue to be shaped and understood. In his chapter he provides such an analysis using a four-part argument. Part one explains how a mass production logic for schooling and teaching was established during the initial phases of the Industrial Revolution as certain organizational habits were consolidated. Part two then shows how this logic is being repurposed in response to recent predictions of a new industrial age. Part three details the problems for schooling and teaching resulting from a mass production logic. Part four responds to these problems by outlining a typology for artistry in and the artistry of teaching. This typology brings together various art-related concepts to elucidate the distinctive features of teaching.

In Chapter 3, 'On Observing Two Pacific Island Poets Teach: Some Reflections on the 'Vā' and the Artistry of Teaching', Shari Sabeti explores the artistry of teaching as a deeply relational practice through detailed observations of two Pacific Island performance poets, No'u Revilla and Selina Tusitala Marsh. Sabeti draws on the Pacific cultural concept of the 'vā' – a relational space between – in order to illuminate how they nurture and navigate relational dynamics in their teaching. Using portraiture as a methodological approach, the chapter contains two written portraits of their practice. Sabeti argues that the 'vā' offers a lens that makes visible what is undervalued in current discourses about teaching: the nuanced, affective labour involved in maintaining the continuously shifting interconnections between teacher, student and subject matter. The chapter also highlights the importance of the modes through which teaching is represented. It uses portraiture to capture the subtleties and dynamism of teaching's relational artistry, resisting reductive views of teaching as technical skill or 'effect'.

In Chapter 4, 'The Art and Artistry of Teaching: Looking beyond the Quantifiable in Initial Teacher Education', Lorna Hamilton takes the discussion about the artistry of teaching to the field of teacher education. She highlights that contemporary views of education are often shaped by behaviouristic understandings of teaching and strongly and unhelpfully influenced by measurement and league tables. As a result, any teaching artistry is overlooked or ignored as it cannot be evaluated by rigid and limited accounts of competency. In her chapter she explores the ways in which we might build a more holistic and relational-humanistic account of teaching where preservice teachers may see and experience artistry as they make choices about who they are as an individual and as a professional. Reflections on the nature of teaching as an art and as artistry, the significance of the language we use in initial teacher education and pertinent concepts such as agency and soul bring such a more relational-humanist model of teaching to the fore. Without dismissing skills-based teaching, she suggests that a hybrid form could be generated in initial teacher education, drawing on both the practical knowledge and skills of established models while also beginning to alter the language of teaching to encompass teaching as a performance art.

In Chapter 5, 'Artful Teaching in the AI Age: Seeing Harm in Artificiality via *Blade Runner*', James MacAllister draws upon the philosophy of Friedrich Nietzsche and the Blade Runner Universe in order to explore what it might mean to be an artful teacher in the AI age. He draws a contrast between artful and artless teaching, suggesting that AI risks fuelling a harmful rise in artless teaching and learning. He argues that poorly regulated use of AI in higher education will foster conditions for academic plagiarism and epistemic mistrust, and will stifle the conditions needed for the generation of long-term well-being. He suggests that three political actions are needed to address the epistemic and ethical issues arising from the emergence of generative AI in education: thought experiments that highlight harms from AI, a reclamation of the autonomy of educational institutions and a democratic debate about how to make AI in education work for human well-being. To close the chapter he proposes ten practice-principles of the artful teacher.

In Chapter 6, 'Art Is the Mother of Resistance: Must Education Resist Too?', Sonia Sjollema explores the parallels between modern art and education, drawing on Theodor Adorno's aesthetic theory and the emancipatory educational philosophies of Philippe Meirieu and Gert Biesta. Sjollema argues that art's resistance to functionalism offers a powerful lens through which to rethink the role of education in democratic societies. Just as art goes beyond utilitarian purposes, education cannot be reduced to mere output measures or functional roles *for* society. Recognizing the artistry in teaching requires an engagement with dynamic processes and relationships that shape educational practice. Educators must navigate the ongoing tensions between control and freedom while fostering student autonomy and safeguarding space for critical reflection and ethical consideration. Ultimately, Sjollema concludes, teaching becomes an act of resistance when it protects the emancipatory aim of nurturing critically thinking, autonomous subjects in a democratic society.

In Chapter 7, 'Challenging Simplistic Storylines: Diversity, Complexity Commonalities and the Artistry of Teaching', Paul McMillan and Mike Jess challenge dominant narratives that cast teachers as deliverers of prescribed policy in standardized ways, and instead argue for a reconceptualization of teaching as complex and adaptive. Drawing on complexity thinking, they introduce four interrelated commonalities – becoming, lived time, boundaries and self-organization – as a lens for understanding the diversity within and across educational settings. Adaptive teaching is explored as a practical expression of teaching as artistry. They also consider implications for leadership and policy. Here McMillan and Jess call for complexity-informed leadership that protects adaptive spaces and fosters teacher agency amid the uncertainty triggered by external political pressures. While they conclude that artistry can act as a counter to reductive political agendas, they try to remain realistic about the systemic conditions required to sustain it.

In Chapter 8, 'Artistry of Teaching as a Practice of Curation: Inviting Possibilities for Knowing and Seeing Anew', Laura Colucci-Gray approaches the artistry of teaching as the ability to curate an environment of relations, in which the 'what' of education gives way to the responsibility of the 'what if'. Following a double movement, she discusses the assumptions guiding education within the confines of the industrial model and the utilitarian logic of the market system. She then draws upon experiences from her own research and practice for approaching the artistry of teaching from an aesthetic stance, opening up to the exploration of what else might be possible in education. The chapter concludes with a tentative statement on teacher artistry. Not to be confused with the prized skill of mastering perfection, the ambition is not to control what the outcomes of the educational process will be, but to evaluate the possibilities for new stories to begin, and to curate the space for these to carry on.

In Chapter 9, 'Aesthetic Tensions and Situated Judgements in Teaching', Ramsey Affifi highlights that teaching is an inherently aesthetic practice that requires making situated judgements within indeterminate educational encounters. Teachers make such judgements when tending, intending and attending to 'aesthetic tensions' common across many arts, such as the interplay between what is happening and has happened, content and context, and risk and safety. However, the aesthetic space that teachers work in is also saturated with tensions shaped by specifically educational concerns and purposes, which in turn colour how these other, more generic tensions appear and are addressed. For instance, he asks how, and to what end, teachers should work with an aesthetic tension that confronts them. And also how teachers should engage their students with tensions they encounter. Affifi concludes by considering opportunities for teacher artistry in the context of teacher education. Beyond theoretical insights, the chapter offers a vocabulary and approach for reclaiming teacher artistry in an age obsessed with evading aesthetic tensions for the anaesthetizing comforts of algorithmic thinking.

In Chapter 10, 'Confucius as a Teacher: On his Artistry of Teaching', Chang Liu presents the unique case of Confucius as a teacher. She explores what kind of teacher Confucius is, how he teaches and what this reveals about the artistry of his teaching. She bases her exploration on a close reading of The Analects, which provides the most authentic teachings of Confucius and is considered one of the most important texts in the Confucian canon. Liu focuses her exploration on the forms of Confucius's teaching as presented in the Analects, as this provides an important way into understanding the way in which Confucius teaches. She argues that the different teaching forms serve his overarching educational purpose, which is the striving for Ren (仁), a humane and significant way of living, and makes the case that teaching in other ways will not be able to achieve this purpose. Through this the artistic inventiveness and aesthetic qualities of Confucius' teaching are brought into view. The 'case' of Confucius thus sheds light on the two main components of teacherly artistry: craft and aesthetics.

In Chapter 11, 'The Aesthetics of Teaching: How Education Really Works', Gert Biesta pursues a suggestion that can be found in the work of Johan Friedrich Herbart (1776–1841), who has argued that education actually works aesthetically, and that it is therefore the main task of the educator to (re)present the world aesthetically to students. The reason for this, so Biesta argues, lies in the fact that in education we should always be after the possibility for the student to exist as subject of their own life and not as object of external forces or interventions. This is why the aesthetic 'register' is important in education, because aesthetics is not a controlling force but rather has the potential to awaken the student, both for the world in which their lives unfold and for their own existence as subject 'in' and 'with' this world. In the chapter he compares aesthetic education with *an*aesthetic education, and provides a range of examples from the arts to give meaning to the idea that education has its own, aesthetic causality. In the final section of the chapter he highlights what it means for teachers' artistry to utilize the aesthetic register in educationally meaningful ways.

The ambition to reclaim the artistry of teaching is not only a matter of articulating different understandings of what the art of teaching entails and why it matters for meaningful education; reclaiming the artistry of teaching is also a matter of resisting the dominance of the image of the teacher as technician, and resisting the whole educational machinery that has been set up to ensure that teachers stay on the narrow, technical path. In the concluding chapter of our book we therefore turn to the political dimensions of our ambitions, which is the issue of teacher activism. However, rather than assuming that the question of teacher activism is 'outside' of and disconnected from the question of artistry, we explore what it might mean to reclaim the artistry of teaching with teacherly artistry and, therefore, with a genuine educational intent. This not just requires hope or, more precisely, the ability to see and sense impossible possibilities: tending and attending to cracks within which seeds may already be taking root and to the hopeful ambiguities that still provide space for manoeuvre. It also requires a different approach to and engagement with one's potential 'opponents' rather than just opposing them, and also with one's allies and one's profession. In that way, saying 'no' can open up a different future, rather than close down all options, which is exactly what makes such political work educational.

An Invitation

The chapters in this book contain our own explorations of the different dimensions and layers of the artistry of teaching. Of course, our texts do not offer recipes for teachers, precisely because thinking in terms of recipes and prescriptions tends to miss the very point of what teaching is, what it is about and what it is to be for. Rather, therefore, we hope that the book will provide inspiration for anyone who wants to take teaching seriously again, in a time in which the teacher is under ongoing pressure from technicist assumptions and technological expectations. In this regard the book can perhaps best be seen as an invitation to readers to continue the conversation we open in this book, and take this conversation into their own practices. It is also, therefore, and invitation to develop new insights, try different ways of doing and being and, in doing so, contribute to the need to reclaim a meaningful account of teaching and sufficient space for teacher artistry.

References

Freud, S. (1937), 'Analysis Terminable and Interminable', *The International Journal of Psychoanalysis*, 18: 373–405.

Stenhouse, L. (1988), 'Artistry and Teaching: The Teacher as Focus of Research and Development', *Journal of Curriculum and Supervision*, 4 (1): 43–51.

CHAPTER ONE

Reclaiming the Artistry of Teaching

Gert Biesta

Introduction

In a chapter from 1984, republished as a journal article in 1988, the British curriculum scholar Lawrence Stenhouse wrote a sentence which, in hindsight, can only be characterized as visionary. It reads as follows: 'Improving education is not about improving teaching as a delivery system [because] crucial is the desire of the artist to improve his or her art' (Stenhouse 1988: 50). The sentence is visionary, because if there is one thing that has characterized educational policy, research and practice over the past decades, it is precisely the ongoing effort to steer the whole educational enterprise towards becoming an effective delivery system of measurable learning outcomes (e.g. see Ball 2012). In this setup the teacher is identified as an important *factor* – there are numerous documents in which it is claimed that research has shown that the teacher is the most important 'in school factor' in the production of measurable learning outcomes (e.g. see King-Rice 2003; McKinsey & Co. 2007; OECD 2005) – but not as a thinking, judging and acting professional who is driven by an ongoing desire to improve his or her own 'artistry' (I will return to this term below).

The keyword in these developments is the notion of 'effectiveness', and the double move that has taken place in many countries over the past decades has been to make the operation of the education system more effective and to do so with regard to the production of an increasingly smaller number of measurable 'learning outcomes' (see Biesta 2010; Hogan and Thompson 2021; Sellar, Thompson and Rutkowski 2017). This line of thought has brought about a worldwide educational evidence 'industry' that seeks to find out, through the conduct of large-scale experimental studies, what allegedly 'works' in education. Moreover, the ambition of such research is to tell teachers what they should do in order to impact effectively on the production of particular 'outcomes'. Some claim that the 'extraordinary advances in medicine, agriculture and other fields' are the result of 'the acceptance by practitioners of evidence as the basis for practice', particularly evidence from the randomized controlled trial, and that it is about time that education embarks upon a similar path (see Slavin 2002: 16). Others, however, have raised fundamental questions about this approach, asking both whether this is a *desirable* way forward for education and whether it is even a *possible* way forward (see Thomas 2021; see also; Biesta 2015; D'Agnese 2017; Davis 2017; for an illuminating conversation see Hattie and Nepper Larsen 2020; and for a critique from within the medical field see Holmes et al. 2006).

The question about the *possibility* of this vision has to do with how we envisage the dynamics of education. In the view of education as a delivery system, teaching is seen as an 'intervention' which, under 'ideal' circumstances, will bring about particular 'outcomes'. We can characterize this as a causal conception of education in which teaching is seen as a cause and learning – or in the lingo of this approach: 'learning outcomes' – as the effect of teaching interventions. In this setup the teacher does indeed appear as a factor in a production-line, and one could say that the only possible role for the teacher here is that of a *technician*, that is, the one who administers prescribed interventions. The question this line of thought raises is whether this is an adequate and accurate understanding of the dynamics of education. In what is to follow I will argue that this is *not* the case.

Yet this also has to do with the question of the *desirability* of this vision. With regard to education itself, the question is whether we should indeed see education as a matter of control, that is, a matter of administering interventions which, under 'ideal' circumstances, will bring about predetermined outcomes. This, in my view, is a problematic and impoverished conception of what education is and should be about. In addition to this, there is also the question of the desirability of the 'figure' of the teacher that is entailed in this vision, that is, of the idea of the teacher as 'factor' or technician who both is controlling his or her students and is being controlled by the prescriptions based on the alleged evidence about what does and what doesn't 'work'. Again, as I will argue, such a conception of the teacher amounts to a misrepresentation of the complex work of teaching and therefore doesn't speak to what this work is about and what is at stake in it.

In several of my publications I have raised questions about the adequacy of a mechanistic or 'quasi-causal' conception of education in which teaching is seen as an intervention, the teacher as a factor and the focus is on increasing the effectiveness of teaching interventions for the production of learning outcomes. Instead, I have made a case for complexity, that is, for seeing education as an open, semiotic and recursive system, that is, a system 'populated' by thoughtful individuals who can make up their own mind and can act accordingly, and whose interaction is a matter of communication and interpretation, not of mechanical 'push and pull' (e.g. see Biesta 2016).

In this chapter I wish to focus on one particular aspect of this discussion, namely the suggestion that we should understand teaching and the work of the teacher as an *art*, first and foremost in the Aristotelian sense in which the arts are about human activity in the domain of the 'variable'. Work in this domain requires 'artistry', that is, the ability to make situated judgements about what are desirable ways of acting, which always entails judgement about the 'how' and about the 'what for'. In this regard, as I will suggest below, teaching can be characterized as a 'double art'. In the three main sections of this chapter I will discuss the question what teaching is which, inevitably, has to engage with the question what teaching is *for*. I will then turn to Aristotle in order to look in more detail at the complexities of work in the domain of the variable. In a third step I will discuss ideas from Lawrence Stenhouse, being one of the authors who has made an explicit case for teaching as an art and for the artistry of teaching.

I do this in order to show that a claim for the artistry of teaching does not have to start from scratch but can build upon ideas that may have been forgotten and definitely have become marginal in the educational conversation. Another author who has made significant contributions to the 'case' for seeing teaching as an art and for focusing on the artistry of teaching is Eliot Eisner (e.g. see Eisner 2002). One reason for focusing on the work of Stenhouse rather than Eisner is that Eisner's contribution stays more closely to the Aristotelian line of argument presented in this chapter, whereas Stenhouse, in a sense, locates the artistry of teaching closer to the (performing) arts. In the concluding section I will say a few words about the intellectual and political work needed for reclaiming a meaningful account of teaching.

The Point and Purpose of Teaching

I wish to take my starting point in the observation that teaching is a relational, intentional and purposeful activity (for a detailed discussion see Biesta and Stengel 2016). First, teaching is not something one can do on one's own but implies a relationship between teachers and (their) students, which means that it takes at least two for teaching to take place. Secondly, teaching doesn't happen by accident; those who teach, or try to teach, do so deliberately. And thirdly, teaching is done with a sense of purpose, which means that it is done for a reason. Teachers have, in other words, good reasons for what they teach and how they teach, and these reasons have something to do with what they hope that their activities will bring about on the side of their students, albeit that it remains open whether or not this will happen, as the 'success' of teaching is not just reliant on what teachers do but also one what students do with what they are being taught.

Over the past decades, the prevalent answer to the question what teaching is *for*, has become 'learning'. This, however, is a rather impoverished idea of what teaching should aim for and actually also a rather unhelpful suggestion. This is not just because learning can happen anywhere, also without teaching. It is also because learning can go in any direction, and therefore just to say that teaching should bring about learning or that the work of teachers is to 'facilitate' learning, says very little, if it says anything at all. The point of education rather is that students learn *something*, that they learn it *for a reason*, and that they learn it *from someone*. Education, in other words, is never about learning in general but always raises questions of content, purpose and relationships. And it is here that teaching comes in, because whereas students can learn all kind of things from being in educational settings – including how to cheat or how to pass an exam with minimal effort – the work of the teacher is to direct the attention of students to particular subject-matter, particular themes, particular issues and particular tasks and, most importantly, to do so with particular reasons and purposes in mind. Teaching, in other words, is always conducted with an orientation.

Elsewhere (e.g. see Biesta 2009, 2010, 2020) I have suggested that there are actually three purposes (or as I prefer to call them: domains of purpose) that are always at stake when education takes place. One important reason why we engage in education is to make knowledge and skills available to our students. We can refer to this as knowledge acquisition, but it is perhaps better to say that one important purpose of education is *qualification*, that is, providing students with knowledge, skills, attitudes and dispositions that makes it possible for them to do something. This 'doing' can either be quite specific and precise, such as becoming qualified for a particular job or profession; but it can also be understood more broadly, such as the way in which schools seek to equip children and young people for their life in complex modern societies.

Some argue that qualification is the sole purpose of education because they are worried that anything else gets education into difficult normative questions, and these are better left to the family or community context. This may sound reasonable, but the problem is that since education is unable to provide children and young people with all existing knowledge and skills, there is inevitable selection going on in education. In everything we do we thus present our students with a particular 'selection' of the world or, more positively formulated, with a particular *representation* of the world. The ways in which we do this inevitably influence our students in some way. Normative questions are therefore inescapable, even if education is confined to the domain of knowledge and skills.

In the literature the (re)presentation of the world, or the presentation of different representations of the world, is known as *socialization*. Some highlight the ways in which this goes on behind the backs of our students – an idea known as the hidden curriculum. Yet we can also think more positively about this and see socialization as an important second purpose of education, where we try to provide our students with an orientation in the world, that is, with a sense of direction. Education as socialization is about providing our students with an orientation into existing cultures, traditions and practices, with the invitation that they locate themselves within them.

Discussions about socialization, particularly strong(er) and (more) directive approaches, raise an important further question, which has been part of the modern educational conversation at least since the Enlightenment. The question here is whether education can and should approach students as 'objects' that need to be(come) qualified and socialized – which seems to be the dominant 'undertone' of the idea of teaching as a delivery system – or whether education always needs to ensure that children and young people can become subjects of their own life. This is partly a very complicated and deeply philosophical question, but it is also a very simple issue which many educators will immediately recognize. After all, in all education we want to make sure that students stop relying on our help and input and become able to think for themselves, make their own judgements, and be able to act and act *well*.

There are different ways in which we can refer to this third domain of educational purpose. I tend to refer to it with the word '*subjectification*', which is perhaps a rather odd word in English, but precisely refers to the ambition that students end up as subjects of their own life and not just as objects of educational 'interventions'. It therefore stands in sharp contrast to education that aims for objectification, that is, education which is only interested in controlling students and their acting, thinking and judgement. Of course, we cannot force our students to be subjects of their own life, but we can, in all kind of ways, 'remind' our students of this possibility to exist as subject of their own life. And we can provide them with opportunities to practice with the complexities of what this means (see Biesta 2020 for more detail).

Dietrich Benner has suggested the phrase 'Aufforderung zur Selbsttätigkeit' as a way to capture the special character of educational work in this domain (see Benner 2015). This can be translated as 'summoning to self-action', although the 'summoning' may sound a bit strict and a word like 'encouragement' might be more helpful. This should not be understood as the encouragement to be *your*self, and also not the encouragement just to become active. It is perhaps best to see this as the injunction to be *a* self, that is, to try to be a subject of your own life, with all the complexities and responsibilities that follow, rather than remaining an object of influences from 'elsewhere'.

Another set of concepts that is helpful here is Benner's distinction between affirmative and non-affirmative education (see Benner 2015: 146–55). Whereas qualification and socialization are, to a large degree, affirmative, in that they start from certain ideas about what education should achieve and where children and young people should end up, the domain of subjectification is precisely the opposite of this, because here it is not for educators to tell children and young people how they should be and become, but rather to provide opportunities for them to figure out for themselves how to live their own lives in the best way possible. That is why the educational work vis-à-vis this domain has to be non-affirmative and has to proceed with caution.

I wish to suggest that qualification, socialization, and subjectification are not only three *legitimate* purposes of education; in a sense they are also three *inevitable* purposes of all education. After all, in all instances of education there is always something for teachers to offer to students and for students to acquire to their benefit. Because qualification always represents (aspects of) the world in a particular way, there is always also socialization going on. And all this also has an impact on the student as subject, to begin with because becoming more knowledgeable or skilled (qualification) and gaining orientation in a particular domain or field (socialization) provides students with increased possibilities for thinking, judgement, and action.

The fact that these three domains of purpose are inevitable, first of all suggests that the three domains are always entangled with each other; they cannot exist separately, because every act of qualification is also an act of socialization and also impacts on the student's subject-ness, positively or negatively. It suggests, secondly that in the design and enactment of education teachers should always consider what they seek their students to achieve in relation to each of these domains. Thirdly, although the three domains are always 'in play' in education, it doesn't mean that they can exist in perfect harmony. There are always potential tensions between, say, what one seeks to achieve in the domain of qualification and what is possible in the other domains. There can be synergy – understanding subject-matter will also provide a degree of orientation and contributes to one's agency – but there can also be conflicts – for example when a too strong push on the domain of qualification undermines students' agency.

The challenge for teachers, therefore, is not just to think and act in a three-dimensional way, that is, with an eye on the three domains of educational purpose. The challenge is also to try to secure a meaningful balance and to think carefully about the costs of emphasizing one domain to the detriment of the other domains. This, as I will argue in the next section, is one important reason why teaching needs to be understood as an art and why teachers need artistry rather than techniques or prescriptions.

The Double Art of Teaching: Craft and Wisdom

One key message emerging from the discussion so far is that teaching cannot and should not be enacted as a form of control or, to be more precise, as a kind of intervention that, under 'ideal' circumstances and based upon the best 'evidence' about what 'works', should be aimed at producing pre-specified learning outcomes. This is not to suggest that everything should be open, which is the mistake of those who denounce teaching in favour of learning. But it is to challenge the view that education is ultimately a causal system (an ontological claim) and that, once we have perfect knowledge about the mechanics of the system (an epistemological claim), teaching can become a matter of administering those interventions that produce the desired outcomes (a praxeological claim). The whole point of teaching is precisely *not* the production of outcomes but a matter of educating human beings so that they become more qualified, that is, able to act thoughtfully, gain a sense of direction in the world, and, through this, take upon themselves the challenge of being subjects of their own lives.

If this is not a matter of implementing evidence-based intervention, how then should we understand the work of teachers, and what do they need to act thoughtfully in educational settings? These questions relate back to a rather old discussion which has been framed, correctly in my view, as the question whether teaching should be understood as a 'science' or as an 'art'. This question surfaces regularly in the educational conversation, including in the quote with which I opened this chapter. In my view, the most helpful engagement with this question can be found in the work of Aristotle, for whom the difference between 'science' and 'art' is not a matter of different kinds of knowledge but actually begins with a proper understanding of the reality we are acting 'in' and 'upon' in such practical endeavours as education.

With regard to this Aristotle makes a very helpful and, in my view, tremendously important distinction between the theoretical life (the 'bios theoretikos') and the practical life (the 'bios praktikos'). The theoretical life is concerned with 'the necessary and the eternal' (Aristotle 1980: 140), that is, with those aspects of reality that do not change (Aristotle mentions such phenomena as the movement of the planets or the stars in the sky). He refers to knowledge about this reality as 'episteme', which is often translated as 'science'. 'Episteme' is knowledge about what is necessary and eternal and because the reality that this knowledge is about doesn't change, the knowledge we have about this reality, once it is accurate, will not change either. From this we have an idea of true knowledge as being 100 per cent stable, secure and certain.

Aristotle's main insight, however, is that most of what our lives are about takes place in the domain of the 'variable' (for this term see Aristotle

1980: 42), that is, the domain of *change*. It is the world in which we act and where our actions have consequences, but where there is no guarantee that our actions will always have the same consequences. It is, in other words, the domain of possibility, not the domain of certainty. Knowledge in this domain is about the relationships between our actions and the *possible* consequences of our actions. This is so for our actions in and interactions with the material world, our actions in and interactions with the living world, and our actions in and interactions with the social world. While we can gain much knowledge about possible relationships between actions and consequences in these domains, there is never a guarantee that when we act in the same way in the future, the same consequences will follow. And precisely there lies the difference between 'science' and 'art', where art refers to our actions in the domain of the variable.

What is also interesting about Aristotle's explorations is that he makes a further distinction between two 'modes' of acting in the domain of the variable and two related forms of judgement. This is the distinction between *poiesis*, which Carr (1987) has helpfully translated as 'making action', and *praxis*, which Carr translates as 'doing action'. *Poiesis* is the art of making things – such as a saddle or a ship – although I prefer to think of it slightly more widely, that is, as action that brings something into existence. We might also call it 'productive action'. As Aristotle puts it, *poiesis* is about 'how something may come into being which is capable of either being or not being' (which means that it is about the variable, not about what is eternal and necessary), and about things 'whose origin is in the maker and not in the thing made' (which distinguishes *poiesis* from biological phenomena such as growth and development) (see Aristotle 1980: 141). *Poiesis* is, in short, about bringing something in existence that did not exist before.

The kind of knowledge we need for *poiesis* is what Aristotle refers to as *techne*, which he defines as 'knowledge of how to make things' (Aristotle 1980: 141). *Techne* is about finding the means that will bring about what one seeks to bring about, to put it in general terms. *Techne* encompasses knowledge about the materials we work with – and we can take 'materials' in the broad sense of the word – and about the techniques we can apply to work with those materials. Yet making something, such as a saddle, is never simply about following a recipe. It involves making judgements about the application of our previous knowledge and experience to *this* piece of leather, for a saddle to fit *this* particular horse, and for *this* particular rider. So we make judgements about application, production and effectiveness in our attempts at bringing something into existence. The best English word for *techne* is probably craftsmanship although in a slightly narrower translation we can also think of it as consisting of the combination of practical knowledge and practical judgement.

The domain of the variable is, however, not confined to the world of things and matters of making, but includes the social domain, that is, the world of human action and interaction. It is here that a second art is called for: the art of *praxis*. The orientation here is not towards the making of things but towards the promotion of the human good (the Greek term is *eudamonia*). *Praxis*, Aristotle writes, is 'about what sort of things conduce to the good life in general' (Aristotle 1980: 142). What we need in order to proceed here is not judgement about how to do things, but rather judgement 'about what is to be done' (Aristotle 1980: 142). Aristotle refers to this kind of judgement as *phronesis*, which is usually translated as practical wisdom. Aristotle defines it as a 'reasoned and true state of capacity to act with regard to human goods' (Aristotle 1980: 143).

Aristotle thus provides a powerful argument for the idea that teaching is an art and not a science and also provides us with precise definitions of 'art' and 'science'. The key insight here is that teaching takes place in the domain of the variable, that is, the domain of actions and possible consequences, and the reason for this, to put it bluntly, is that in teaching we work with 'living material', that is, with human beings who are capable of their own thought and action. What is also interesting about Aristotle's approach, is the distinction he makes between two different arts: the art of making, for which we need *techne*, which is the practical knowledge and practical judgement about how to brings something into existence, and the art of doing, for which we need *phronesis*, the practical wisdom we need to judge what is to be done. In this regard we could say that teaching is a 'double art', which requires both educational craftsmanship – the 'techne' of teaching – and educational wisdom – the orientation of what teaching is *for*.

The final point to make here is that the 'how' of teaching and the 'what for' of teaching should not be seen as disconnected from each other. It is not that in education we can first set the goals and then just find the most effective and efficient way of getting there. The reason for this lies in the simple fact that the ways in which we proceed in education, the ways we teach, the ways we engage with our students, the ways we focus their attention, the ways we encourage them, are not just more or less effective interventions that happen behind the backs of our students. On the contrary, they are in full view of our students and contain important messages for our students as well. This means that in addition to judgements about the purposes of our teaching, judgements about the way we try to balance the different domains of purpose, and judgements about possible trade offs in achieving a balance, we also need to judge the ways in which we teach. And this judgement is not just technical – which is the question of effectiveness – and also not just moral – 'Are the ways in which we teach morally acceptable?' – but also needs to be *educational*, that is, to be judged in terms of the ways in which they may or may not contribute to the overall ambitions we have with our teaching.

If teaching is an art and, more specifically a 'double art' of craft and wisdom, then it is important that teachers keep working on their own educational 'artistry', that is, their ability to make situated judgements about educationally desirable ways of acting in the always new situations they encounter. It is here that the whole question of the ongoing improvement of education finds its 'home', so to speak, because, to quote Lawrence Stenhouse once more, 'improving education is not about improving teaching as a delivery system [because] crucial is the desire of the artist to improve his or her art' (Stenhouse 1988: 50). And I wish to reiterate that to think of teaching as an art in the nuanced way in which I have discussed it in this section, provides a way to distinguish it from technicist accounts that seek to do away with the need for complex educational judgement and ongoing inventiveness in the educational situation.

Lawrence Stenhouse on the Artistry of Teaching

I have given this chapter the title '*reclaiming* the artistry of teaching' because I wish to highlight that the insight that teaching is an art (in the Aristotelian sense of the word) which requires artistry from its artisans, so to speak, is not a new insight. It partly goes back to the very origins of Western philosophy and, more specifically, to the work of Aristotle who, unlike Plato, can be seen as one of the first philosophers within the Western 'canon' who had a keen interest in the practical life of change and possibility. The particular connection with the practice of teaching is also not new, and can, in a sense, be seen as an important 'thread' in modern educational thought. Think, for example, of the idea of 'tact' in the work of Herbart (for an excellent discussion see Van Manen 1995; see also Van Manen 1991), Wiliam James's comments on the art of teaching quoted at the beginning of this chapter, or the work of Joseph Schwab on the idea of 'the practical' (e.g. Schwab 1969; see also Reid 1999 on the 'deliberative tradition'). We could even say that modern educational thought and practice are characterized by an ongoing tension between those who seek to push teaching towards the technicist end of the spectrum and those who make the case for teaching as thoughtful inventive situated action. One author whose work is clearly positioned within the latter approach and who has not just made the case for seeing teaching as an art but also has connected this explicitly to the idea of 'artistry' is, as mentioned, Lawrence Stenhouse. In this section I wish to take a closer look at some of his ideas.

Lawrence Stenhouse locates the discussion about the artistry of teaching in the context of questions about 'the relation of research to educational action' (Stenhouse 1988: 43). Acknowledging that the contribution from disciplines such as history, philosophy, psychology and sociology provide 'a context in which to plan intelligent action' but that such disciplines 'do not tell us how to act' (Stenhouse 1988: 43), he notes that 'the yearning toward a form of research which might guide educational action [has] led educational researchers to look enviously at agricultural research' (Stenhouse 1988: 43). Such research is characterized by 'field trials which [utilize] random sampling ... in order to recommend to farmers those strains of seed and crop treatments which would maximize yield' (Stenhouse 1988: 43). Stenhouse argues, however, that this approach – which nowadays is more commonly referred to in education as the 'medical model' – is not appropriate for the field of education, both because of the idea of 'random sampling' and because of the talk about 'yield'. Not only does he make the interesting point that 'it is the teacher's job to work like a gardener rather than a farmer, differentiating the treatment of each subject and each learner as the gardener does each flower bed and each plant' (Stenhouse 1988: 44). He also highlights that 'the variability of educational situations is grossly underestimated' in the agricultural approach, which means that 'sampling procedures cannot be related to educational action except on a survey basis rather than an experimental basis' (Stenhouse 1988: 44), and he points out that the intentionality of educational action is not a matter of having a goal that should be 'produced', but that 'purpose in education is having an agenda' (Stenhouse 1988: 44).

Stenhouse also rejects the suggestion that for teachers to know what to do should be a matter of following instructions 'laid down for us in the form of curricula and specifications of teaching methods' (Stenhouse 1988: 44). This is partly because of the totalitarian character of such a suggestion which, in his view, goes against the very point of education as 'learning in the context of a search for truth' (Stenhouse 1988: 44). It is not only that 'truth cannot be defined by the state even through democratic processes', and if the state were to do this it would be as problematic as 'the totalitarian control of art' (Stenhouse 1988: 44). Stenhouse also argues – and the point is entirely correct in my view – that teaching requires 'situational professional judgement' because 'prescriptions will vary according to cases' (Stenhouse 1988: 44). 'We do not need doctors if all they are going to give us is a treatment laid down by the state or suggested by their professor without bothering to examine us and make a diagnosis' (Stenhouse 1988: 44).

For Stenhouse, then, the key argument against attempts to control teaching, either by state mandates or through particular forms of research that are supposedly able to tell teachers 'what work', lies in the simple statement that 'good teaching is created by good teachers' (Stenhouse 1988: 45). Stenhouse acknowledges that this statement may seem 'self-evident to the point of absurdity' (Stenhouse 1988: 45), yet he also stresses that 'the implications of this self-evident proposition do not seem to be widely grasped' (Stenhouse 1988: 45) – to which I wish to add that they are *still* not widely grasped, given the ongoing desire by many policymakers, politicians and others, including educational practitioners, to push the field of education and the work of teachers towards technicism. All this doesn't mean that teachers should not welcome 'access to ideas created by other people at other places or in other times', but they do know – and so should those who generate such ideas – that all this is 'not of much real use until [it is] digested to the point where [it is] subject to the teacher's own judgement' (Stenhouse 1988: 45). And this is so because education cannot be done 'behind the back' of teachers. As Stenhouse puts it, '[O]nly teachers are in the position to create good teaching' (Stenhouse 1988: 45).

It is at this point that Stenhouse brings forward the claim of teaching as art, and art as 'an exercise of skill expressive of meaning' (Stenhouse 1988: 45). He explains: 'The painter, the poet, the musician, the actor and the dancer all express meaning through skill'. Some are geniuses, but claiming teaching as art is not meant to elevate teachers inordinately, but rather to diagnose 'the nature of their job in order to discern how performances might be improved' (Stenhouse 1988: 46). What is distinctive about the art of teaching is that it 'expresses in a form accessible to learners an understanding of the nature of that which is to be learned' (Stenhouse 1988: 46). Stenhouse makes this point in order to emphasize that teaching is not about the mere transmission of knowledge or skill, but always involves what he refers to as 'the epistemology' of a particular discipline or field, that is, 'the nature of its tenure on knowledge' (Stenhouse 1988: 46). 'Teaching tennis is about understanding the logic and psychology and techniques of the game and about expressing that understanding through skill in teaching' (Stenhouse 1988: 46). Whether teaching is concerned with knowledge, the arts of with practical skills, makes no different with regard to the requirement that 'the teacher should aspire to give learners access to insight into the status of what they learn' (Stenhouse 1988: 46). This is as much a requirement for the teacher as it is for the student, as 'good learning', as Stenhouse puts it, is 'not mere doing [but] is about constructing a view of the world' (Stenhouse 1988: 47).

When, against this background, Stenhouse then (re)turns to the question of research, it is to highlight research as an inextricable dimension of art, not something that comes to it from the outside, tries to steer and direct it from the outside, and thus seeks to gain control over teaching from the outside. 'All good art', Stenhouse writes, 'is an inquiry and an experiment' (Stenhouse 1988: 47). Yet is it important to see that such inquiry and experiment is not the inquiry and experiment of the so-called 'scientific method' – the agricultural approach which Stenhouse clearly rejects – but is the ongoing investigation of the complexities of one's own practice and one's own art. And the reason for this is not to increase control over education as a process of production but, as already mentioned before, to improve one's own artistry. Stenhouse makes the interesting claim that 'the purpose of the artist's research is to improve the truth of his performance' (Stenhouse 1988: 47). Artists – Stenhouse mentions Leonardo, George Stubbs, Nureyev, Solti and the Chicago Symphony Orchestra, and Derek Jacobi – are all 'engaged in inquiry, in research, in development of their own work' (Stenhouse 1988: 47). And while this will involve 'improvement of technique, it is not for the sake of technique [but] for the sake of the expression of a truth in a performance' (Stenhouse 1988: 47). Teaching needs technique, so we might say, but the technique is never more than a means for enhancing one's teacherly artistry. Improving teaching – improving one's own teaching – is therefore a matter of 'the development of understanding expressed in performance: understanding of the nature of knowledge expressed in the art form of teaching and learning' (Stenhouse 1988: 50).

The final point Stenhouse makes is for teachers to work together in the pursuit of enhancing their artistry. 'I can exercise my art in secret, or even in a small group of consenting adults', Stenhouse writes, but 'if I want the support of a movement, I need to make alliances and develop some political power' (Stenhouse 1988: 48). In this context Stenhouse mentions the 'teacher-as-researcher' movement in Britain, suggesting that ideally universities and colleges of education should work together with teacher groups. What is required for this to happen, so Stenhouse argues (and we shouldn't forget that he is writing in the beginning of the 1980s), 'is that [universities] break the stranglehold of the "psycho-statistical and nomothetic paradigm" of educational research' (Stenhouse 1988: 48). Stenhouse proposes case study as a much more appropriate 'form' for enhancing one's art, also because it 'turns one toward one's professional work rather than away from it' – a 'gesture' he also recommends for teachers' further study and development. His ideal – which, as he concedes, may be 'so radical that I may not be communicating it' (Stenhouse 1988: 50) – is for the emergence of communities of teachers 'whose attention is primarily focused on the art of teaching', just as 'a company of actors does' (Stenhouse 1988: 50). This means that any inquiry that may take place should express itself 'in performance of his or her art rather than (or as well as) in a research report (Stenhouse 1988: 51).

Concluding Comments: Reclaiming the Artistry of Teaching

In this chapter I have tried to make the case for seeing teaching as an art and for the importance of putting the artistry of teachers at the very centre of our understanding of what teaching is about. I have tried to make this case in a clear and in a sense rather 'basic' manner. I have done so by setting out the main characteristics of teaching, by reconstructing Aristotle's insights about the domain of the 'variable' and the roles of (the art of) *poiesis* and (the art of) *praxis* in this domain, and by exploring insights from Lawrence Stenhouse about the particular artistry of teaching. In one way I would say that the case is clear and straightforward and difficult to contest; but in another way I am acutely aware that many forces in contemporary educational theory, research, policy and practice are strongly moving or have already strongly moved into the opposite direction, that is, constructing teaching as a 'delivery system' and making sure that the delivery of the desired 'outcomes' is done in the most effective and efficient way which, so it is claimed, requires that teaching becomes evidence-based.

While such arguments sound neat and attractive – also because they often come with the promise that they can 'fix' education – they amount, in my view, to a misunderstanding but also a misrepresentation of the complexities of education and the work of teachers. Whereas Lawrence Stenhouse was still able to point a finger at researchers based in universities as having a problematic conception of what 'real' research was supposed to be, in our times I am worried that many teachers have actually adopted the agricultural logic of interventions and outcomes as the way to engage with and enhance their own practice. In this sense the ambition to reclaim the artistry of teaching is not just directed against particular strands of policy and research but also entails a difficult but nonetheless important conversation with the teaching profession itself – and to speak in the singular here is perhaps no longer adequate.

I am also aware that my case for 'reclaiming' refers back to older discussions and older scholarship, and may, in this sense, be perceived as a nostalgic move; a longing for a past that no longer exists and also no longer should exist because 'the times have moved on'. In response I would like to suggest that 'the times' may move on, but that there is always the need for us to judge whether 'the times' are moving in a desirable or in a problematic direction. This point is not just political, but it is, in my view, also profoundly educational. After all, parents who just say 'yes' to anything their children want will most likely turn them into spoilt brats, rather than helping them to come into a relationship with their desires and acknowledge that not everything that 'arrives' as a desire is automatically desirable. Education has, in other words, always also a 'duty to resist', as Philippe Meirieu has called it (see Meirieu 2007). Rather than just keeping up with 'the times', there may be good reasons for teachers to see themselves as 'untimely' professionals, as professionals who are 'out of time' (on this idea see Kelchtermans 2012), precisely so that they can keep a perspective on all the desires that policy makers, politicians, researchers, but also parents and students and society at large project onto education. In this regard, reclaiming the artistry of teaching may be the very act of resistance education may need in order to keep a sense of direction in turbulent times.

Acknowledgements

An earlier version of Chapter 1 was published as Biesta, G. (2023). Reclaiming the artistry of teaching. In R. Tierney, F. Rizvi, K. Ercikan & G. Smith (Eds), *The international encylopedia of education (4th edition). Section 4: Teachers lives, work and their professional preparation* (Ed. D. Mayer) (pp. 648–54). Oxford: Elsevier. https://doi.org/10.1016/B978-0-12-818630-5.04034-3

References

Aristotle (1980), *The Nicomachean Ethics*, Oxford: Oxford University Press.

Ball, S.J. (2012), *Global Education Inc.*, London/New York: Routledge.

Benner, D. (2015), *Allgemeine Pädagogik. Eine systematisch-problemgeschichtliche Einführung in die Grundstruktur pädagogischen Denkens und Handelns. 8. Auflage*, Weinheim: Beltz/Juventa.

Biesta, G. (2009), 'Good Education in an Age of Measurement: On the Need to Reconnect with the Question of Purpose in Education', *Educational Assessment, Evaluation and Accountability*, 21 (1): 33–46.

Biesta, G. (2010), *Good Education in an Age of Measurement: Ethics, Politics, Democracy*, Boulder, CO: Paradigm Publishers.

Biesta, G. (2015), 'Resisting the Seduction of the Global Education Measurement Industry: Notes on the Social Psychology of PISA', *Ethics and Education*, 10 (3): 348–60.

Biesta, G. (2016), 'Improving Education through Research? From Effectiveness, Causality and Technology, to Purpose, Complexity and Culture', *Policy Futures in Education*, 14 (2): 194–210.

Biesta, G. (2020), 'Risking Ourselves in Education: Qualification, Socialisation and Subjectification Revisited', *Educational Theory*, 70 (1): 89–104.

Biesta, G. and B. Stengel (2016), 'Thinking Philosophically about Teaching', in D.H. Gittomer and C.A. Bell (eds), *Handbook of Research on Teaching, Fifth Edition*, 7–68, Washington, DC: AERA.

Carr, W. (1987), 'What Is an Educational Practice?', *Journal of Philosophy of Education*, 21 (2): 163–75.

D'Agnese, V. (2017), *Reclaiming Education in an Age of PISA: Challenging OECD's Educational Order*, London/New York: Routledge.

Davis, A. (2017), 'It Worked There. Will It Work Here? Researching Teaching Methods', *Ethics and Education*, 12 (3): 289–303.

Eisner, E. (2002), 'From Episteme to Phronesis to Artistry in the Study and Improvement of Teaching', *Teaching and Teacher Education*, 18 (4): 375–85.

Hattie, J. and S. Nepper Larsen (2020), *The Purposes of Education: A Conversation between John Hattie and Steen Nepper Larsen*, London/New York: Routledge.

Hogan, A. and G. Thompson, eds. (2021), *Privatisation and Commercialisation in Public Education. How the Public Nature of Schooling Is Changing*, London/New York: Routledge.

Holmes, D., S.J. Murray, A. Perron and G. Rail (2006), 'Deconstructing the Evidence-Based Discourse in Health Science: Truth, Power and Fascism', *International Journal of Evidence Based Healthcare*, 4 (3): 180–6.

James, W. (1899), *Talks to Teachers on Psychology: And to Students on Some of Life's Ideals*, New York: Henry Holt.

Kelchtermans, G. (2012), *De Leraar als (On)Eigentijdse Professional. Reflecties over de 'Moderne Professionaliteit Van Leerkrachten,' Van Leerkrachten*, Den Haag: Onderwijsraad.

King-Rice, J. (2003), *Teacher Quality: Understanding the Effectiveness of Teacher Attributes*, Washington, DC: Economic Policy Institute.

McKinsey & Co. (2007), *McKinsey Report: How the World's Best Performing School Systems Come Out on Top*. Available online: https://www.bing.com/sear

ch?q=McKinsey+Report%3A+How+the+world%27s+best+performing+school+
   systems+come+out+on+top.&cvid=ce9e2544fd98491082e83d5975a00c7b&aq
   s=edge..69i57.317j0j4&FORM=ANAB01&PC=U531.
Meirieu, P. (2007), *Pédagogie: Le Devoir de Résister*, Issy-les-Moulineaux: Éditions
   Sociales Françaises.
OECD (2005), *Teachers Matter: Attracting, Developing and Retaining Effective
   Teachers*, Paris: OECD.
Reid, W.A. (1999), *Curriculum as Institution and Practice: Essays in the
   Deliberative Tradition*, Mahwah, NJ, & London: Lawrence Erlbaum.
Schwab, J.J. (1969), 'The Practical: A Language for Curriculum', *The School
   Review*, 78: 1–23.
Sellar, S., G. Thompson and D. Rutkowski (2017), *The Global Education Race:
   Taking the Measure of PISA and International Testing*, Edmonton: Brush
   Education.
Slavin, R. (2002), 'Evidence-Based Educational Policies: Transforming Educational
   Practice and Research', *Educational Researcher*, 31 (7): 15–21.
Stenhouse, L. (1988), 'Artistry and Teaching: The Teacher as Focus of Research and
   Development', *Journal of Curriculum and Supervision*, 4 (1): 43–51.
Thomas, G. (2021), 'Experiment's Persistent Failure in Education Inquiry, and Why
   It Keeps Failing', *British Educational Research Journal*, 47 (3): 501–19.
Van Manen, M. (1991), *The Tact of Teaching: The Meaning of Pedagogical
   Thoughtfulness*, Albany, NY: SUNY Press.
Van Manen, M. (1995), 'Herbart und der Takt im Unterricht', in S. Hopmann
   and K. Riquarts (eds), *Didaktik und/oder Curriculum. Grundprobleme einer
   international vergleichenden Didaktik*, 61–80, Weinheim: Beltz.

CHAPTER TWO

Teaching under the Spectre of a New Industrial Revolution

Stephen Sowa

Introduction

In the previous chapter, an eloquent case was made for reconceiving teaching as an art as opposed to a science. While recent arguments for and against conceptualizing teaching as a science have generated valuable insights, these studies have largely analysed problems in their abstract configuration rather than scrutinizing the historical developments shaping schooling and teaching (Biesta this volume, Chapter 1; Roediger 2013; Stenhouse 1988). This is not to say that these studies have ignored contemporary trends in educational policy and research. But as teaching is an activity that has been and remains intimately tied to the institution in which it commonly occurs (e.g. school system), to analyse the conceptual foundations of teaching, both actual and ideal, it is equally important to attend to the historic and institutional conditions that have and continue to shape teaching.

Contemporary organizational practices and conceptions of schooling and teaching have roots dating back at least to the establishment of mass schooling during the nineteenth century (Davis, Conroy and Clague 2020; Tyack and Cuban 1995). Presently, conceptions of schooling and teaching are evolving as new socio-economic conditions and technologies emerge. This includes conceptual and policy responses to predictions of a new Industrial Revolution and advances in artificial intelligence (Doucet et al. 2018; OECD 2023). Reflecting upon these historic and emerging socio-economic conditions, I provide a broader analysis of teaching using a four-part argument.

Part one explains how a mass production logic for schooling and teaching was established during the initial phases of the Industrial Revolution. Part two then shows how this logic is being repurposed in response to recent predictions concerning the world of work. Part three details the problems for teaching resulting from a mass production logic. Part four then responds to these identified problems by detailing a typology for the artistry in teaching. This four-part argument begins with an analysis of the development of mass schooling, primarily in Great Britain and the United States. Although the points made in this first part are not necessarily generalizable to other country contexts, because of the substantial geo-political influence of Great Britain during the nineteenth century and the United States in the twentieth century, these two countries have significantly shaped the trajectory of schooling in many countries across the world.

A Mass Production Logic for Schooling and Teaching

The Industrial Revolution marked a profound moment in the evolution of human social organization and economic arrangements. Dated from around 1760 to 1840, the Industrial Revolution was initiated by the construction of railroads and the invention of steam power (Schwab 2017). These innovations gave rise to mechanical production processes for the first time. Subsequent technological developments led to a second phase in the Industrial Revolution. By the end of the nineteenth century, mass production was made possible through the introduction of electricity and the assembly line (Schwab 2017). At this time industrializing countries such as Great Britain required a workforce that was approximately 80 per cent manual labour and 20 per cent professional (Becker, Hornung and Woessmann 2011). With large numbers of people transitioning from agrarian lifestyles to work in new industrial centres, an imperative arose to develop a well-disciplined workforce possessing physical skills and mental capacities corresponding to the demands of the industrial economy (Kliebard 1999).

During this period of rapid socio-economic change, nation-states in Western Europe began developing systems of mass schooling from the late eighteenth and into the nineteenth century (Davis, Conroy and Clague 2020). Responding to skill demands coming from industry, mass schooling during the nineteenth century placed increasing emphasis on vocational subjects alongside literacy and arithmetic, including textiles, metals and other trades (Becker, Hornung and Woessmann 2011; Caruso 2015). In the United States, the prioritization of vocational subjects and skills tied into its period of accelerated industrialization and expansion of mass schooling from the 1870s to the 1910s. Summarizing this period Kliebard (1999: xiv) explains that 'job training as an educational ideal, beginning with the drive to install manual training in American schools and proceeding to vocational education and vocationalization ... incorporates the idea that the curriculum as a whole, not just a part of it, exists for the purpose of preparing students to get and hold jobs'.

The institutionalization of mass schooling in industrial societies necessitated the teaching of large groups of children who had been brought together from across the country (Caruso 2015; Davis, Conroy and Clague 2020). To educate large numbers of pupils a systematization of classroom instruction was considered important by government officials and inspectors (Caruso 2015). In Great Britain, as reflected in the reports published by the government's Committee of Council on Education between the 1840s and the 1880s, an emphasis on well-ordered schools was underpinned by a rationale of securing learning outcomes through efficiently organizing educational space and time to manage the largest number of pupils (Committee of Council on Education 1842–89). Competent teaching was often understood as the 'production of good classroom and institutional order' and a response to the 'technical imperatives of the workplace and of ideological and political concerns generated by industrialization and urbanization' (Grace 1985: 7). A drive to massify schooling thus became closely intertwined with a production-like mentality to efficiently generate learning outcomes to meet growing industrial demands.

Whereas character and moral education were afforded a high priority by school inspectors in the 1840s (Grigg 2021), by the 1880s, following a new payment by results era, encapsulated in the Revised Code of 1862, schooling had become significantly incentivized by and focused on, managing attendance rates and achieving examination success in reading, writing and arithmetic (Arnold 1908). With learning outcome measures given elevated importance, the British government's school inspectorate, Her Majesty's Inspectorate of Schools, increasingly viewed teaching quality through the narrow lens of exam results and teachers' excellence in terms of adherence to predefined criteria (e.g. 'modelling professional behaviours' and 'maintaining an orderly classroom conducive to learning') (Grigg 2021: 766). These institutional developments began to cement mass production norms for the organization of schools and set narrow limits within which teaching could proceed. Even the Inspector of Schools, in his observations of elementary schools from 1852 to 1882, repeatedly reported that the results-driven era had led to a 'mechanical turn to the school teaching' and was 'trying to the intellectual life of a school' (Arnold 1908: 112–13).

Systems of mass schooling thus began to converge around a certain kind of organizational logic. To efficiently manage large groups of students and produce measurable outcomes, standardized ways of organizing schools became widely adopted and quickly taken for granted (Tyack and Cuban 1995). In maintaining orderly classrooms and adhering to predefined quality criteria, teaching became increasingly subject to proceduralization. That is, teachers tended to routinely follow established organizational conventions, including the organization of classroom space and time, with diminished conscious consideration of their educational merits (Tyack and Cuban 1995). This proceduralization served the efficient production of learning outcomes – particularly outcomes with work-related value (Caruso 2015; Grace 1985).

A crucial reason in support of the claim that a mass production logic underlies schooling and teaching is to note the remarkable continuity in the way schools have been organized since the end of the nineteenth century. As Tyack and Cuban (1995: 85) elucidate in their book reviewing the history of public school reform, 'the basic grammar of schooling, like the shape of classrooms, has remained remarkably stable over the decades … little has changed in the ways that schools divide time and space, classify students and allocate them to classrooms, splinter knowledge into "subjects", and award grades and "credits" as evidence of learning'.

Such continuity for over a century implies the early consolidation of organizational habits and norms. As these habits became ingrained and taken for granted, they turned into unspoken rules which set bounds to the organization and operations of schools and teachers (Tyack and Cuban 1995). Similar to the way people speak without being conscious of following the rules of grammar or employ deductive reasoning without being aware of following the rules of formal logic, the logic of mass schooling need not be consciously recognized by school management or teachers for it to operate efficiently (Eisner 2003; Tyack and Cuban 1995). The logical conditions underlying mass schooling and teaching can be summarized thusly: (1) the securing of predictable learning outcomes and credentialization; (2) efficient school organization concerned with massification; and (3) standardization of schooling procedures (Davis, Conroy and Clague 2020).

This argument for a mass production logic does not imply schools are a mirror image of industrial factories or solely determined by economic forces. The history of schooling and conceptions of teaching have been shaped by many factors. These include nation-states projecting their ideals, class conflicts, religious and moral philosophies, scientific theories, applications of technologies and unique socio-political influences across different countries (Davis, Conroy and Clague 2020; Grigg 2021). Nonetheless, if other commonly cited explanatory factors were principally responsible for the state of contemporary schooling, such as the direct application of experimental science or political developments such as neoliberal reforms in education, then it would be reasonable to suppose that significant changes would have occurred to the prevailing form of school organization in the intervening decades since the end of the nineteenth century. Yet, this has not been the case. This is not to say that there has been an absence of innovations in mass schooling. Innovations were indeed tried out. For example, flexible scheduling and class sizes, variable-space classrooms, team teaching and individualized instruction. But such innovations tended to fade out or were often hybridized within the existing delivery system (Tyack and Cuban 1995).

Recent global education policy has largely been characterized by reforms that align with a mass production logic. These reforms include the rise of a standardized testing culture across national education systems and international attempts to monitor and quantify educational inputs and learning outcomes using the Programme for International Student Assessment (PISA) and Global Education Monitoring Reports (Alexander 2015; Biesta this volume, Chapter 1). Efforts to define and raise educational quality have focused global attention on a narrow range of measurable learning outcomes rather than attending to the intricate processes of teaching (Alexander 2015). A production logic is also consistent with trends during the twentieth and twenty-first centuries to prioritize experimental evidence and evidence-based policymaking in education (Thomas 2021). The recurring emphasis on experimentally validated teaching interventions derives from a logic that prioritizes the securing of predictable outcomes and prescribed procedures for teachers to implement.

In summary, it has been argued that a mass production logic for schooling was established during the initial phases of the Industrial Revolution as certain organizational habits and norms were consolidated and came to function as unspoken rules. Moving forward with this understanding, part two of the argument examines predictions for a new phase in the Industrial Revolution and proposed educational responses to it. In doing so I consider how a production logic for schooling and teaching might proceed or be challenged.

Teaching in a New Industrial Age

The last decade has seen various influential voices spanning intergovernmental organizations, big business and academia claim that a new industrial age is beginning to unfold (Brynjolfsson and McAfee 2014; Frey and Osborne 2017; Schwab 2017). Following on from the third phase in the Industrial Revolution, which began in the 1960s with developments in electronics, this purported new phase has been varyingly referred to as the Fourth Industrial Revolution, Industry 4.0 and the Second Machine Age (Brynjolfsson and McAfee 2014; Schwab 2017). What makes this fourth phase distinct is the development and integration of cyber and physical systems in increasingly sophisticated ways (Schwab 2017). New technologies based on machine learning, mobile robotics and artificial intelligence are at the forefront of this change (Frey and Osborne 2017). Some suggest these technologies will radically alter production and consumption patterns, significantly changing how human beings partake in work, entertainment and education (Brynjolfsson and McAfee 2014; Schwab 2017).

In response to these predictions of a new industrial age, a growing number of countries are devising revised forms of education and teaching (Bazić 2017; Gleason 2018). Unlike early phases of the Industrial Revolution, the imperative is no longer to supply a workforce equipped for routine or manual labour-intensive work. Rather, an emerging imperative, arising from the projected automation of routine and some non-routine tasks, is for a workforce possessing more domain-general skills such as creativity and social intelligence (Frey and Osborne 2017), skills and tasks that cannot be easily carried out by advanced algorithms. It is the production of domain-general skills and meta-level learning outcomes that is increasingly attracting the attention of educational policymakers, including learning-to-learn as an essential capacity (Bazić 2017; OECD 2023). In one of the leading books on the subject, with forewords from the chairman of the World Economic Forum and the director for Education and Skills at the OECD, it is argued that education should support students in 'developing profoundly human skills such as leadership, socio-emotional intelligence and critical thinking … to impart students with a new flexible and adaptable mindset about learning' (Doucet et al. 2018: 1–2).

Proposed instructional approaches for teaching in the Fourth Industrial Revolution include various learner-centred approaches such as problem-based learning and experiential learning (Ally 2019; Doucet et al. 2018). These approaches are advocated on the grounds that they are evidence-based and well-specified to impart twenty-first-century skills and self-regulated learning among students in a predictable manner (Doucet et al. 2018). For similar reasons, classroom space is to be organized in such a way as to ensure group learning and project work (Stehlik 2018). A competence-based curriculum is thought of as being important for promoting transferable skills, interdisciplinary thinking and taking students beyond the foundational subjects of language, mathematics, science and ICT (Gleason 2018; World Economic Forum 2017). Further emphasis is placed on integrating digital competencies and new technology subjects into school curricula, including robotics, data analytics and cybersecurity (Gleason 2018; World Economic Forum 2017). The intent behind these proposed reforms is to prepare students for future workplaces and societies infused with advanced digital technologies and tasks requiring higher-order cognitive skills.

Many of these educational proposals, some of which have been trialled in the past, may follow a similar fate to historic innovations. They may tend to fade out or become hybridized within existing delivery structures (Tyack and Cuban 1995). While appearing to depart from past and contemporary school organizational norms and teaching practices in several respects, such as group work-friendly spatial arrangements and problem-centred rather than knowledge-based learning, these proposed innovations remain implicitly tied to mass production principles. There remains a tendency to standardize schooling procedures through pre-specified organization of educational space and time, curricular design and prescribed evidence-based instructional approaches. Justifications for these approaches continue to rely on experimental or scientific evidence and the securing of predictable outcomes for stakeholders (Doucet et al. 2018; OECD 2023). This repurposed production logic assumes that general and meta-level learning outcomes can be reliably produced at scale using approaches that are uniformly applied across contexts. It is only on the surface then that these proposed learner-centred reforms appear to offer something more adaptive than past schooling practices. In actuality, they similarly presuppose that pre-specified instructional or organizational approaches can be precisely tested and routinely applied irrespective of contextual intricacies.

A renewed focus on securing predictable learning outcomes is also evident in the proposals to incorporate advanced AI technologies into classrooms of the future. One of the most widely anticipated applications of AI technologies involves each learner having access to a highly intelligent, virtual personal tutor (Doucet et al. 2018). Future AI tutors are predicted to deliver highly personalized content and tailored feedback to each student which a human teacher may eventually find difficult (if not impossible) to match. The technological promise of very precisely monitoring learner progress and automatically adjusting content to fit students' ongoing cognitive development ties into a logic of producing learning outcomes in a predictable and efficient manner. Whilst the role of the teacher in most AI-informed visions of schooling is acknowledged to remain important due to the superior social and emotional support a human teacher still offers students (Ally 2019; Doucet et al. 2018), there looms a risk of proceduralizing teaching.

A teacher's active decision-making may enter less into educational processes (i.e. away from subtlety and purposively adjusting forms of content representation and organization according to circumstance). Instead, in service of securing learning outcomes that are pre-programmed into the AI technology, the teacher may be drawn into routinely filling in missing procedural inputs, such as giving socio-emotional prompts for learning. With the teacher's attention centred on bringing the AI-driven procedure to fruition, the teacher may become less alert to take advantage of emergent features embedded in the educational process. This includes openings for improvised meaning-making, fluidly responding to shifting group dynamics or attentively nurturing authentic relationships with students. As discussed more in the following parts, despite the promise of AI programs being highly adaptive to learners or educational contexts, I argue that the rule-governed nature of AI programs means that they will distinctively lack the capacity to employ forms of representation that fittingly convey contextualized meanings.

Thus far I have argued that conceptions of schooling and teaching for a new industrial age remain implicitly tied to a mass production logic. Yet, there is an evolving shift in focus from the production of domain-specific outcomes to general skills and meta-level learning outcomes. In the following section, I provide an analysis of the problems associated with a mass production logic for schooling and teaching.

Problems with a Mass Production Logic for Teaching

Conditions Underlying the Production of Learning Outcomes

For over a century, schools' production of learning outcomes has often proceeded on the basis of ensuring predictability for stakeholders and standardizing organizational procedures (Davis, Conroy and Clague 2020). On the surface such logical conditions do not raise obvious concerns. But they have come to limit the meaningful practice of teaching in various ways. As described in part one, organizational habits and norms for schooling, which were consolidated during the industrial era, have come to function as unspoken rules which teachers have tended to automatically follow (Tyack and Cuban 1995). Similar to the experience of factory workers working on a standardized and fast-moving assembly line, an automaticity and detachment from one's craft quickly sets in (Shepard 1977). Rather than being imaginative and attentive to the organizational, purposive, and emergent features of the teaching process, conditions in favour of automaticity leave teachers less flexible to employ new forms of organization or respond to the ever-changing circumstances and diverse human subjects that characterize educational encounters (Biesta this volume, Chapter 1; Eisner 2003).

Studies with both experienced and newly qualified teachers suggest practising schoolteachers often demonstrate qualities associated with automaticity. This is shown in the discrepancies between teachers' initial intentions to teach in a certain way and their actual teaching behaviours in the classroom. A longitudinal study with science and mathematics teachers revealed that despite initially reporting their teaching actions were student-centred, most teachers automatically reverted to teacher-centred actions during lessons and failed to discover and reconcile this discrepancy (Simmons et al. 1999). Similar inconsistencies are apparent in teachers' organization of educational space and time, which in practice tend to routinely (re)align with standard operating procedures (Doyle and Redwine 1974; Feldon 2007; Simmons et al. 1999). The point of issue here is not that teachers must entirely avoid automatic modes of thinking and acting (since this is impossible for any human being). Of concern are the institutionalized norms which move teachers towards a reflexive following of organizational and procedural conventions. The net result is the inhibiting of teachers' imaginative thinking and purposive educational action.

Another problem stemming from a production logic involves the tendency to reduce the complexities of teaching to well-specified interventions on the basis of securing predictable outcomes. There have been multiple trends in the twentieth and twenty-first centuries towards experimentally verified teaching interventions and evidence-based educational policymaking (Thomas 2021). Education policymaking for a new industrial age continues to elevate experimentally derived interventions, as well as promote AI-based tutoring approaches (Doucet et al. 2018; OECD 2023). While objections to experimental approaches in education have been previously raised (Stenhouse 1988; Thomas 2021), to expand on these critiques, a more general case is made against teachers automatically or rigidly following any well-specified procedure or rule-governed approach to teaching. In the case of experimentally derived teaching approaches, to attain construct validity and generalize in a contextually invariant way, the intervention (e.g. direct instruction or reciprocal teaching) needs to be tested without deviation from a well-defined series of steps (known as intervention fidelity). Under conditions presupposed by experimentalists, not necessarily what actually happens in real-world classrooms, teachers are then meant to 'string together' and rigidly implement these experimentally verified approaches. While other rule-governed approaches include routinized forms of school organization and AI programs delivering personalized tutoring.

To make a case against rule-governed approaches to teaching, I employ a prominent philosophical argument originally made against strong AI claims in computer science. This argument contends that an expert could instantiate any highly advanced rule-governed computer program, without additional causal powers equivalent to a human brain, and this program could still never achieve the conditions sufficient for producing the semantics necessary for human understanding (Searle 1980). Searle (1980) makes this case by describing a thought experiment named the 'Chinese Room' argument. Even though this argument was formulated several decades ago, the core claims remain applicable to modern forms of AI, such as those based on large language models (Coeckelbergh and Gunkel 2024). A simplified version of the argument is described here. I use first-person pronouns for better readability. First, imagine that I am locked in a windowless room and have been given batches of Chinese symbols. I understand no Chinese, written or spoken, and the Chinese symbols are meaningless to me. After receiving a set of rules/instructions in English from someone outside the room, I am able to follow the English instructions and give back appropriate Chinese symbols in response to questions written in Chinese writing.

Next, suppose the instructions I receive get so advanced and I get so good at following the instructions for manipulating Chinese symbols, that from the point of view of another person external to the room, my observable Chinese symbol outputs are indistinguishable from a native Chinese speaker. Yet, while I can give back Chinese symbols in a way that is observably equivalent to a native Chinese speaker, as acknowledged at the beginning, I still do not *understand* Chinese. In essence, though evidence for learning can be observed in this Chinese room scenario and it describes an intervention or rule-governed procedure with optimal inputs and outputs, because it does not introduce linguistic meanings or semantics into the instructional process, only syntax, it does not make a significant contribution to human understanding (Searle 1980).

What might this argument mean for teaching? Let's translate this thought experiment into educational terms. The optimal computer program/English instructions can be considered the experimentally derived or rule-governed instructional approach rigidly delivered by the teacher. The Chinese symbols are the subject matter to be taught. The person answering with Chinese symbols is the student, while the outsider observer measuring the quality of the Chinese outputs represents an objective assessment. When put in these educational terms, the argument points to, albeit does not definitely refute, the idea that even in cases where a teacher faithfully delivers an experimentally verified instructional approach or optimal rule-governed procedure, by rigidly following the specified steps of the decontextualized instructional approach, and without actively attending and responding to emergent happenings in the classroom, a teacher is unlikely to significantly evoke context-specific meanings which are crucial to human understanding and the educational process. Put another way, as human minds require both syntax and semantics to make sense of linguistic representations, including implicit and contextually derived meanings (Todorov 1986), teaching in a way that automatically or narrowly follows the syntax of interventions, even seemingly highly advanced interventions, will likely result in significant omissions of semantics or contextualized meanings.

Similar to myself in the Chinese room, a common observation of contemporary schooling is that students more often achieve surface-level learning. That is memorizing and giving back basic pieces of information on tests rather than achieving deep learning, that is, learning with understanding (Dolmans et al. 2016). This is not to say experimental or rule-governed teaching approaches do not contribute anything to understanding. Indeed, in response to the points hitherto raised, some may retort that because experimentally derived teaching approaches are tested in classrooms with real students, they are, to some extent, generalized instantiations of classroom semantics. Such a counterargument would hold significant weight if the meanings humans derive from language and other forms of representation were not highly dependent upon the unique contexts in which words and signs are interpreted. The meanings humans interpret from different forms of representation do not merely come from context-independent or direct expressions of meaning (i.e. as understood by linguistic rules). They notably include indirect or suggested meanings taken from their context, for example those based on prior circumstances, emergent situational features and unique interlocuters (Todorov 1986).

Contextualized or suggestive meanings are far from peripheral in education. To evoke educationally significant meanings in particular circumstances, it is not merely the prescribed instructional approach or content that matters, but equally the *form* of representation brought to bear by the teacher at specific moments (Eisner 2003; Stenhouse 1988). These include the use of tonal inflections to signify a key point, adjustments to spatial or temporal arrangements to situate students in immersive scenarios, conveying culturally resonant examples and timely interjections of silence. Despite the importance of semantics to education, prevailing conditions for schooling often disable teachers from purposively evoking contextual meanings and instead promote automatic following of standardized organizational procedures and prescribed interventions. This does not mean that teachers cannot benefit from learning about general principles of human psychology which are uncovered through experimentation or other empirical research. But it is the attempt to reduce teaching to well-specified procedures that poses a significant problem for a semantically rich education.

Teachers in the Production Process

While operating within mass production conditions, teachers are themselves impacted in various ways. In addition to the reduced autonomy discussed in the previous chapter (Biesta this volume, Chapter 1), a production logic conveys a strong expectation that adhering to organizational procedures or experimentally validated approaches will produce predictable outcomes. However, upon noticing partial or inconsistent results from the implementation of prescribed interventions (Thomas 2021), the teacher is put in a position to conclude they are at fault. This is a likely consequence because prescribed evidence-based interventions carry the expectation that they are a reliable means by which to secure desired outcomes irrespective of contextual variations. Thus, rather than there being room to accept the limitations of the prescribed interventions, the teacher is forced to conclude that *their* actions are the source of the problem and that they have failed to execute properly. By imposing unwarranted expectations on teachers and a heightened emphasis on securing outcomes, there is a risk of teachers feeling harried and guilty; accepting responsibility for all failures in learning (Scheffler 1960). These openings for negative self-attribution may compromise teachers' self-efficacy beliefs and realistic outcome expectations. Yet, both matter for self-expressive teaching and are positively associated with teachers' motivation and autonomy (Min 2019).

Learning Outcomes as the Primary Foci

Another set of problems associated with a mass production logic stem from a heightened focus on producing measurable learning outcomes. In response to recent predictions for the world of work, a shift in focus is taking place from producing domain-specific outcomes to general or meta-level learning outcomes (OECD 2023). While these learning outcomes are not necessarily unimportant for schools to attend to, in practice the institutional imperative to produce learning outcomes with measurable work-related value has often encroached on other domains of purpose (Grigg 2021). Frequently, a narrow band of measurable outcomes are treated as proxies for quality. This tends to direct teachers' efforts towards imparting content that is expected on standardized assessments rather than attending closely to the intricate processes of teaching (Alexander 2015). Beyond procedural questions, teaching also involves important and unavoidable moral considerations in both means and ends (Biesta this volume, Chapter 1).

There thus remain a wider range of values and purposes to attend to, those of relational, social, democratic and existential significance. Because different educational aims can sometimes be in competition, a teacher's professional judgement is required to manage trade-offs in purposes, balance curricular content and meet diverse stakeholder demands (Alexander 2015; Biesta this volume, Chapter 1). A frequently neglected purposive question for schools, particularly as discussion of a new industrial age grows, is whether teachers' actions should be directed towards preparing students for a predetermined vision of a future technological society or to guide students to shape the future anew. Both may be important and require balancing in judicious ways.

A Typology for the Artistry in Teaching

Up to this point I have explained a range of problems associated with a mass production logic for schooling and teaching. Given that some of these problems are strongly tied to historic and emerging institutional developments, a truly comprehensive solution will ultimately require mutually supportive actions across multiple levels of educational policymaking, management and practice. For the purpose of this chapter, I limit the scope of my response to reconceiving four fundamental features of teaching. To do this I bring together distinctive art-related concepts detailed by past scholars in combination with my personal contributions (see Biesta this volume, Chapter 1; Eisner 2003; Humphreys and Hyland 2002; Noddings 2018; Stenhouse 1988). These concepts cover imaginative, semantic, relational and judgement qualities of teaching which often remain obscured by a production logic. This serves as a valuable contribution to past scholarly efforts by unifying previously disparate ideas into a single classification system. In setting out a typology for the artistry in teaching, it is important to stress this conceptualization is not intended as a set of well-specified approaches for teachers to follow. It does, however, aim to elucidate a new language game, imagery and an indicative mode of thinking about the distinctive aspects of teaching.

Art of Imaginative Observation

In the initial phase of teaching, before engaging in any act, a teacher must observe and make sense of the educational reality before them. Unlike the work of a technician or a scientist who may directly observe their environment or phenomena, a teacher operates in a domain that is not readily reducible to direct observations or well-defined procedures. As Eisner (2003) explains, educational environments contain rapidly changing, interdependent and sometimes hidden features. Instead of reducing educational complexities to observable phenomena, the art of imaginative observation brings forth the educationally significant possibilities to the teacher's consciousness through their imagination. Teachers are call upon to imagine the educational process through the eyes of their audience. To picture the experiences students will resonate with such that they may stretch them beyond their comfort zone or even evoke surprise. When fuelled with insights from personal experience and empirical observations, a teacher's imagination can serve to visualize which courses of action are more or less likely to evoke meaningful responses from the human subjects they interact with. This artistry enables the teacher to anticipate moral issues of concern and envision how interrelated pedagogical acts can contribute to a wide range of educational purposes.

As brought out through the prior institutional analysis, a production logic often leads to automaticity and an oversight of contextual meanings. Conversely, imaginative observation promotes teachers' alertness to new possibilities for situated meaning-making. It is the art of playing out the educational hypotheticals. To imagine how alternative forms of organization and content representation will breathe new meanings into classroom life. This mode of thinking prompts teachers to transcend organizational norms and institutionalized routines to conceive of new forms of representation – making them curious to seek out different ideas and to ask new questions (Eisner 2003). The contextual meanings and unifying narratives that were once hidden can be pictured in the teacher's mind. A teacher can recognize uncertainties in their imagined educational scenarios and prepare contingencies accordingly. This art does not necessarily involve a rejection of scientific principles or schooling conventions. Instead, mediated through the teacher's imagination, there remains an openness to conceiving new combinations of established practices and pedagogical innovations according to circumstance.

Art of Purposive Evocation

After observing the educational situation and its imagined possibilities, the next phase in the teaching process is to act in such a way that expresses that which is educationally significant. A production logic often conditions teachers into routinely following organizational procedures or prescribed interventions, neglecting the emergent features and semantics embedded in unique educational contexts. This automaticity can instil a sense of detachment over their actions. Indeed, students can often notice when a teacher is on autopilot mode, inattentive to their responses and absentminded from the material they present. Conversely, if a teacher feels and exhibits a sense of ownership and conscious control over their teaching, this will likely be noticed and potentially modelled by students as they interact with a teacher who radiates a passion for their craft. Stenhouse (1988) notes this mental outlook can reinvigorate the desire of the teacher to improve their art. In this sense the art of purposive evocation has its source in the teacher, in *their* intentional act to evoke a cognitive or emotional response from their audience and accentuate its significance.

Teachers are not merely teaching students something, they are simultaneously teaching students *so what*. The subject matter a teacher presents is not perceived neutrally by the student. A teacher must, therefore, accentuate or gesture towards its significance using symbolically rich forms of representation and organization. It is not simply the content and prescribed instructional approach that matters then. But equally the *form* of representation brought to bear by the teacher. Eisner (2003) reminds us form and content are inextricably linked; by changing the intonation in a line of poetry one changes the poem's meaning. Teachers are required to bring together content and forms of representation in ways that are accessible to students and which evocatively signal values or ideas of educational significance. Both explicit and suggestive expressions of meaning can be evoked using language and other forms of representation (Todorov 1986). Suggestive meanings depend on the context (e.g. prior circumstances and unique interlocutor). Such meanings are evoked by the teacher in the sense that they associate something present, such as an idea or object in the classroom, with something absent. This serves to induce wonder about the world or one's inner self rather than a simple cognitive perception (Todorov 1986).

One of the most important ways of conveying suggestive meanings is through structuring students' school experience in the form of a narrative. Historically, schools have organized educational space, time, and curricula in a largely rigid and symbolically empty manner. In contrast, teachers and schools may consider framing students' educational experiences around a narrative. Sequencing and representing curricular as meaningful plot lines to actively partake in and encounter new ways of thinking and being. For example, this could mean building up to moments of suspense that surprise, spark curiosity or prompt divergent thinking. Educational space and time can also be purposely (re)organized to situate students in stories and narrative arcs that move them towards individually and collectively valued ends.

Art of Relational Accessibility

During the process of engaging with and evoking meaningful responses from students, teachers and students enter into certain kinds of relations. Noddings (2018) explains that teachers are called upon to be receptive and attuned to students' situational responses and self-expressions. Yet, within the conditions afforded by a mass production logic, an automaticity means that teachers are less attentive to students' spontaneous self-expressions. With a heightened focus on the efficient production of learning outcomes, teachers are disposed to act on students in an instrumentalist manner rather than being personally available to students in authentic and accessible ways. In contrast, the art of relational accessibility forefronts a teacher's intention to enter into mutually accessible relations with students – embodying a receptiveness to their responses. Teacher–student relationships involve a reciprocity of giving and receiving responses (Noddings 2018). This reciprocity is based on an underlying sense of trust in each other and the integrity of the educational process. Within this relationship the teacher is still implicitly understood to possess a certain authority. For this reason teacher–student trust must include the recognition that the teacher will not use their authority to engage in exploitive acts (Tom 1980).

In caring for the student a motivational displacement takes place from the teacher to the student as they will the good to be realized in the student (Noddings 2018). A teacher may equally show an openness to the contributions students bring to the educational encounter. They come to reassure the student that they are not being acted upon, but are being embraced as unique persons with something valuable to offer the educative process and the teacher themself. This is not to say that teachers should accept all forms of student behaviour. When exercises of authority and discipline are required, the teacher, through their demonstration of good character and trustworthiness, typically encourages students to return to reciprocal relations on the basis of their perceived qualities rather than being induced by the teacher's power or the status granted by the school institution (Macleod, MacAllister and Pirrie 2012).

Art of Contextualized Judgement

The final expression of teachers' artistry is the art of contextualized judgement. Within a mass production system, institutional conditions tend to limit a teacher's autonomy and professional judgement by directing their attention towards efficiently producing a narrow set of measurable learning outcomes (Alexander 2015). But as Biesta (this volume, Chapter 1) astutely notes, there nonetheless remain important moral and pragmatic considerations in both the means and ends of teaching. Because a teacher cannot cover all subject matter, value judgements must be made about what content to cover and when. This also applies when upholding certain standards of behaviour in the classroom. For these reasons the act of teaching cannot be treated as merely procedural or disconnected from the purposes of education. Teachers are required to weigh up and make trade-offs in competing educational purposes, balance curricular content and manage diverse stakeholder demands (Biesta this volume, Chapter 1).

Teachers must be mindful of the educational purposes in their actions. However, they should also not be rigidly attached to predefined aims when the possibility of better ones emerge (Eisner 2003). Teachers may at certain times need to surrender to what the work in progress suggests. In what Dewey (1938) referred to as flexible purposing, a teacher may judiciously apply their professional judgement to shift aims during the teaching process to opportunistically capitalize on emergent features in the classroom or explore new lines of enquiry with students (Eisner 2003). Many teaching acts and judgements are rapid and situational. They sometimes require intuitive thinking and improvisation (Humphreys and Hyland 2002), while at other moments they allow for a deliberative mode of decision-making. In making complex professional judgements, there is a need to reflect on the decisions made during the teaching process, including their moral quality and likely contribution to the overarching educational purposes. Considered collectively, the four forms of artistry making up this typology are closely interlinked. Teachers are called upon to move fluidly between these different kinds of artistry as the educational situation unfolds.

Conclusion

Upon reaching the climax of this chapter it may seem as though I have merely dressed up different features of teaching in pleasant metaphorical language. Indeed, what is the point of using the metaphor of art when considering teaching? In this analysis, taking into perspective historic and emerging developments in schooling, I have argued that there is a kind of imagistic impoverishment in the way we have and continue to view schooling and teaching. In serving a mass production logic, we are in a sense trapped in an automatic and symbolically vacuous mode of thinking that is often blind to the forms of representation and organization being employed in schools. What vibrant metaphors can do then is shake us out of our institutionalized habits and help to form powerful images of teaching in the mind of the teacher (Eisner 2003). By reframing the debate against teaching as a science, moving to a mass production conception, I have illuminated new problems and constructed a unified framework of concepts that illustrate the artistry in teaching. This typology serves as an initial reference point for teacher educators and teachers to engage in visualizing, articulating, trialling and reflecting on how the distinctive features of teaching can be artfully expressed.

References

Alexander, R. (2015), 'Teaching and Learning for All? The Quality Imperative Revisited', in S. McGrath and Q. Gu (eds), *Routledge Handbook of International Education and Development*, 138–52, New York: Routledge.

Ally, M. (2019), 'Competency Profile of the Digital and Online Teacher in Future Education', *International Review of Research in Open and Distributed Learning*, 20 (2): 303–18.

Arnold, M. (1908), *Reports on Elementary Schools 1852–1882*, London: Wyman and Sons.

Bazić, J. (2017), 'Trends in Societal and Educational Changes Generated by the Fourth Industrial Revolution', *Sociološki Pregled*, 51 (4): 526–46.

Becker, S., E. Hornung and L. Woessmann (2011), 'Education and Catch-Up in the Industrial Revolution', *American Economic Journal: Macroeconomics*, 3 (3): 92–126.

Brynjolfsson, E. and A. McAfee (2014), *The Second Machine Age: Work, Progress, and Prosperity in a Time of Brilliant Technologies*, New York: W. W. Norton.

Caruso, M. (2015), *Classroom Struggle*, Berlin: Peter Lang Verlag.

Coeckelbergh, M. and D.J. Gunkel (2024), 'ChatGPT: Deconstructing the Debate and Moving it Forward', *AI & Society*, 39: 2221–31.

Committee of Council on Education (1842–1899), *Minutes and Annual Reports*, London: HMSO.

Davis, R., J. Conroy and J. Clague (2020), 'Schools as Factories: The Limits of a Metaphor', *Journal of Philosophy of Education*, 54 (5): 1471–88.

Dewey, J. (1938), *Experience and Education*, New York: Free Press.

Dolmans, D., S. Loyens, H. Marcq and D. Gijbels (2016), 'Deep and Surface Learning in Problem-Based Learning: A Review of the Literature', *Advances in Health Sciences Education*, 21 (5): 1087–12.

Doucet, A., J. Evers, E. Guerra, N. Lopez, M. Soskil and K. Timmers (2018), *Teaching in the Fourth Industrial Revolution: Standing at the Precipice*, New York: Routledge.

Doyle, W. and J. Redwine (1974), 'Effect of Intent-Action Discrepancy and Student Performance Feedback on Teacher Behavior Change', *Journal of Educational Psychology*, 66 (5): 750–5.

Eisner, E. (2003), 'Artistry in Education', *Scandinavian Journal of Educational Research*, 47 (3): 373–84.

Feldon, D. (2007), 'Cognitive Load and Classroom Teaching: The Double-Edged Sword of Automaticity', *Educational Psychologist*, 42 (3): 123–37.

Frey, C. and M. Osborne (2017), 'The Future of Employment: How Susceptible Are Jobs to Computerisation?', *Technological Forecasting & Social Change*, 114 (C): 254–80.

Gleason, N. (2018), 'Introduction', in N. Gleason (ed), *Higher Education in the Era of the Fourth Industrial Revolution*, 1–11, Singapore: Springer Singapore.

Grace, G. (1985), 'Judging Teachers: The Social and Political Contexts of Teacher Evaluation', *British Journal of Sociology of Education*, 6 (1): 3–16.

Grigg, R. (2021), 'Ofsted Says We Are Outstanding: HMI Conceptions of Teaching Excellence in the Nineteenth- and Twentieth-Century Primary School', *British Journal of Educational Studies*, 69 (6): 753–71.

Humphreys, M. and T. Hyland (2002), 'Theory, Practice and Performance in Teaching: Professionalism, Intuition, and Jazz', *Educational Studies*, 28 (1): 5–15.

Kliebard, H. (1999), *Schooled to Work: Vocationalism and the American Curriculum, 1876–1946*, New York: Teachers College Press.

Macleod, G., J. MacAllister and A. Pirrie (2012), 'Towards a Broader Understanding of Authority in Student–Teacher Relationships', *Oxford Review of Education*, 38 (4): 493–508.

Min, M. (2019), 'School Culture, Self-Efficacy, Outcome Expectation, and Teacher Agency toward Reform with Curricular Autonomy in South Korea: A Social Cognitive Approach', *Asia Pacific Journal of Education*, 43 (4): 1–17.

Noddings, N. (2018), *Philosophy of Education*, New York: Routledge.

OECD (2023), 'OECD Future of Education and Skills: OECD Learning Compass 2030: A Series of Concept Notes', *OECD*. Available online: https://issuu.com/oecd.publishing/docs/e2030-learning_compass_2030-concept_notes?fr=xKAE9_zU1NQ (accessed 18 February 2025).

Roediger, H. (2013), 'Applying Cognitive Psychology to Education: Translational Educational Science', *Psychological Science in the Public Interest*, 14 (1): 1–3.

Scheffler, I. (1960), *The Language of Education*, Springfield: Charles C Thomas.

Schwab, K. (2017), *The Fourth Industrial Revolution*, New York: Portfolio Penguin.

Searle, J. (1980), 'Minds, Brains, and Programs', *Behavioral and Brain Sciences*, 3 (3): 417–24.

Shepard, J. (1977), 'Technology, Alienation, and Job Satisfaction', *Annual Review of Sociology*, 3: 1–21.

Simmons, P., A. Emory, T. Carter, T. Coker, B. Finnegan, D. Crockett and K. Labuda (1999), 'Beginning Teachers: Beliefs and Classroom Actions', *Journal of Research in Science Teaching*, 36 (8): 930–54.

Stehlik, T. (2018), *Educational Philosophy for 21st Century Teachers*, Cham: Springer International Publishing.

Stenhouse, L. (1988), 'Artistry and Teaching: The Teacher as Focus of Research and Development', *Journal of Curriculum and Supervision*, 4 (1): 43–51.

Thomas, G. (2021), 'Experiment's Persistent Failure in Education Inquiry, and Why It Keeps Failing', *British Educational Research Journal*, 47 (3): 501–19.

Todorov, T. (1986), *Symbolism and Interpretation*, New York: Cornell University Press.

Tom, A. (1980), 'Teaching as a Moral Craft: A Metaphor for Teaching and Teacher Education', *Curriculum Inquiry*, 10 (3): 317–23.

Tyack, D. and L. Cuban (1995), *Tinkering toward Utopia*, Cambridge, MA: Harvard University Press.

World Economic Forum (2017), 'Realizing Human Potential in the Fourth Industrial Revolution: An Agenda for Leaders to Shape the Future of Education, Gender and Work', *World Economic Forum*. Available online: http://www3. weforum.org/docs/WEF_EGW_Whitepaper.pdf (accessed 18 February 2025).

CHAPTER THREE

On Observing Two Pacific Island Poets Teach: Some Reflections on the 'vā' and the Artistry of Teaching

Shari Sabeti

Introduction

In response to current trends in educational policy and research which repeatedly posit the teacher as a technician employed to bring about certain 'effects' in their students, Biesta (Chapter 1, this volume) has called for a re-appraisal of teaching which acknowledges it as a complex, situated endeavour involving 'artistry'. Drawing on the Aristotelian concepts of poesis and praxis, he outlines the 'double art' of teaching as both 'educational craftsmanship' and 'educational wisdom' (Biesta, Chapter 1, this volume). Biesta aligns himself with others before him, notably Stenhouse (1988) and Eisner ([1984] 2005), who have made similar arguments about the necessity for a new discursive language about teachers and teaching centred on art or artistry. Their efforts to articulate this have involved reaching for an array of other, more specific, metaphors. For example, writing about the dominant scientific modes of understanding and researching the work of teachers, Stenhouse uses the imagery of the 'farmer' and his agricultural 'yield' to show how teaching is often talked about as a mechanistic activity leading to production. He contrasts this with a different metaphor which he argues is more attuned to the work of the teacher – that of the gardener, because teaching, like gardening, is about nurture, attention and intuition (Stenhouse 1988: 43–4). Eisner too insists on the need to move away from the scientific language of proposition, control and experiment, and acknowledge that teaching is a variable, qualitative activity requiring interpretation, judgement and sensibility. On one occasion he turns to a musical metaphor and writes:

> It is increasingly recognized that teaching in many ways is more like playing in a jazz quartet than following the score of a marching band. Knowing when to come in and take the lead, knowing when to bow out, knowing when to improvise are all aspects of teaching that follow no rule, they need to be felt.
>
> (Eisner 2005: 201)

Definitions of 'artistry', whilst pointing to notions such as 'creative skill' or 'workmanship', also hint at something that is *not* able to be captured in language: words and phrases such as 'talent', 'wizardry', 'virtuosity', 'flair' and 'a magic touch' abound in these definitions. This language also suggests that artistry is performative, something that is also implied by Eisner's jazz musician and Stenhouse, when he draws on another metaphor and makes a parallel with the work of actors (Stenhouse 1988: 50).

In this chapter I am interested in these notions of intuition and sensibility; in how teachers *feel their way* through their teaching. What is it that they pay attention to? What kinds of judgements are they making, and what is at stake in these? How do they themselves describe what they are doing? I explore these questions by drawing on ethnographic material collected as part of a project centred on exploring the legacy of the Scottish writer, Robert Louis Stevenson. The research involved collaborations with 'teaching artists' (Booth 2003: 5)[1] who, as part of a community-based participatory research approach (Stanton 2014), were asked to undertake a series of workshops with young people across locations relevant to Stevenson's legacy (Hawai'i, Sāmoa and Scotland). If teaching is like an artistic performance, then how do artists teach? Here I focus on the workshops of two Pacific Island performance poets: No'u Revilla and Selina Tusitala Marsh. I have picked these two artists for the simple reason that I admired their teaching: I believed I saw 'artistry' in it. What follows is my attempt to understand the impression they made on me; to draw out the qualities of the teaching I observed and appreciated.

Rather than bringing theories from outside the research context to frame this analysis, I take up an offer made by one of the artists themselves when they spoke to me about 'the vā as a teacher'. The vā in Samoan and other Pacific cultures is often described as 'the space between' (Wendt 1999) or the context in which relationships of different kinds unfold. The vā needs to be nurtured, kept alive and flowing for the interconnected web of relations that constitute life to continue. To speak of teaching as 'artistry' or to draw on metaphors about jazz and gardening might help to emphasize some of the neglected dimensions of the complex work that teachers do, but they also elide the fact that teaching is profoundly relational: it is something that happens *in the spaces between* the teacher, the student and the subject matter. The concept of vā is helpful here both because it foregrounds that relationality and because it is *not* a metaphor; it is part of the lived reality of Pacific peoples' lives. In order to emphasize its distinctiveness in the discussion section later in the chapter, I do briefly draw some comparisons with relational theories of teaching which exist in the Euro-American research literature. However, for the most part I take my cue from the poet: I *work (think) with* the concept of vā to explore the insights it can provide about teaching and/as artistry.

In making my argument, I also set myself a writing challenge: that of trying to represent or describe the vā that I observed being nurtured in these poets' workshops. In this I am prompted also by Eisner who called for educational researchers to become 'intimate with practice', 'capture nuance' and 'develop methods of inquiry that do not squeeze the educational life out of what we study' ([1984] 2005: 93). For him, ethnographic approaches and 'thick description' (Geertz 1973) came closest to doing this within the social sciences. But they also did not go far enough: he pushed for more artistic, more courageous modes of inquiry and representation. More specifically, I draw on the methodology of 'portraiture' (Lawrence Lightfoot and Hoffman 1997) and employ vignettes to present portraits of Revilla and Marsh's teaching artistry. If, as Biesta (Chapter 1, this volume) has argued, teaching is both misunderstood and misrepresented, then what follows is an attempt to understand, *and* represent, it differently.

The va¯ and 'teu le va¯' – Looking after the Space in Between

The concept of vā exists across a number of Pacific Island (specifically, 'Polynesian') cultures and is alternately transcribed as vā (Sāmoa), vā/va'a/vaha (Tonga) and wā (Hawai'i, Aotearoa). The writer Albert Wendt has described the vā as central to Samoan views of reality in which everything, both animate and inanimate, is related

> Vā is the space between, the betweenness, not empty space, not space that separates, but space that relates, that holds separate entities and things together in the Unity-that-is-All, the space that is context, giving meaning to things. The meanings change as the relationships and the contexts change.
>
> (Wendt 1999: 402)

Wendt also underlines the need to nurture the vā.

A well-known Samoan expression is 'Ia teu le vā'—cherish, nurse, care for the vā, the relationships. This is crucial in communal cultures that value group unity more than individualism, that perceive the individual person, or creature, or things in terms of group, in terms of vā, relationships.

(Wendt 1999: 402)

I'uogafa Tuagalu (2022) draws out two interrelated notions of vā in the Samoan context which help nuance the concept further: the *vā fealoaloa'i* (social space) and *vā tapua'i* (sacred space). The former 'is about knowing one's position in relation to others', including the need to attend to 'social responsibilities towards, and communication protocols with', those others (Tuagalu 2022: 39). In a village setting in Sāmoa today, these others would include kin and relations formed through chiefly hierarchies, or ones' position in a village or district. *Vā tapuai'i* (sacred space), on the other hand, has to be 'activated via prayer or ritual' (Tuagalu 2022: 40). It involves actions that sanctify the space between people and their God, or between bodies which are not in physical contact with each other. The example Tuagalu gives is of prayers that might be made for the safe return of travellers: even though they are geographically distant, the travellers and supporters are in what might be called 'contagious magical contact' (Tuagalu 2022: 40).

The vā offers a different understanding of both space and relationship from those we might be familiar with in a Euro-American context. First, the space of the vā is not a literal one; nor is it space which divides individuals from each other; rather it is a space of relation. 'Everything is related,' writes Wendt, 'That connectedness is holistic, so to alter any part of it alters the whole Unity, re-transfigures it' (Wendt 2015: 34). In Pacific worldviews relations between people, and between people and things, are already there; they have ontological precedence over the individual entities that they relate (see Strathern 1988). Indeed, these entities are constituted *by the relations*, rather than the other way around as our understanding of the word 'relationship' – a bridge between two pre-existing entities – might suggest. This also explains why the focus is on *looking after the relation*, and not the people or objects that relate. To 'teu le vā', to look after the vā, is not an act of care for an individual but for constantly shifting context in which those individuals are held together.

The vā and the need to 'teu le vā' have been important concepts in a range of scholarly work by Pasifika academics, including those working in education (see Anae 2010; Māhina 2008; Reynolds 2016; Thaman 2002, 2007; Ualesi 2024). In these the vā is most often used as a way of emphasizing the pivotal importance of relationships (with both students and their families) in the education of diasporic Pacific Islanders. To my knowledge, however, the concept of vā has not been applied to a close-up study of *teaching*. The vā, in *both* the social and sacred iterations outlined by Tuagalu, I will argue, provide a lens through which we can re-describe the act of teaching. Importantly so in the context of teaching, the vā is both dynamic *and* structured: it contains hierarchies, protocols and responsibilities. In the following sections I outline the context of these observations before going on to describe my own methodological approach in detail.

Research Context

The teaching that I focus on in this chapter formed part of a broader series of workshops undertaken by visual artists and poets for a three-year research project called 'Remediating Stevenson'.[2] The project provides Indigenous Pacific writers and artists opportunities to creatively re-work some of Stevenson's Pacific stories within a contemporary context. The arts workshops provided a means through which the artists collaborated with, and consulted, the intended audience of their future work – students and teachers in school contexts across three locations pertinent to Stevenson's travels and writing: Hawai'i, Sāmoa and Scotland.

The two poets discussed here, No'u Revilla from Hawai'i and Selina Tusitala Marsh, who is of Samoan ancestry and lives in Aotearoa New Zealand, delivered creative writing workshops to young people in schools. Revilla's workshops took place in Honolulu and Marsh's in both Sāmoa and Scotland. The portraits of their practice later in the chapter focus on a series of workshops by Revilla in which she worked with students on writing 'Aloha Odes', and a workshop by Marsh in North Berwick, Scotland which engaged students directly with Stevenson and with the Samoan language. Both poets have positions within higher education contexts where they teach literature and/or creative writing. Marsh also had considerable experience of working with school-aged children through her outreach work in Aotearoa New Zealand.

Writing Portraits: Bringing Artistry into View

As a researcher, my dominant (and preferred) methodological approach is an ethnographic one. Textbook ethnography involves the building of relationships over time, engagement in participant observation and the conduct of informal interviews; it involves a lot of writing – fieldnotes, transcription, description and argument (Emerson et al. 2011; Hammersely and Atkinson 2019). As a former student, and teacher, of literature, its emphasis on writing as a mode of collecting and working with research materials appeals to me. As does its slowness ('doing ethnography'[3] properly takes time), its attention to everyday practice, its carefulness and its ease with its own subjectivity. The project I am discussing here aligns with previous projects which have also involved ethnographies of artists' teaching and of creative practice and process (see Sabeti 2019, 2023). As well as being an ethnographer, I am a teacher educator; before that, I had a career in teaching in secondary schools for which I, of course, had to undertake an education in how to teach. I have spent – and continue to spend – a lot of my time observing, reflecting on and writing – in a number of different modes – about teaching. These experiences, as well as the fact that evaluating teaching is part of my job, inevitably lead me to believe that 'I know good teaching when I see it'.[4] In a project focused on revisiting Stevenson's work and biography in collaboration with Indigenous Pacific artists, the fact that I am not a Pacific Islander, but also not white, is also worth noting here, even if I do not have time to dwell on it at any length. It positioned me in particular ways in my relationships with these poets.

The next two sections of this chapter are 'portraits' of two poets teaching. In order to write these, I am drawing on my fieldnotes, reflections, informal interviews and conversations; I am also drawing on 'portraiture' methodology (Lawrence Lightfoot and Hoffman Davis 1997). Portraiture methodology was originally conceived as a response to precisely the kind of 'scientism' in educational research criticized by Stenhouse, Eisner and Biesta, as well as the tendency of educational researchers to document failure, rather than what was 'good' in education. It situates itself within phenomenological and ethnographic paradigms but also pushes these into the aesthetic realm, aspiring to speak to audiences beyond academia. The portraitist must produce:

> subtle description in context [...] developing a convincing and authentic narrative [which] requires careful, systematic, and detailed description developed through watching, listening to, and interacting with the actors over a sustained period of time, the tracing and interpretation of emergent themes, and the piecing together of these themes into an aesthetic whole.
>
> (Lightfoot and Davis 1997: 12)

Rather than writing *about* the poets in these portraits, I write *to* them. The decision to do so is based on a number of reasons: methodological, personal and conceptual. First, it emphasizes my subjectivity – this is what *I* see/saw – which is, as I have outlined above, important here. Secondly, the second person is an 'address' to the poets. An address opens the possibility of response – keeps them (stylistically at any rate) – as active subjects, rather than objects of what I describe. Thirdly, it brings to the foreground again the notion of vā; it highlights the vā between me (as researcher/teacher) and them (as poets, colleagues, teachers, friends), as well as attempting to convey the vā of their teaching. The portraits reflect my growing relationship with both of them over time: in the case of Marsh, this developed over extended and intense periods of time working on the project in both Sāmoa and Scotland. We stayed in the same place, took morning walks together; we shared meals and jokes. My relationship with Revilla extended over a week or so in her home city of Honolulu. There was nevertheless a strong sense of connection which emerged particularly during our interview. In this interview she also articulated her relationship to Marsh, whom she had never met in person at the time, as someone she considered as a role model.

When it came to composing the portraits, I followed a layering process. I relied first on my memory; in this, I assumed, were the kernels of what had affected me most deeply, or that I had thought most important. As I wrote, I remembered more details so added these too. The relationships – between the poets and their students, between myself and the poets – unfolded through the process. Secondly, I consulted my fieldnotes: what had I forgotten, how did these notes revise what I had written down? What were the differences between the first and second stage of writing; which details did I want to keep and which to remove? Why? I then turned to my interviews with the poets. In these we discussed a number of issues but their teaching, based on my observations, constituted a large part of our conversation. I have drawn threads from these into the portraits and I have also used them in the discussion which follows. Finally, I tried to finesse the portraits with minor revisions: have I captured the vā successfully? How is my reflection on their teaching also explicating the vā? What has changed over time and space, between then and now, there and here?

First Portrait: 'Love poems we wrote' – No'u Revilla[5]

On a humid, cloudy morning in Honolulu, I stand in the doorway of a school looking out into the car park where a grey SUV has just drawn up. You step out: tall, composed. You hold your head up high. Your hair is arranged neatly in a dark bun; it bobs gently as you open the back door, take out a bag, some books. You look over at me, catch my eye and smile. I do not recognise you. Even though I've watched videos on your website and seen your photograph; even though I've read your words and I've written words about you. I think you are another teacher coming to work for the day.

Then I see you standing with arms folded, talking to one of the other artists. You break into a smile at something the artist says, toss your head back and laugh. In the photographs you were stern, defiant; you were waving a Hawaiian sovereignty flag. Here you are full of laughter and love and twinkles. You meet peoples' eye when you speak to them. I am here. You are here. We are here together. This is what you say without saying anything at all.

I watch you at work over the next few days: see how you get a 'sense of their rhythm as a group', quiz them on similes and metaphors. You work out what they know, what you (and they) can do, where you should start. Then one morning they are sitting with four small pieces of blank white paper and a sharpened pencil in front of them. They are making their own writing booklets. You guide them step by step through the folding and design. On the front cover you tell them to make two boxes along the fold. 'When you get bored, or distracted', you say, 'focus on your notebook: decorate it'. In the top box you ask them to write: 'Poems and Writing by Name and Grade'. 'This is your notebook', you say, 'This is officially your notebook, and you are going to put all your work from our workshops in it.' Then you tell them to go to the back of their notebooks and place their non-dominant hand on the page. As the students trace around it, they laugh at their clumsiness and discuss who has/hasn't cut their fingernails recently. You ask: 'Are we all good with our hands?' Somewhere on each of the five fingers, either at the tip or the side, you tell them to write the name of someone they love. On each finger, the students write 'something they love to do'. 'Listen to this Hawaiian proverb', you say, '*Aia nō ka pono – 'o ka ho'ohuli i ka lima i lalo, 'a'ole 'o ka ho'ohuli i luna. That is what it should be – to turn the hands palms down, not palms up.* No one can work with the palms of his hands turned up. When a person is always busy, he is said to keep his palms down. 'On your palm, where you carry things', now you turn your own palm upwards and place your other hand's fingers into it, 'write five things you would love to do'.

Then you speak more about love. About odes. About 'aloha' and what it *really* means: to breathe in the presence of someone or something else, to share breath. You open your bag and take out a big block of a book; you smooth your hand over its lime green cover. It is *All the Odes* by Pablo Neruda. You say, 'He wrote odes to bees, and fruits and water – he loved so many things. Love is expansive; it goes outwards.' As you say this your right hand touches your chest and moves outwards in a circle which encompasses all of them. 'You are going to write an ode to somebody you love.'

Another day and we are in a space with a whiteboard. There are fewer bodies today. It is the afternoon. We catch each other's eye as we sense their reluctance, see a resistance in their bodies, a sloping. You use the white board. You talk about the 'gentle comparison' that is a simile, about specificity, about 'growing metaphors'. What is love like? They begin to tell you things slowly and you write 'beautiful', 'strong' and 'safe' on the board. Underneath it the students come up and write down things under each heading: 'tulips', 'cherry tree', 'my Dad'. You give them an example metaphor about your own grandmother: 'Your love is a jar of pickled mango.' I realize they are calling you 'auntie' when they need help; I see you high fiving them and whooping in celebration when you read what they have written. They are buoyed by this. Little heads of dark hair bob up and down as they continue to write. I look up at the board and the scaffold you have constructed for them. I remember the examples you have given them about yourself, your grandmother: a book whose 'skin feels like old paper'. They tell you things you would never have imagined being told. One girl lets you read her sentence: 'I love you like my brother loves you in heaven.' You falter. You realize she is telling you her brother is dead. 'If you do poetry right, and you teach right,' you tell me later that day as we sit watching the ocean under the booming engines of planes ascending from the nearby airport, 'you earn a really beautiful kind of trust'.

In the class we keep reaching what I think is the obligatory plenary, but you can see further than I can. You write, 'LOVE POEMS WE WROTE' in capital letters on the board. You invite them to come up and write their first lines. You have given each of them a different coloured pen. When they are finished, it says: 'You are a key./You are a stone./You are an orchid./You are sunlight'. Then their second lines, their third, and so on. We are still not finished; now you ask them to each speak their own lines and their own poems; they do this and doing it they realize that their love poems are also one love poem written by all of them in this room today. Those hands they drew around, turned down to write, are now turned inwards to clap, held up to high five each other.

Second Portrait: 'Little bodies' and 'binnacles' – Selina Tusitala Marsh

In the quiet staffroom it's the period just after lunch. You sit on the low chair in the corner by a bookcase, writing into a jotter with a sharp pencil. I can hear it gently scraping on the paper. The fluorescent lights, activated by movements in the room, come on and off every now and then. You are busy: thinking, planning, scribbling. I've seen you teach before – at Vailima in Sāmoa, when you had flowers on your dress and in your hair. Here, in a Scottish November, cold, and damp, you wear olive green leather boots.

Later, in a classroom shaped like a box, neat and ordered, you stand at the white board. You are a disruption in this space – a tall brown woman with unruly corkscrew curls tumbling over your shoulders. The teacher stays in the room with us. Proprietorial. You speak English with a New Zealand accent; instead of 'pen' you say 'pin'. I watch two students notice this: one of them picks up a pen and shows it to another. They both titter. You see it too. 'Yis', you say, emphasizing your accent, 'I say "pin"; you say "pen"'. You feed this into your plan to get them thinking about sound and about meaning. On the board you write, in large capital letters, your own middle name: 'TUSITALA'. You know this Samoan word will be strange here. You make them play with it. They say it out loud in different ways which you model: quickly, slowly, softly, in a deep bellow and going up in pitch towards the end. Then you get them out of their seats, and they move their bodies as they say the word; bodies jump and crouch, arms go up, down or out like stars. Then it's time for the 'pins'. We all smile. They are with you now.

There is silence in the classroom as the students think and write. They are making a list of words out of the word TUSITALA. 'Us', 'it', 'I', 'sit' they tell you, taking their raised arms down once you've pointed to them. But every now and then, it bubbles over, and one of them forgets. Someone shouts out, 'ta', another 'la' and you respond to these ones too. These are English words they are making out of a Samoan one. You don't tell them what Tusitala means, you let them feel the word and its sounds. You get them to work their imaginations in and around the word. You ask them to write five answers to five questions you put on the board. What does a Tusitala look like? What does a Tusitala sound like? And so on. They write and they share. Tusitalas become monsters, cakes, the whistling wind and someone's cuddly best friend. 'Words are worlds,' you tell me later.

'A "tusi" is a writer; a "tala" is a story. A tusitala is a writer of stories, a teller of tales. It is what the Samoans called Robert Louis Stevenson, and it is my middle name. It was passed down to me by my grandfather, but I don't know why, or how, he came to be called by it.' You tell them this story about yourself, about who you are and what you do. At this point. You tell them at *this* point. After they've copied you, moved for you, danced with you and imagined with you. After they've had your middle name wrapped round their tongues and metamorphosing in their minds.

Out comes the Stevenson – the first page of his story *The Beach of Falesá* – handed round to these ten-year-olds on a drizzly Tuesday afternoon. Its setting and its genesis are nine and a half thousand miles away on a Pacific Island, and one hundred and thirty years in the past. 'I saw that island first', it begins, 'when it was neither night nor morning'. You ask them to read through the page and to circle the words they like. You have primed them to do this. They are not scared of mysteries. There is a hush in the room. I can see some of their mouths move in silent articulation as eyes scan the text. Next, you ask them to connect the circles with a pencil line which flows through the black and white words, backwards and forwards, in swerves. This nineteenth-century text suddenly becomes theirs and each piece of paper on each desk is different. You tell them this. Now for the black markers. They are to 'black out' the words they have *not* chosen, the words that are *not* part of their flow. They do this enthusiastically. The class teacher is flustered. She is hastily putting blotting sheets under the extracts to make sure the ink doesn't come through and stain the desks. They are new, you see. You carry on speaking to them, as you black out Stevenson's words on your own copy and the students black out Stevenson's words on theirs.

What is left is poetry.
These 'stars of words left to pinprick on the page'.

Finally, they are standing in a circle with you. A few individuals read out their poems, made of what shone – for them – out of Stevenson's words. Then we go through the text chronologically so that each person can speak the words they have kept; often, we notice a word which everyone – or almost everyone – has chosen. Sometimes it is one lone voice. At 'binnacles' it is almost the whole class. They don't even know what a binnacle is. Doing this, you say later, they hear the 'connective tissue of repetition'. The class breathes through the spaces of the text. 'It works for me when it *moves* people, *opens* people ... ', you say about teaching and about poetry and about writing.

When we are tidying up to leave, I find the jotter in which you scribbled lying on the table in the staffroom. I open it up. The paper inside is like the classroom – a grid through which your arrows, circles and words run. 'It's my job as a poet to enliven the words,' you tell me. 'You've got these *little* bodies, reading these *massive* lines about binnacles; you know, it's just ... you know ... it *moved* me'.

Discussion: The va¯ and the Artistry of Teaching

What is it that teachers do when they teach? How do they use themselves? How do they move? What level of tension, of affect, of spontaneity do they display? To what extent do they reveal themselves as persons to the students with whom they work? Are they approachable? In what ways? What kinds of values, ideas, and covert messages do they emphasize? How, given questions such as these, can the qualities to which such questions guide us be disclosed? How can they be disclosed in a way that does not rob them of their vitality as experienced?

(Eisner 2005: 53)

In the portraits above I have tried to disclose the qualities of both Revilla's and Marsh's teaching through *my own experience* as an observer of it. I have tried to capture the ways in which they moved, and were moved by, the students whom they taught. I have tried to show the ways in which they both moved *me*; indeed, the way these portraits are written is an outcome of these affects. In many ways, their practice contains elements that are typical of what good teachers do: there is a purpose (to demystify poetry and to re-mystify words, to decolonize literary texts and forms, to empower young people as writers) and there are pedagogical structures (warm up exercises, scaffolds, stagings, plenaries). These things are part of their 'educational craftsmanship' – knowing how to plan a lesson that 'works'. But it is also clear that there is more going on here than the 'techne' of teaching.

In this section, I want to return to the questions I began with by drawing out some common threads in the two observations. What was it exactly about these poets' teaching that made such an impression on me, and how does the concept of vā help to illuminate this? In what ways does the fact that they are artists matter? And finally, what does all of this add to our understanding of teaching as a form of artistry?

I focus on three remarkable (for me) aspects of the teaching I observed. First, the speed (in a matter of hours) in which relationships of trust and care were established between these poets and their students. This happened in Revilla's case in her home context of Hawai'i, but it also happened for Marsh in a context – Scotland – which was entirely new to her. The important point here being that it happened in the *context of teaching*. Secondly, in both cases, the climax of their lessons – in something communal and performative – was not one I had anticipated or imagined; it took the teaching to a plane outside of my experience of most classrooms. Lastly, both poets had an extraordinary 'presence' in the room; their position as 'the teacher' was never in doubt.

When I asked Marsh about her relations with the students, she told me:

> I'm thinking of vā as a teacher. How we nurture, adorn and beautify the space between us and our students, between our students and knowledge, the book, the story.
>
> (Interview, 11 July 2023)

Though Revilla did not explicitly mention the vā, the emphasis she placed on attending to relations (the eye contact, the high fives, the encouragement), including kin relations (her grandmother; the fact that the students called her 'auntie') suggest the 'social vā' and the importance of 'knowing ones' position in relation to others' (Tuagalu 2022: 39). Her lesson, on writing odes to what we love, deliberately resurfaced the social and emotional networks in which her students (and herself) were already embedded. Marsh too spoke to the students about her grandfather, his name and the possible relationships with Stevenson. There is something of the sacred vā here too: the task of the teacher is, on one level, the dilemma of how one might bring students into 'contagious magical contact' with an ode, or a nineteenth-century text about 'binnacles'. Both lessons ended with performances that showcased this contact and the exchanges that had taken place. Revilla turns the lines she has helped them to construct into a group poem through the ritual of writing in different coloured pens and reading individual lines in succession. Marsh brings students into a circle to perform their black out poems in concert; to feel what she calls 'the connective tissue of repetition'. To understand vā as a teacher is to read the classroom space as the context in which relationships unfold and are held together. But it is also to understand and respond to the fact that these relations are in constant flux. They need to be nurtured and rearticulated as positions change and new 'spaces between' are created; these need to be acknowledged and validated in turn. We can see this when both poets draw on themselves in different ways which communicate their positions as either with, or apart, from the students. When Marsh notices the students laugh at her accent, she acknowledges it as a difference but then she takes it up and uses it in the flow of her lesson; it becomes a shared joke, a shared position. Anae writes of the vā:

> Where there is tension or disagreement, to teu le vā means to soothe, mute and/or attenuate these, in order to correct or realign priorities to ensure the dialogue is kept intact and moving forward.
>
> (Anae 2016: 122)

There are clear resonances here with theories of teaching in the literature. These have recognized both 'presence' (Rodgers 2020; Rodgers and Raider Roth 2006) and 'relationality' (Aspelin 2021; Frelin 2013; Noddings [1984] 2003a, b) as vital – albeit elusive – elements in good teaching. Drawing on Dewey's notion of 'heightened vitality' ([1934] 2005: 18) and Greene's 'wide-awakeness' (1973: 162), Rodgers and Raider Roth (2006) argue that the 'presence' of a teacher is constituted of attentive relations with the world, the student and also with one's self. Marsh told me that she needed 'the students to be present and curious' so that she could 'bring them into the same space' as herself. The emphasis she placed on vocal, physical and imaginative actions – getting students to move in, and around, the word 'tusitala' did precisely this: it brought them into relation with words and into relation with their teacher. Noddings has argued that 'teaching is thoroughly relational' and can involve:

> a growing intellectual enthusiasm in both teacher and student, the challenge and satisfaction shared by both in engaging new material, the awakening sense (for both) that teaching and life are never-ending moral quests.
>
> (Noddings 2003b: 249)

There is an emphasis here on mutuality of experience, but it suggests something non-hierarchical. More recently, Aspelin drawing on Martin Buber's work (in which position *is* acknowledged) goes further and argues that teaching is, in fact, a process of 'bonding'. Aspelin writes that through Buber's concept of 'inclusion' a teacher:

> [b]ecomes directly involved in the student's reality, while remaining active as a pedagogical subject [...] the teacher, on the basis of inclusion, enables the student to stand in relationship to the world, that is, to be present 'in between'.
>
> (Aspelin 2021: 591)

However, Aspelin's notion of 'bonding' strongly implies that relationships still need to be built. These show important differences with the vā: in the vā relations are present in hierarchical structures. Attention goes on 'teu le vā';

on tending to the spaces ('not empty space, not space that separates') that are already full of these relations.

Let us circle back to 'artistry' and its relationship to teaching. It is telling that Marsh talks of the need to 'adorn', to 'beautify' these spaces in between. In my interviews with them, I was continually struck by how both Marsh and Revilla drew their practice as poets and their practice as teachers (of writing) together. Writing poetry depends on carefully chosen words, carefully placed and on gaps, silences – spaces in between. This is what makes poetry; to paraphrase Eisner, poems use words to say – paradoxically – what words cannot say (see Eisner 2005: 152). These 'spaces between' words and lines are not empty spaces; they are full of relations with other words present and absent – otherwise the ecology of the poem would be broken. Poems are also about rhythm and movement. The lessons I observed – this teaching – was also *like* poetry, was it not? It was more than the sum of its parts. The reason we often explain or describe things as 'magic' is because we cannot see what is in the space between. Another important point to note is that both Marsh and Revilla are *performance* poets: poets who address live audiences. Biesta has argued, that teaching is 'the "event" of "being addressed"' (Biesta 2017: 43). Any kind of relation has recognized modes of address – ways in which one calls out/attracts the attention of the other. Part of caring for the vā is caring for the modes of address that go with that relation (the use of the second person in my portraits is part of *my* care for the vā). For Marsh teaching is not just about sharing her enthusiasm for the subject matter; it involves a modality of address that ensures the students attend to her (it gives her authority), but it also reinforces the fact that, in turn, *they* deserve to be noticed *by her*.

Conclusion

For these Pasifika poets the vā constitutes part of a decolonial pedagogy; it articulates and enacts a distinctly Pacific understanding of a classroom context inherited through colonization. We might ask then what the vā has to do with us? What are the implications of this discussion for teachers and teaching in other kinds of contexts? We might also ask if artful teaching is only possible when teaching (poetry in this instance) something the teacher is already in relation with? Could an occupational teacher (given all the constraints they work under) attend to spaces between in the same way? The artistry of these poets' teaching lay in how they nurtured and navigated the spaces between the normal apparatus of a classroom – the teacher, the student, the text, the outputs. It is *where* their attention was placed and *what* was looked after that, I think, made it artful for me. 'I'm thinking of vā *as* a teacher,' said Marsh; from this position – the one who teaches – specific relations must be acknowledged and nurtured. I am not suggesting that teachers everywhere adopt the vā as a framework or a 'toolkit'; it is important to acknowledge its situated nature in Pacific worldviews. But we can also learn from it. Looking through the lens of the vā makes visible the kinds of relations that are often ignored, or elided, in teacher education programmes and discourses about teaching. What if we came at teaching differently? Rather than thinking of classrooms as spaces in which relationships are problems to be solved, or issues that need to be 'managed', why not think of them as contexts in which already existing relations are continually unfolding? Here teacher artistry is not an act of cultivation and growth (gardening); nor is it a performance (acting), or an improvisation (jazz); it is the ability to constantly attune and reattune relations in order to 'keep the dialogue intact and moving forward'.

Notes

1   Booth's definition of a 'teaching artist' is someone with the 'complementary skills and sensibilities of an educator, who engage[s] people in learning experiences in, through, or about, the arts' (2003: 11).

2   The project is funded by the Arts and Humanities Research Council, UK. Grant No: AH/W007010/1.

3   See Green and Bloome (2004: 184).

4   To use Eisner's terminology, I put myself in the position of both a 'connoisseur' and 'critic' of teaching ([1977] 2005: 48–50).

5   The portrait of Revilla draws on fieldnotes taken between 4 and 6 July 2022 and an interview on 6 July in Honolulu, Hawai'i. The portrait of Marsh is based on field notes taken on 14 November 2023 in North Berwick, Scotland and on two separate interviews conducted on 11 July 2023 in Apia, Samoa and on 29 January 2024 on MS Teams. Excerpts in citation marks in these portraits are taken from the interviews.

References

Anae, M. (2010), 'Research for Better Pacific Schooling in New Zealand: Teu le va–a Samoan perspective', *MAI Review*, 1 (1): 1–24.

Anae, M. (2016), 'Teu le va: Samoan Relational Ethics', *Knowledge Cultures*, 4 (3): 117–30.

Aspelin, J. (2021), 'Teaching as a Way of Bonding: A Contribution to the Relational Theory of Teaching', *Educational Philosophy and Theory*, 53 (6): 588–96.

Biesta, G.J.J. (2017), *The Rediscovery of Teaching*, London: Routledge.

Booth, E. (2003), 'Seeking Definition: What Is a Teaching Artist?', *Teaching Artist Journal*, 1 (1): 5–12.

Dewey, J. ([1934] 2005), *Art as Experience*, New York: Perigree Books.

Eisner, E. (2005), *Reimagining Schools: The Selected Works of Elliot W. Eisner*, London and New York: Routledge.

Emerson, R.M., R.I. Fretz and L.L. Shaw (2011), *Writing Ethnographic Fieldnotes*, Chicago, IL: University of Chicago Press.

Frelin, A. (2013), *Exploring Relational Professionalism in Schools*, Leiden: Brill Publishers.

Geertz, C. (1973), *The Interpretation of Cultures: Selected Essays by Clifford Geertz*, New York: Basic Books.

Green, J. and D. Bloome (2004), 'Ethnography and Ethnographers of and in Education: A Situated Perspective', in J. Flood, S.B. Heath and D. Lapp (eds), *Handbook of Research on Teaching Literacy through the Communicative and Visual Arts*, 181–202, New York: Macmillan Publishers.

Greene, M. (1973), *Teacher as Stranger: Educational Philosophy for the Modern Age*, Belmont, CA: Wadsworth.

Hammersley, M. and P. Atkinson (2019), *Ethnography: Principles in Practice*, London: Routledge.

Lawrence Lightfoot, S. and J. Hoffman Davis (1997), *The Art and Science of Portraiture*, San Francisco, CA: John Wiley and Sons.

Māhina, H. (2008), 'From Vale (Ignorance) to 'ILO (Knowledge) to Poto (Skill) the Tongan Theory of Ako (Education): Theorising Old Problems Anew', *AlterNative: An International Journal of Indigenous Peoples*, 4 (1): 67–96.

Noddings, N. ([1984] 2003a), *Caring: A Feminine Approach to Ethics and Moral Education*, Berkeley, CA: University of California Press.

Noddings, N. (2003b), 'Is Teaching a Practice?', *Journal of Philosophy of Education*, 37 (2): 241–51.

Reynolds, M. (2016), 'Relating to Va: Re-viewing the Concept of Relationships in Pasifika Education in Aotearoa New Zealand', *AlterNative: An International Journal of Indigenous Peoples*, 12 (2): 190–202.

Rodgers, C. (2020), *The Art of Reflective Teaching: Practicing Presence*, New York: Teacher's College Press.

Rodgers, C. and M.B. Raider-Roth (2006), 'Presence in Teaching', *Teachers and Teaching: Theory and Practice*, 12 (3): 265–87.

Sabeti, S. (2019), 'Making Murals in the Marshall Islands and Hawai'i: An Exploration of the Possibilities and Limits of Artistic Agency in a Community Arts Education Project', *Crossings: Journal of Migration & Culture*, 10 (1): 71–87.

Sabeti, S. (2023), '"You Think You Know, but You Have No Idea": On Anger, Critical Pedagogy and the Dilemmas of Being a Teaching Artist', *Pedagogy, Culture & Society*, 33 (2): 633–53.

Smith, L.T. ([1999] 2012), *Decolonizing Methodologies: Research and Indigenous Peoples*, London: Bloomsbury.

Stanton, C.R. (2014), 'Crossing Methodological Borders: Decolonizing Community-Based Participatory Research', *Qualitative Inquiry*, 20 (5): 573–83.

Stenhouse, L. (1988), 'Artistry and Teaching: The Teacher as Focus of Research and Development', *Journal of Curriculum and Supervision*, 4 (1): 43–51.

Stevenson, R.L. ([1892] 1996), 'The Beach of Falesa', in R. Jolly (ed,) *South Seas Tales*, 3–72, Oxford: Oxford University Press.

Strathern, M. (1988), *The Gender of the Gift: Problems with Women and Problems with Society in Melanesia*, Berkeley, CA: University of California Press.

Thaman, K.H. (2002), 'Va'a: A Pacific Foundation for Education for Inter-cultural Understanding', paper delivered at UNESCO/APCEIU workshop on Education for International Understanding, Suva, Fiji.

Thaman, K.H. (2007), 'Partnerships for Progressing Cultural Democracy in Teacher Education in Pacific Island Countries', in T. Townsend and R. Bates (eds), *Handbook of Teacher Education: Globalization, Standards, and Professionalism in Times of Change*, 53–66, Dordrecht: Springer.

Tuagalu, I. (2022), 'The Energetics of the Vā and the Samoan Faletele', in A. Engels-Schwarzpaul, L. Lopesi and A.L. Refiti (eds), *Pacific Spaces: Translations and Transmutations, Vol. 10*, 37–53, Oxford and New York: Berghahn Books.

Ualesi, Y.M. (2024), 'Lessons from a Vā Relational Approach: Embedding Indigenous Constructs for Classroom Practice', *New Zealand Journal of Educational Studies*, 59 (1): 125–39.

Wendt, A. (1999), 'Tatauing the Post-Colonial Body', in V. Hereniko and R. Wilson (eds), *Inside Out: Literature, Cultural Politics, and Identity in the New Pacific*, 399–412, Lanham, MD: Rowman & Littlefield.

Wendt, A. (2015), *Out of the Vaipe, the Deadwater: A Writer's Early Life*, Wellington: BWB.

CHAPTER FOUR

The Art and Artistry of Teaching: Looking beyond the Quantifiable in Initial Teacher Education

Lorna Hamilton

Introduction

In this chapter I wish to share my concerns about a common overemphasis on developing teachers via technical and overly standardized Teacher Education programmes. In looking for an alternative way of thinking about the early professional development of teachers, I believe that a more holistic approach is necessary. This does not entail abandoning skills and knowledge but instead looks to the uniqueness of the individual teacher, their professional identity development and possible agency and through these to engage with teaching as an art and the teacher as a creator of artistry within diverse contexts.

In order to do this, I will discuss the current attempts to generate future teachers through a formulaic approach using benchmarks or similar as a means to achieve a standardized and 'effective' teacher. I also introduce ideas about an alternative view of teaching, as a form of artistry and how this might be conceptualized and understood. This is followed by consideration of the ways in which traditional models of teaching can promote use of language which reduces teachers and teaching to technical skills and competencies and then question whether it is possible to enhance and extend the language of Teacher Education as we look for a more complex and holistic conceptualization of teaching.

The struggle for an alternative language which might capture the less tangible aspects of teaching and its development in ITE (Initial Teacher Education) is important but there is a need to explore and think critically about what this might look like. Next, I consider the early professional development of teaching in the twenty-first century and in particular within the competency regimes located within Scotland and elsewhere. The significant managerialism which has come to dominate the field and the dominance of competency narratives (Ball 2003, 2016; Hickey and Riddle 2025) have been considered a threat to the teacher's soul. It has to be acknowledged that the skills focus may reflect a harmonious interplay of some key elements which the teacher can draw upon to facilitate learning but this often produces a reductionist model of teaching. Instead, embracing an alternative relational-humanist perspective and viewing teaching as a performance art can provide a new way of conceptualizing teaching. My holistic multi-dimensional view reflects the art of teaching as part of the everyday artistry of the classroom as the player/conductor shapes and is shaped by the interactions, relationships and subject knowledge and skills that contribute to artistry. Beyond the immediacy and improvisational qualities of teaching as an art, are relational imperatives which form part of professional narratives and contribute to the success or otherwise of the artistry pursued by the teacher; nurturing relationships and building trust.

The possibility around a hybridized model of Teacher Education is exciting: one which does not exclude the skills and knowledge that inform the teacher's art but which present a more holistic and humanistic approach that can help to challenge accepted wisdom. This is contrasted with some of the issues that have been raised about the vulnerabilities of the student teacher who is evaluated and judged by traditional ideas of the 'good' teacher through benchmarks. The almost inevitable power asymmetry faced by student teachers as they move into diverse schools, subject to assessment of their teaching and of their character can encourage conformity within existing norms but there may be spaces available for quiet rebellion. Finally, I reflect on the way forward if we are to embrace teaching as an art and its performance as artistry.

Standardization versus Artistry

Popular views of education today are often shaped by behaviouristic understandings of teaching and education policy emphases on the need for measurement of student outcomes and the reductionist tendencies in defining and supposedly capturing teaching as a combination of competencies (Hickey and Riddle 2025). International league tables also continue to encourage such views of teaching and learning, with the result that any teaching artistry is overlooked or ignored as it cannot be evaluated by rigid and limited accounts of competency. A more relational-humanistic approach to teaching and learning is likely to take us into the realms of fusions or syntheses of diverse qualities, relationships and purposes, infused by personal-professional uniqueness. Through authentic performances in the classroom, the embrace of an orchestral metaphor may help to capture a vivid fusion of teaching artistry. Here, use is made of a performance analogy – where the teacher is both conductor, crafting, shaping rhythms, influencing pace and modulating tones (Ivie 2020) and co-participant, focused on the building of relationships and trust as a basis for successful experiences. It is argued here that when unique syntheses of the above occur in classrooms and in similar spaces, artistry is manifested. The challenge, however, is to explore how such uniqueness can be understood and developed during the early years of student teacher and new teacher development.

In striving to understand the uniqueness of the individual teacher and the artistry generated, we immediately face the problem of a political desire for standardization and reductionism. However, it could be argued that uniqueness can carry with it, shades of universality (Hamilton et al. 2024; Simons 1996) in that although we may draw on key skills and attitudes to shape teacher education experiences, we need to acknowledge that the fusion of such qualities, the nature of contexts and the ambience of classroom spaces and people, creates something original and new, a form of artistry, which models and resonates for those learning to teach. The challenge, however, is to explore how such uniqueness can be understood and developed during ITE.

The current popularity of competencies or benchmarks in many countries reflects a striving for certainty in relation to a 'recipe' for building the effective teacher. However, my position is that each student teacher is unique in past experiences and responses, in relationship to subject and in the idiosyncratic identity negotiations which help shape the kind of teacher they may be becoming (Hamilton 2013; Tsakalou et al. 2018). Yet the challenge of such a perspective is that it is not easy or perhaps even desirable to determine a formulaic protocol for the production of teachers. To challenge accountability narratives is risky when artistry may be marginalized in a world which seems to idealize traditional notions of 'scientific methods'. The concept of artistry is often viewed as intangible and unmeasurable and consequently can be considered to be in conflict with educational structures and policy controls. This led me to reflect on how the uniqueness of the individual might lead to Teacher Education experiences that can promote the uniqueness and universality of the new teacher professional and promote discussion of teaching as an art in conjunction with open discussion of the uncertainty, unpredictability and risk-taking inherent in teaching along with ongoing teacher identity development during ITE. I am drawing here on the work of Helen Simons (1996) whose work in case study engages with the dilemma of seeking a particular uniqueness while also recognizing the need to be able to apply findings more generally in research. This also captures the paradox of trying to combine the established skills of teachers with the uniqueness of teaching as a performance art. How can we reconcile the need for certainty found in established competencies with the unique qualities found in the enactment of artistry? The answer perhaps lies in not seeing these as antagonistic towards each other but in accepting the paradoxical unity (Simons 1996) of their value in a more holistic view of early professional development.

Of particular interest is the emerging new teacher and the challenges encountered in the face of national and supranational efforts to claim the linguistic, policy and ITE arenas and curricula with implicit messages about the nature of the teacher and the measures of success considered necessary for the production of 'effective' teachers (Ball 2003, 2016; Zeichner 2014). An alternative model embracing the uniqueness of the teacher with the possibility of universal resonance for others is a possible way forward, especially if combined with a consensus over key skills. Here the individual may stir a ripple of challenge to conventional thinking or may actively rebel against the dominant language of the Global Education Reform Movement (GERM) and National competency frameworks which often crave formulas for successful teacher creation.

The Language of Teaching and Teacher Education

It is important to consider first some key aspects of teaching as an art including the language we use. Does the language we use exclude us from conceptualizing teaching as an art? Policy obsessions with the measurability of teaching (Menter and Flores 2021) often reduce teaching to specific skills and outlooks. The emphasis is on the technical versus the aesthetic. We need to consider the kind of changes that would be necessary to encourage both a technical and artistic enactment of teaching. Bryant (2009) complains about the pseudoscientific jargon applied in education with the purpose of having teaching 'masquerade' as a science and therefore as warranting legitimacy in the academy and wider society. In submitting to this 'false' narrative and ignoring teaching as an art, he argues that we have denied the importance of idealism and the importance of questioning and believing in the 'creative potential and possibilities of the human spirit' (Bryant 2009: 163). In the continual pursuit of ever 'higher standards' (Zeichner 2014), those that are easily measurable and quantifiable, we are in danger of creating a perpetual loop of language and practice which is reductionist but also dangerous to the genuinely artistic teaching we seek. If we can reclaim the language of education, we might empower new teachers to challenge rather than simply assimilate as so often happens. However, given the tendency towards competency-based teacher education we would need to ask where are the spaces for counter-narratives and how can pre-service teachers find and make use of them? It would seem counter-intuitive to expect student teachers to actively find or make such spaces, but this then means that part of challenging the established narratives of standards and accountability, would need to include the collective agency of Teacher Educators (TEs) and the persuasion of educational policymakers to help formally bring about change in concepts and language used. Moreover, there would need to be a collaboration between TEs and student teachers to support spaces for artistic rebellion and alternative ways of thinking about the orthodoxies of educational practice. This is not to say that the directional agency for this innovation needs to start at the top but it acknowledges that in order for Teacher Education systems to change the language and reconceptualizations of the development of the new teacher, an important element would need to be the translation of the language used in policies and programmes. Transforming the language of teaching might require some artistic agency and an acceptance of the need for risk taking in the unpredictable world of the classroom.

Becoming a Teacher in the Twenty-First Century: Agency and Soul

In light of powerful attacks internationally on teacher professionalism and on ITE itself through pejorative media narratives and political posturing on the part of politicians, how can we begin to argue for a more complex understanding of teaching and teacher self that can coexist with or excise delimited versions of teacher competency? Stephen Ball's article (2003) and Zeichner's work (2014) on the struggle for the teacher's soul have argued that the performativity and accountability agendas in the GERM have endangered and eroded teacher agency and instead promoted a technicist and conformist profession under a restrictive, standardized competency framework. Standardization does not encourage creativity and complexity or dynamic processes and the uniqueness of the individual. A space, therefore, is needed to contest and challenge the very nature of the teaching self despite competency-based straitjackets. Our hope lies, I believe, in the support for critical and imaginative student teachers who are empowered to manifest agency in their teaching choices and relationship building with school students and communities of practice. Thus, ITE becomes a vital space both for the generation of expertise and for the discovery of possible ways in which agency can be manifested and it is perhaps in agentic spaces that teachers can bring artistic choices to bear. The prescient Lawrence Stenhouse (1988), forty years ago, warned us that our priority needs to be towards encouraging teachers to want to change their understanding of the nature of their role and to extend their knowledge and understanding beyond the instrumental and limited versions permitted within traditional models. This further underpins the importance of ITE and the holistic or restricted paths that may be encouraged in the early professional development of teachers if we do not encourage agency and artistry in our TEs and student teachers.

Lupton (2013: 163) highlights that the structured experiences of GERM are attempts to 'teacher proof' and 'student proof' the system when we focus on limited skills-based models of teachers. She contends that we need to look to qualities that reflect teacher identity through beliefs and values, the customization of teaching and learning processes and the willingness to take risks. However, teacher identity is a highly debated area. Here I would suggest the need to view teacher education and the development of teacher identity as an artistic endeavour in which we are dealing with the creation and recreation of a multitude of teaching moments, relationship building, dynamic emotional support and potentially transformative learning. For those supporting the teacher-as-artist model, there may be an acceptance of the need for skills development and so a more hybrid approach could be embraced but there would also need to be either some kind of reconciliation or acceptance of the possible contradictions that might emerge.

Those student teachers in ITE inhabit a space where survival is key and as part of that survival, conformity and compliance are often seen as the most prudent way forward. Britzman (1993: 29) captures this potential narrow path succinctly, describing it as 'imitation, recitation and assimilation'. That is not to say that there is no space for agency from student teachers but it does acknowledge the restrictions that many student teachers find which we know have tended to lead to particular short-term survival strategies. With this imperative, we need to consider what possibilities there are for the development of artistry and agency during this period and whether the concept of the art of teaching is fully absent from ITE and accompanying experiences in practicum. Research (Britzman 1993: 75) highlights the fact that post ITE, new teachers can be faced with, 'diversity of the actual landscapes in schools', and how new teachers may be, 'dismayed by the extent to which those landscapes worked against their being able to perform prescribed teacher scripts as well as they had', during practicums. Immersion in other landscapes led to concern over the dominance of policy and system restrictions and the emphasis on conformity to the status quo. We are left with a number of conflicts between what may be seen by some student teachers as the survivalist and conformist narratives that may hold sway during ITE and the need for improvisational, adaptive and critical mindsets within schools when they emerge as newly qualified teachers.

Teacher Educators and Student Teachers: Possible Catalysts for Hybridity?

Teacher Education then sits in a key space and Teacher Educators (TEs) may provide an impetus for change and encourage agentic movement by new teachers but only if they are able to counter the dominant narratives of competencies or benchmarks and conformity. Attempts to change the narrative by TEs and student teachers might suggest their voices are less likely to be heard in regard to change and challenges to the norm on the broader stage. We then need to consider if change needs to begin at the local level within ITE programmes where spaces for cultivation might allow the beginning of an appreciation of the artistic with acceptance of the uncertainty of the improvisational in encouraging a critical but exciting engagement with teaching as an art and the potential for new teacher artistry. Artistry is seen here not only as an aspect of the highly experienced teacher and the result of a 'successful' lesson but also as something which can be achieved in moments within spaces, in interactions that shine a light on an idea and in improvisational melodies that may or may not influence learning in a new way for emerging teachers and those at the beginning of their professional journey.

If Teacher Education and teaching can be perceived as an aesthetic experience (Hall 1983) and one which is dynamic, processual, flexible and improvisatory but also, potentially, dangerous or risky, there is no formulaic certainty but at the same time there are elements of scientific modelling in the framework for learning generated through curriculum guidelines and important skills and knowledge. It might then be possible to reconcile a hybrid vision of teaching as both an art and a skills-based approach. Embracing the concept of teaching as artistry, holding at its centre the teacher and the learner, where teacher qualities, often nebulous, intangible, dynamic, emotional, and spiritual, reflect the soul of the teacher, then our systemic focus on LOs and scores is weakened by a lack of attention to the other side of the teaching stories our student teachers can tell. To what extent can we encourage student teachers to make explicit their teaching journeys as artists rather than technicians and what form might these take? Lupton (2013) refers to Da Vinci's description of an arch – it consists of two weaknesses, which leaning one against the other, make a strength. This captures the wonderful image of the accountability/performativity part of the arch as teetering on the verge of collapse as it tries to succeed without its supporting narratives of teacher artistry. I would like to see a project built around the student teacher as a burgeoning artist using storytelling and other forms of artistic expression to more readily capture the being and becoming, creation and re-creation of significant moments and processes at the heart of teaching and learning in order to explore this further. Eisner's suggestion of a teacher's studio (2002) for experiential learning and improvisation may provide one way of developing a deeper understanding of the artistic self and the artistry of teaching. Working towards a more artistic framing for teaching while acknowledging the necessity of skills development, may be a way of generating a hybrid model in ITE.

Teachers' Voices

For pre-service student high school teachers, there is a powerful connection between the form of professional identity that may emerge and the type of subject-specific framing that occurs. This hybridity is one specific to high school subject teachers as it can be such an essential component of the teaching self. For these becoming teachers, there are questions to be asked about the extent to which science-oriented subject teachers can engage with the possibility of their teaching as an art. Makedon (1990, 3) suggests this would not be problematic, 'a teacher may hold the view, as did John Dewey, that students should learn through the scientific method, but consider his own teaching more his creatively designed art, than his empirically pretested science'. Yet when the language of policy and that of benchmarks seems to fixate on a technical and compartmentalized accounting of specific skills and attitudes, we need to consider how TEs can take an artistic approach in the language used to help create a sense of the art of teaching in addition to any scientific element in a hybrid and fluid notion of the teaching self.

Drawing on both skills and the art of teaching there is a need to acknowledge a much more complex and artistic concept that accepts the 'scientific' grounding of many skills but then imagines an expression of teaching as unique, unpredictable and unmeasurable. It has variously been described as a site of orchestral synthesis or the interweaving of a multitude of threads of knowledge, skills and expertise and, of course, learners. To embrace such metaphors can be seen as lacking the accountability of the skills and knowledge-based technician promoted in much modern policy. Eisner (1983) highlights the need for prediction and control within such prescribed formulas for teachers and the challenges felt in applying a prescribed script which relies on specific and limited responses. In the multiplicity of interactions and the many decisions taken by the artist-teacher each day, each unique encounter may reflect the unique artistry of the teacher. But my next consideration is if there are moments of artistry but a practicum lesson as a whole has been patchy, how do we use our desire to recognize artistry to evaluate the quality of the teacher? Or is there a need to see artistry across the entirety of a lesson? Should the nature of artistry be open to evaluation? This leaves us with the challenge of trying to determine whether artistry must reflect a high level of interaction and 'orchestral' quality at all times or in part and how can we evaluate such moments of artistry. Specific teachers may have diverse strengths, and additionally, the unpredictability of school and classroom landscapes mean that artistry may be more difficult to achieve in some spaces than others. It also raises questions about how TEs and mentor teachers evaluate student teachers' teaching beyond the competencies. As our language moves through metaphors and intangible qualities, the more challenging evaluation becomes. This returns us to my earlier point regarding hybridity in PSTs' ITE experiences. We need to consider how hybridity might conceptualize the technical and the artistic elements of teaching as well as reflecting on what should be evaluated and in what ways. Currently, student teachers are the focus of concentrated observations and evaluations by different mentor teachers and university tutors. Such intense scrutiny against set competencies can inhibit their teaching and interactions and this can potentially subdue their artistry. With limited scope for agentic manoeuvring at this stage in their early professional development it is unclear to what extent PSTs may be able to move beyond a safe place, meeting competency requirements and towards the riskier artistry of teaching. I would like to highlight some examples of reflexive commentaries from students. One in which the struggle between certain orthodoxies and personal beliefs can be at odds during the ITE transition and another where the PST's subject can lend itself towards a hybrid stance but where she opts for seeing teaching as an art.

For this first student studying to become an English teacher, we can see that as she gained new experiences in classrooms, reflected and argued about contrasting ideas, she began to show that she found there were possible spaces for change and adaptation, from what might have seemed the safer traditionalist approach to the more risky and at times, more improvisational position involving subtle engagement with teaching as a more fluid and dynamic form. Transforming her view of her role and the underlying priorities that come with trying to meet the needs of her assessment by schools and university tutors, she was able to rearrange the composition of her teaching and to shift her positionality in order to synthesize more complex and melodious teaching moments. More than this it acknowledges the complex relationships and emotions involved in orchestrating her lesson.

> I realized the complexity of behaviour management; there's not just a problem and a solution. You have to live with some uncertainty. I think before I had the idea of the perfect classroom, children at desks, working away in silence but I had to change expectations, look below the surface. I learned to let go of the academic a little. I had to let go of my selfish needs. Yes, I had a crit to pass, yes, I had this and that to do but I had children. In some classes, the focus had to be making a connection. I had one girl, it was a struggle to work with her. She was damaged and aggressive and I was thinking how am I going to get them doing things

for my crit, for me. But then I thought no – what do *they* need from *me*? That's what I have to give if I want to build up real trust.

Annie's interview (Hamilton 2013)

Annie's emerging prioritization of relationships and her acceptance of the complexity of practice and the importance of uncertainty reflect a movement away from the illusion of control and predictability which can restrict conceptualizations of teaching. For this second PST, she shows a belief in her subject area which quite naturally seems to reflect teaching as an art, having changed her view since experiencing teaching on placement. Her subject was design and technology and I had thought she might look to a hybrid view. As it was, she acknowledged the skills and knowledge needed but highlighted that teaching itself is an art. (PGDE Secondary subject Design and Technology)

> I now understand the various layers a teacher needs to build into a lesson to ensure success for all pupils which is why I think teaching is more like an art. I think my opinion [at the beginning of the programme] would have been more neutral in the beginning, edging towards it being a science, as I was coming to uni to learn simply how to teach, rather than appreciate the needs and lives of the people I am teaching. I think there are a set of skills and knowledge you need as a teacher, and also the way you apply these which is inherently something that can't be taught. Teaching is definitely not a science as there is no formula to follow to guarantee correct results. The nuances and individuality of every pupil make it more like an art where the end product is subjective to the viewer looking at it. Some things will work and some will not, but from another's perspective the opposite will occur.
>
> —Lisa's interview (from an ongoing research project, New Teacher Professional Identity)

It is interesting that she highlights that teaching itself cannot be taught but that you can learn the skills and knowledge necessary to begin to create teaching artistry. Bringing teaching to life and acknowledging how dynamic and improvisational it can become perhaps points towards the idea that the foundational elements are a necessary component but that the orchestration and conducting of teaching are unique to each teacher. We may find that we are more successful in our artistry at certain times than at others but this simply underlines the unpredictable and risky nature of teaching. In conversation with an experienced teacher (Sara) who has worked with student teachers in her classroom, I asked about whether she saw teaching as an art and to what extent there were spaces for teaching artistry during her career.

I would say when I was at college and certainly in my early years of teaching [1990s] my artistry was the main emphasis and focus. I think that, yes, everything else was important, but unless you had that artistry, it wasn't going to work. And I think what I noticed was there was then more of a shift towards a scientific side at the expense of the artistry. And I think that's been a loss. There's definitely been a loss in teaching because of it. Now, on paper, you have to produce everything on paper, and it's almost as if you have to produce the perfect teacher on paper as well. And it is a loss to professionalism, to artistry. I think a lot of the scope for imagination and scope for developing your own ideas and running with them has maybe been lost a wee bit … It's definitely something that I've noticed.

—Conversation with Sara (from ongoing research project, New Teacher Professional Identity)

She highlighted her concerns about the almost formulaic approach to teaching encouraged nowadays in ITE, leading to seeing teaching as an academic subject rather than an applied one.

But when you come out of university, you're not doing these detailed lesson plans anymore. These, you know, you can become experienced in them more than you can in the actual performance of the lesson. And I think it's the performance and what you do with the results of the performance of the lesson that are more important than actually, writing up beforehand. You don't have that luxury of time to spend on these details, so you need to be a much faster thinker, thinking on your feet, altering things very quickly, changing things. And if you're used to sort of set lesson plans and lessons, are you going to be able to do that? Yes, when you are dealing with multiple decisions and the ability to change things when it's not working or things happen or interruptions … what then?

—Conversation with Sarah (from ongoing research project, New Teacher Professional Identity)

Sarah's story recognizes the changing nature of teaching and reinforces her concerns about the almost scripted nature of classroom performance where risk and uncertainty are to be avoided. Her own teacher education had taken place long before the dominance of competencies and the freedom she describes created spaces for risk and responsiveness, creativity and imagination and allowed her to put her own stamp on her teaching artistry. We should perhaps start our conversations about teaching as an art and what that means within our ITE programmes as well as reflecting on the place of artistry within national frameworks. However, most importantly, we need to encourage our student teachers to consider teaching more holistically moving away from the instrumental notion of teaching to pass tests or other assessments and towards a more philosophical bent. What is their philosophy of teaching and how does it evolve through the year in ITE? What are the multiple threads or notes they draw upon to conduct the complex and unique compositions inherent in the unpredictable and the unique in diverse classrooms? These questions may be seen as a luxury in a world where the rush to put new teachers in classrooms is given primacy and yet we may need to find the spaces where student teachers can engage with their own subjectivities in a deeper way to enable them to negotiate a more holistic and artistic identity.

The Way Ahead

I recently listened to a discussion on the nature of consciousness and was interested to learn of the very many diverse ideas about what this might mean, although it was noted that there had been great confidence in subject-based definitions. Some decades before, a Nobel laureate Roger Penrose, had attempted to propose a revolutionary alternative to the more traditional conceptualizations in which he suggested that consciousness could be described as quantum in nature. This had been dismissed at the time but more recently in two separate projects, scientists had inclined towards the idea of the quantum nature of consciousness involving the ebb and flow of quantum crystalline waves. This transformational understanding of the brain and consciousness brought with it a new analogy for the brain: not as a supercomputer but instead as an orchestra. Could it have elements of both? Penrose's ideas were radical and flew in the face of accepted wisdom. In trying to conjecture something so different without proof, traditional science was reluctant even to consider this proposition. However, in moving away from the view of the brain as a computer and towards an even more complex and subtle understanding could undermine the cumulative wisdom achieved. Revolutionary thinking can become, at the very least, very uncomfortable but could, with time, lead to new understandings.

Thinking of teaching as a performance art, supported by skills and fleshed out by relational insights which manifest in moments of teaching and learning as artistry, we may be challenging teaching orthodoxies too strongly. In this chapter I have engaged with the idea of teaching as an art and the dynamic and responsive quality of artistry with an improvisational element reflecting the myriad interplay of beliefs and values, knowledge and skills, interactions and responses. How might this way of thinking impact ITE programmes in the future? If we maintain and reinforce competences, are we not in danger of omitting that key part of the individual which will help to provide a catalyst for teachers living and engaging with teaching in a meaningful way? This chapter has focused on the solitary artist within policy and competency restraints and for the student teacher, becoming a teacher can, at times, feel isolating and the creation of artistry, a nebulous but abstract concept which carries little currency within ITE. Yet it is perhaps incumbent on us to consider the communities of practice (Wenger 1998) or artistic colonies inhabiting schools which can potentially provide support and stimulus for artistry in teaching. However, we need to consider our next steps in beginning to quietly rebel rather than expecting an overnight revolution. Returning to Bryant (2009), he highlights the importance of language in beginning to challenge the accepted orthodoxies. A quiet rebellion might start with a shift in vocabulary and an acknowledgement of the artistic in ITE. The alternative might call for a louder claim to artistry. Bryant argues:

> Boldly and proudly proclaiming to the world that teaching is nothing less than an art is itself a revolutionary ideal. This linguistic change matters because it provides this profession that we all love so much with a voice. We must not forget or belittle the fact that every true, meaningful revolution begins with words. Revolutions are born in the minds of thinkers and are then committed to paper. Eventually, these words spring to life in the streets. (…) We must begin immediately the work of reclaiming the vocabulary of education. We must re- establish the true meanings of words like *pedagogy* and *praxis* in our classrooms and in the hearts and minds of our students, who themselves are future teachers.
> (Bryant 2009: 163)

Conclusion

This is my starting point then for the creation of a subtle revolution in ITE aligned with a more holistic view of teachers and teaching and including an important acknowledgement of the intangible elements which help to inform the unique compositions conducted within our classrooms. Through a renewed embrace of the concepts and language around what it means to be a teacher and the kind of teachers we hope to encourage, we can move away from the formulaic conceptualization of cloned individuals and instead look to enjoy the skilled professional who creates unique compositions within diverse contexts and interactions. This does mean that there needs to be a fundamental shift in how we view teaching and the education of future teachers. If teaching is in part a performance art with an emphasis on the relational-humanistic qualities inherent in the role, then ITE would need to be 'oriented towards performance-oriented training' (Crutchfield 2015: 104). Crutchfield also draws on Eisner (2002) and the idea of a 'teaching studio' where the intention is to 'train teachers experientially in their craft and provide a framework for professional feedback, critique and reflection. … teachers learn to think like artists … the ability to move, speak, think, feel, sense, imagine and react authentically in the present moment with clarity of intention' (Eisner 2002: 384).

Stenhouse (1988) argues for the need to spread the word of the teacher as artist (TAA) to support a transformation if we want to move beyond teachers exercising their art in secret. However, to generate a more powerful movement, there is a need to create alliances and conversations with those in positions of power to generate an impetus for change. Change, though, must be nurtured in part through teachers themselves who will need their ITE and in-service experiences to begin to engage with the idea of the teacher as artist. Recognizing the uniqueness of the teacher as artist, the uniqueness of each lesson and classroom, will likely seem risky to those in power. However, seeking a more holistic, relational and humanistic vision of teaching is to embrace uncertainty and messiness; to find artistry there is a need to look to an 'aesthetic fusion' of intuition and performance while building emotional bonding and care with the young people we are teaching (Ivie 2020). These are not measurable in the modern vocabulary of teaching but if we intend to go beyond the formulaic and to seek a fuller understanding of teaching as a performance art, then we need to stray from orthodoxies and tangle with an added aesthetic of teaching to help us to look beyond simple competencies.

References

Ball, S. (2003), 'The Teacher's Soul and the Terrors of Performativity', *Journal of Education Policy*, 18 (2): 215–28.

Ball, S. (2016), 'Subjectivity as a Site of Struggle: Refusing Neoliberalism?' *British Journal of Sociology of Education*, 37 (8): 1129–46.

Bellezza, A. (2020), 'Developing Performative Competence and Teacher Artistry: A Pedagogical Imperative in the Multicultural Classroom', *L2 Journal*, 12 (3): 23–42.

Britzman, D. (1993), 'The Terrible Problem of Knowing Thyself: Toward a Poststructuralist Account of Teacher Identity', *Journal of Curriculum Theorizing*, 9 (2): 23–46.

Bryant, J. (2009), 'B.S.: Reclaiming the Language of Education', *The Clearing House: A Journal of Educational Strategies, Issues and Ideas*, 82 (4): 161–4.

Campbell, L. (2018), 'Rupturing the Contract: Performative Pedagogy, Power Relations and Interruption', *Spark: UAL Creative Teaching and Learning Journal*, 3 (2): 104–15.

Crutchfield, J. (2015), 'Fear and Trembling. The Role of "Negative" Emotions in a Performative Pedagogy', *Scenario*, 9 (2): 102–14.

Eisner, E. (1983), 'The Art and Craft of Teaching', *Educational Leadership*, 40 (4): 4–14.

Eisner, E. (1998), *The Kind of Schools We Need*, Portsmouth, NH: Heinemann.

Eisner, E. (2002), *The Arts and the Creation of Mind*, New Haven, CT: Yale University Press.

Eisner, E. and L. Cuban (2013), 'On Teaching', *National Educational Policy Center*, 3 April. Available online: https://nepc.colorado.edu/blog/teaching-elliot-eisner (accessed 3 April 2025).

Federičová, M. (2021), 'Teacher Turnover: What Can We Learn from Europe?', *European Journal of Education*, 56 (1): 102–16.

Hall, W. (1983), 'The Aesthetics of Teaching', *The South Pacific Journal of Teacher Education*, 11 (1): 15–21.

Hamilton, L. (2013), '"Silence Does Not Sound the Same for Everyone": Student Teachers' Narratives', *SAGE Open*, 3 (3): 1–12.

Hamilton, L., G. Beauchamp, M. Hulme, L. Clarke and J. Harvey (2024), 'Challenges for School Leadership and Management in the Four Nations of the UK during the Pandemic: Conceptual Shifts and Implications for Future Thinking', in S. Brookes (ed), *Research Handbook on Public Leadership in a Post Pandemic Paradigm*, 80–96, Cheltenham: Edward Elgar Publishing.

Hickey, A. and S. Riddle (2025), 'Performative Enactments of Pedagogy in the Classroom: Strategies and Tactics of Relationality', *Pedagogy, Culture and Society*, 33 (1): 69–84.

Ivie, S. (2020), 'The Artistry of Teaching', *Excellence in Education Journal*, 9 (2): 121–38.

Jenkins, R. (2015), '4 Properties of Powerful Teachers', *The Chronicle of Higher Education*, 29 October. Available online: https://www.chronicle.com/article/4-properties-of-powerful-teachers/ (accessed 3 April 2025).

Kelchtermans, G. (2017), '"Should I Stay or Should I Go?": Unpacking Teacher Attrition/Retention as an Educational Issue', *Teachers and Teaching*, 23 (8): 961–77.

Lang, J. (2015), 'Waiting for Us to Notice Them', *The Chronicle of Higher Education*, 19 January. Available online: https://www.chronicle.com/article/waiting-for-us-to-notice-them/ (accessed 3 April 2025).

Lupton, M. (2013), 'Reclaiming the Art of Teaching', *Teaching in Higher Education*, 18 (2): 156–66.

Lutzker, P. (2007), *The Art of Foreign Language Teaching: Improvisation and Drama in Teacher Development and Language Learning*, Tubingen: Francke Verlag.

Lutzker, P. (2016), 'The Recovery of Experience in Foreign Language and Learning', in S. Even and M. Schewe (eds), *Performative Teaching, Learning, Research*, 222–40, Berlin: Schibri Verlag.

Lynch, S., J. Worth, S. Bamford and K. Wespieser (2016), *Engaging Teachers: NFER Analysis of Teacher Retention,* Slough: National Foundation for Education Research.

Makedon, A. (1990), *Is Teaching a Science or an Art? Paper presented at the Annual Conference of the Midwest Philosophy of Education Society*, Chicago, IL, 10 November.

Menter, I. and M.A. Flores (2021), 'Connecting Research and Professionalism in Teacher Education', *European Journal of Teacher Education*, 44 (1): 115–27, DOI: 10.1080/02619768.2020.1856811.

Ovenden-Hope, T. (2021), 'Teacher as Commodity versus Teacher as Professional: An International Status-Based Crisis in Teacher Supply', *Impact – Journal of the Chartered College of Teaching*, (11): 71.

Palmer, P. (1998), *The Courage to Teach: Exploring the Inner Landscape of a Teacher's Life*, San Francisco, CA: Jossey-Bass.

Patterson, C.H. and W.W. Purkey (1993), 'The Preparation of Humanistic Teachers for the Next Century Schools', *The Journal of Humanistic Education and Development*, 31 (4): 147–55.

Rubin, L. (1985), *Artistry in Teaching*, New York: Random House.

Sarason, S.B. (1999), *Teaching as a Performing Art*, New York: Teachers College Press.

Simons, H. (1996), 'The Paradox of Case Study', *Cambridge Journal of Education*, 26 (2): 225–40, DOI: 10.1080/0305764960260206.

Simpson, D., M. Jackson and J. Aycock (2005), *John Dewey and the Art of Teaching: Toward Reflective and Imaginative Practice*, Thousand Oaks, CA: Sage.

Stenhouse, L. (1988), 'Artistry and Teaching: The Teacher as Focus for Research and Development', *Journal of Curriculum and Supervision*, 4 (1): 43–51.

Tsakalou, D., L. Hamilton and J. Brown (2018), 'Institutional Narratives and the Struggle for Inclusive Communities in the Greek Context', *International Journal of Inclusive Education*, 24 (4): 395–413.

Wenger, E. (1998). *Communities of Practice: Learning, Meaning, and Identity*. Cambridge: Cambridge University Press.

Zeichner, K. (2014), 'The Struggle for the Soul of Teaching and Teacher Education in the USA', *Journal of Education for Teaching*, 40 (5): 551–68.

CHAPTER FIVE

Artful Teaching in the AI age: Seeing Harm in Artificiality via *Blade Runner*

James MacAllister

Prologue

Over the past twelve months I have felt a growing sense of unease over the impact of technological developments in my own teaching context of higher education (HE). My unease relates to the use of generative AI in assessed coursework. In the past when I marked a student essay, I assumed I was engaging with the thoughts of a person. Now I assume I am may not be. Many colleagues share my sense of unease, and with good reason. A recent survey suggested that nine in ten undergraduate students at UK universities use generative AI tools like ChatGPT in their assessments (Freeman 2025). The rise of AI use in HE has been nothing short of meteoric. In this chapter I will explore some of the pedagogical implications of the ascent of generative AI in HE drawing upon the realm of *Blade Runner* and the aphorisms of Nietzsche in the process. I draw a contrast between artful and artless teaching, expressing concern that AI could fuel a harmful rise in artless teaching and learning. I also argue that unless properly regulated, AI will foster conditions for a rise in academic plagiarism and epistemic mistrust, on the one hand, while also stifling the conditions needed for generation of long-term human well-being, on the other. Much more needs to be said to establish the validity or otherwise of these claims. In the rest of the chapter, I will try to show why there are *good reasons* for thinking that these risks of AI are very real.

A Note on *Good* Reasons

The great question would still remain whether we can *do without* illness, even for the development of our virtue; and whether especially our thirst for knowledge and self-knowledge do not need the sick soul as much as the healthy.

(Nietzsche 2001: 120)

What does it mean to have a good reason? My contention here is that *good* reasons for thinking or doing something always have an ethical dimension. More specifically, good reasons prioritize realization of well-being. Amongst other things real individual and collective well-being requires that knowledge be sought and shared in reliably sincere and accurate ways.[1] Given generative AI (GenAI) has potential to undermine these epistemic conditions of well-being perhaps one question should inform choice and action in respect to AI in education. Is this new technology or usage of AI more likely to enhance the well-being prospects of the individuals and collectives impacted or is it more likely to lead to their ill-being? I do not defend a specific and certainly not an essentialist conception of well-being here. Instead, it is my argument that students ought to be afforded opportunities to explore what well-being might look like for them, so that they might work on their own well-being. It is my contention though that employing AI as a shortcut to understanding may well lead to prolonged ill-being if deception is involved or if knowledge is only held in appearance, not truly grasped. Persevering in study may be a surer path to prosperity. Experiencing a little short-term ill-being for the sake of long-term well-being might sometimes be educationally beneficial. A degree of honest slog in search of understanding may be good for the soul (as Nietzsche implies). Of course, well-being prospects cannot be *known* in advance but well-informed, ethical choices are still possible absent certainty of the future. Some may also not see well-being as their primary ethical consideration – they may value having freedom of choice (even if choices lead to ill-being) over well-being considerations. However, freedom of choice is one of the conditions needed for real well-being. If it transpires that AI is increasingly shaping our choices, perhaps even making them for us, then we will be ill-beings not well-beings, ill for being less free.

A Note on Form and Style

What style of academic writing does the generative AI age call for? Large Language Models have after all opened up possibilities for academic plagiarism on an unprecedented scale. As coasting through writer's block has now become easy for the unscrupulous or the under pressure, perhaps now is a good time to remember there can be value in staying in a stuck state, at least for a while, if one can work through it, learn from it. Writing can after all be seen, perhaps should be seen, as a craft, an art to be learned, over time. Patient, thoughtful academic writing can be of educational value to the author/s – it can help them work out what they really think about something. Perhaps even help them work out who they are and what they stand for. Over time I have learned that writing about cinematic artworks can help me develop my thinking on a topic. I draw on the fictional world of *Blade Runner* to support my thinking in this chapter. This chapter also takes some inspiration from Nietzsche. Janaway (2014) claims that Nietzsche's writing involved more than just personal expression. His aphorisms and literary flourishes exemplify a distinct type of philosophical argumentation – an emoting rhetoric. His arguments were articulated with feeling to prompt his readers to feel the force in his arguments, not just think about them. This chapter includes aphorisms, and I have communicated some of my own worries about AI in education (in an at times rhetorical style) so that readers may feel the force of my arguments and not just think about them.

Learning from Artists and Artworks

Only artists ... have given men eyes and ears to see and hear with some pleasure what each himself is, himself experiences, himself wants; only they have taught us ... the art of regarding oneself as a hero, from a distance and as it were simplified and transfigured. (...) Only thus can we get over certain lowly details in ourselves. Without this art we would be nothing but foreground, and would live entirely under the spell of that perspective which makes the nearest and most vulgar appear tremendously big and as reality itself.

(Nietzsche 2001: 78)

The account of artful teaching developed here is inspired by Nietzsche, and particularly his insights on what can be learned from art and artists in *The Gay Science*. In this text he intimated that art can teach some people to be and become themselves by prompting them to transform their own desires beyond mere baselessness (2001: 78). Nietzsche famously thought it desirable to regard oneself as a work of art. He reserved the highest praise for those who were able to imagine an artistic plan for themselves and then mould themselves into this plan through sustained practice (2001: 290). Nietzsche suggested that artworks can profitably distance us from our desires. Art can inspire people to work on themselves until their souls become well. He implied that those who are well in soul will first and foremost be content in themselves rather than ashamed of themselves. As he puts it – only 'one thing is needful: that a human being should *attain* satisfaction with himself – be it through this or that poetry or art' (Nietzsche 2001: 290). Artists show us how to look upon the world with fresh eyes and from multiple perspectives, rendering beautiful, what appears not to be (Nietzsche 2001: 299). Nietzsche insists we *ought to learn from artists* but also go beyond them by taking their teachings into our lives (Nietzsche 2001: 299). If artworks and artists do have potential to teach people to see themselves and be themselves and look upon the world anew perhaps there are good reasons (in the well-being sense) for thinking that teaching ought to be artful, at least at times? What might artful teaching look like though and what might it aim at?

Artful and Artless Teaching

Artful teaching involves supporting students to look upon self and world under a different aspect. Artful teaching however aims not just at new student seeing, but also at new student being, and especially student well-being. Artful teaching aims to inspire students to a wellness in soul. Artful teaching is only a part of teaching – it is the side of teaching especially concerned with student self-making and student well-being. Artful teaching supports self-making and well-being by (amongst other things) encouraging students to both recognize their own desires and study what they love, slowly, carefully and over time. Artful teaching favours exposure to multiple perspectives and careful exploration of authentic student desire. Through its concern with artful living and student well-being, artful teaching is much more than a preparation for the world of work. Artful teaching prizes truthfulness, honesty, and deep knowledge of self and world. In contrast, artless teaching prizes efficiency over student well-being and self-making. Indeed, artless teaching conceals students from themselves by rushing to the preordained learning outcome.

Artless teaching cares little for truth or whether knowledge of self or world is held in the head and heart or simply regurgitated and then forgotten. Artless teaching thinks little of carelessly exposing students to ideologies or the whims of new technologies and capitalist corporations. Artless teaching obscures student discovery of self so that the inauthentic self (the artificial self?) can be put to work as quickly as possible or commodified and ideally both. Over the course of this chapter, I will expand further upon the challenges that AI presents for artful teaching in HE. For now, it is perhaps enough to note that though AI runs a very real risk of fuelling artless teaching and learning at a grotesque and previously unseen scale, I do not think AI must be inevitably complicit in artless teaching and learning. AI might in some circumstances support artful teaching and learning – if great care is taken in how it is used. However, unless it is properly regulated AI might represent an enormous (near and vulgar) barrier to artful teaching in HE.

The First Question Is Not *How* to Use AI in Education but Whether *It Should Be* Used

In late 2022, OpenAI 'gave' ChatGPT3 to the world. ChatGPT is significantly impacting assessment of learning in universities, for significant ill. It has made it incredibly easy for students to commit hard-to-detect academic plagiarism. Students can now submit sophisticated essays based on copy and pasted text generated by AI (Bower et al. 2024) – and it can be very hard for markers to determine if these essays are written by a person or AI (Cotton et al. 2024). How should teachers respond to this new challenge? Bower et al (2024) claim that more face-to-face teaching and assessment may be needed with a shift onto group presentations. Cotton et al. (2024) suppose that students could present drafts of their writing in class and that universities could invest in AI detection tools and be taught about the limitations of AI. Universities have been hastily drafting up guidance on AI use too. Edinburgh University, where I work, has for example recently published guidance which suggests it is 'generally acceptable' and 'positive' for students to use GenAI for:

- 'Brainstorming ideas through prompts
- Getting explanations of difficult ideas, questions and concepts
- Self-tutoring through conversation with the GenAI tool
- Creating practice questions and self-tests
- Organising and summarising your notes
- Planning and structuring your writing
- Summarising a text, article or book' (University of Edinburgh 2024)

There are some sensible practical suggestions being put forward here. However, some aspects of the university guidance also trouble me. Perhaps the situation demands *political* action, not just *pedagogical* action.[2] Perhaps some democratic resistance is needed until AI can be made to work more responsibly in education. I am particularly uncomfortable with the last point of the guidance as it normalizes the notion that it is acceptable to let AI read, think and write for students. Opportunities for valuable learning will be lost though if students utilize AI summaries and don't themselves write about what *they* have read. What capacities will students develop if they increasingly depend on AI to read, plan and even write coursework for them? It might be *time efficient* but will regular use of GenAI inhibit *student development*?

Might AI Reveal Its Inhumanity by Encouraging Student Shame?

And what about students who use AI in non-sanctioned ways – for academic plagiarism? What lessons and habits will students who plagiarize take into their life beyond education? That you don't need to *know* or work at anything when AI can do this for you? That the *appearance* of knowledge or skill is enough? That faking it to make it is *good*? That educational institutions approve of the fast (maybe fake) fix or are powerless to prevent plagiarism? Or perhaps those who cheat will be haunted with shame? Some students who have used AI to plagiarize have after all admitted feeling shame – that their degrees felt tainted (Coldwell 2024). If humanity involves sparing someone shame might AI reveal its inhumanity by creating optimal growth conditions for academic plagiarism and student shame? And what about students who play it straight, studying the old way? Is this fair on them? Their qualifications are being downgraded – their future employment prospects diminished. Reports of mistrust on campus are on the rise with staff not trusting students have produced work and students not trusting each other (Coldwell 2024). Whose agenda and well-being interests are being served by all this mistrust? Instead of stopping to ask if it would be *good* for students, staff, society if GenAI is used extensively in higher education, or *if it should be used at all*, the sector has been rushed into (and is also rushing into) thinking about *how to use it*. The ethical implications are it seems being lived with after the horse has bolted rather than thought through carefully, democratically.

Ethical Education Research and Practice in the AI Age

Those who work or study in universities today are guinea pigs in mass market research experiments for GenAI – but they did not choose to be. ChatGPT3 and similar tools violate a fundamental principle of ethical research – consent – and in two ways. GenAI first trained on research papers without the consent of the researchers involved before being secondly dropped on the sector (and the wider world) without consent. It is worth remembering that consent is a basic principle of ethically respectful social life and not just research. GenAI presents epistemic issues too. GenAI is not only making it easy to commit academic plagiarism, the content in AI generations quite often contains unreliable misinformation.[3] Epistemic trust should only be given to sources that reliably provide accurate information. Yet, GenAI tools can be unreliable and readily used for deceiving others. So long as this continues, they merit epistemic mistrust rather than trust. GenAI is opening up issues of academic freedom for teachers too. Teachers should be free from undue political or commercial influence over their practice – yet GenAI tools are eroding this basic freedom. Currently the autonomy and credibility of educational institutions are being undermined by profit-seeking tech companies that want to insert their products into what they see as the 'education market'.[4] However, these products may well foster conditions for a rise in epistemic mistrust and a degeneration of real well-being.[5]

Given all this there are good reasons for concluding that it is deeply problematic for educational institutions to endorse use of GenAI in education until these ethical and epistemic problems are worked through. However, at the moment formal university guidance gives staff and students a green light to use knowledge and images (which may or may not be accurate) obtained by ethically questionable means. I believe at least three actions are urgently needed to address the ethical and epistemic issues arising from the emergence of GenAI in education:

1) thought experiments that highlight possible harms to well-being arising from GenAI
2) a reclamation of the autonomy of educational institutions
3) democratic debate about how to make AI in education work for the real long-term well-being interests of students and society.

Thought experiments are much more ethically justifiable than mass live experiments on a non-consenting public with little thinking through of risks. Unlike actual experiments, thought experiments have the advantage of being unlikely to harm any participants and they don't violate principles of consent. Thought experiments might be the most ethically appropriate way of understanding possible harms of AI in education. Thought experiments might also be used to inform democratic debate about AI in education, debate that might helpfully focus on a core question: under what conditions might the majority of staff and students in educational institutions have justified confidence that any use of AI in teaching, learning and assessment is ethically responsible and epistemically trustworthy? Teachers ought to be able to discern the difference between real human creations born from student endeavour and artificial generations whisked up in an instant. Everyone in education should also have assurance that any platforms they are using are epistemically reliable and not exploitative of others.

Of course, educators will need to adapt some practices in the short term to try to make the best out of a bad situation. However, I believe they also need to collectively call on governments to legally require three responsibilities from companies that develop GenAI tools that can be used in formal educational contexts. That all content in AI generations must be (1) based only on data that has ethical approval for use from the original creators; (2) be accurate and not misleading and (3) include an unremovable kitemark (this could be hidden but it would need to be capable of being made visible by anyone who wants to check) that highlights its artificial mode of production. If these three principles of consent, accuracy and verifiability were consistently applied in educational institutions I believe they would provide much better grounds for confidence and trust in AI. It may well be very difficult to bring about the realization of these principles in practice though. These principles may not be the best ones either – they may well need amendment. It is therefore vital that all involved in higher education debate how to make AI work for the long-term good of students and society and not just the interests of profit-seeking tech companies. It is crucial that tech companies be held accountable for the social consequences of their creations. Legal actions may be required. At the moment there are simply not good reasons to think that GenAI can be used ethically and trustworthily in education. The current situation necessitates more (ethical) research, political debate and legislation – not swift adoption of unregulated GenAI in education practice.

Who Ought to Bear Responsibility for a New Technology That Creates Social Problems?

The artful teacher knows that artworks can open up educational conversations about complex topics, topics like the ethical implications of AI. The fictional realm of *Blade Runner* is relevant here. In *Blade Runner* the Tyrell Corporation has created artificial human replicas (called replicants) for slave labour on off-world colonies. The most advanced replicant model (the Nexus 6) is physically and intellectually superior to humans and virtually indistinguishable from them. A Voigt-Kampff test can be employed to separate human from replicant. This assesses the empathic powers of subjects by measuring speed of pupil dilation and blush response to a series of questions, questions often involving the torture of living beings. It is supposed that, unlike real humans, replicants lack empathy for other living beings – the test is designed to reveal humanity by the presence of empathy or inhumanity via its absence. However, this test is imperfect. In *Do Androids Dream of Electric Sheep?* (the novel that inspired *Blade Runner*) psychiatric patients known to be human, fail the test due to a 'flattening of affect' (Dick 1968: 30). Deckard is a bounty hunter charged with 'retiring' any violent replicants who pose a threat to humans. Knowing the test of humanity that his work relies on is flawed, Deckard suggests that corporations that create new technologies ought to bear responsibility for ensuring there is a reliable way to detect AI from the human. Hear! Hear!

Seeing Humanity in Artificiality and Inhumanity in Capitalism

'More than human' is the creed of the Tyrell Corporation. Over the course of *Blade Runner* Deckard learns that replicants may be *more human* than he initially credits. Through seeing Rachel's pain on learning she is a replicant (she was unaware of this until Deckard subjects her to the Voigt-Kampff test) he grasps that replicants can experience human-like emotions. Roy Batty teaches him that replicants and humans alike fear death and can empathize with others, in their sufferings, longings and joys (Mulhall 2002). Deckard's education is completed when he falls in love with Rachel and she with him (Mulhall 2002). When he uncovers that he is likely a replicant too Deckard has little reason to doubt replicants can empathize, love, fear, suffer – for he has experienced these very things first hand in his own (replicant?) body. Through all this the audience also sees that artificial beings can (at least in film) exhibit humanity. Possession of human-like bodies is central to the possibility of artificial beings possessing humanity (Mulhall 2002). Deckard's moment of self-recognition is made feasible by his awareness that artificial memories are implanted into some replicants (including Rachel). When Deckard sees an origami unicorn at his apartment door, he understands that this is Gaff's (a police officer) way of telling him that he is a replicant, and that his vision of a unicorn is a memory implant. The implanted memory of a horse is also central to the development of self-understanding in the hero of the sequel to *Blade Runner*.

In *Blade Runner 2049* (BR2049), K is a Blade Runner, who knows from the outset that he is a replicant. However, when he discovers his memory involving a wooden toy horse might be real rather than implanted, he starts to believe he may have been born rather than made. K had earlier unearthed compelling evidence that Rachel miraculously (for replicants cannot reproduce) gave birth before she died. Believing he could be the 'miracle' child, K embarks on a quest to find Deckard. K discovers that he is not Rachel's daughter. However, the experience of a quasi-father–son relationship with Deckard reveals the profound 'value of the parent child-bond' to K (Mulhall 2020: 39). Indeed, K is moved to sacrifice his own life to ensure that Deckard is reunited with his actual daughter, Ana. She makes memories for replicants and by the end of the film, it becomes clear that Ana set in motion the events that led to reunion with her father when she illegally implanted her own real memory of the (trojan?) horse into K. BR2049 opens up a range of philosophical, political and pedagogical questions. For the purposes of this chapter, I will focus on only two: what might BR2049 show audiences about (1) how AI can distort understanding and desire in ways that harm well-being and (2) the economic behaviour and priorities of tech companies in the AI age? Mulhall (2020: 46) claims there may be a hint of 'villainy' in Ana as she implicitly encourages K to believe *her* memory implant really happened to *him* – and this misunderstanding costs K his life. Ana deceives and enslaves K for her own purposes (Mulhall 2020).

Mulhall's reading of BR2049 does not do justice to the possibility that K may have freely chosen his fate, and it is perhaps a bit harsh on Ana. She may not (at least not consciously) have had such malignant intent. However, her memory-making does cinematically depict how misinformation can be artificially implanted into sentient beings distorting their thoughts, desires and actions, causing harm to well-being. Smart (2020) suggests K is also manipulated and enslaved by the Wallace corporation. He maintains BR2049 generates novel philosophical insights about the impact of AI on commerce and capitalism. In the film K is not just a Blade Runner, he is also an economic agent. He produces economic goods by retiring harmful replicants but he also consumes them. K may even have been programmed to feel loneliness – intentionally fitted with the desire and means to pay for the company of his AI hologram partner Joi (Smart 2020). His longing for Joi is manufactured so as to line the pockets of the Wallace Corporation. Wallace may have built a tragic flaw (the feeling of isolation) into K so that they could sell him the 'technological fix' to his problem (in the form of Joi, their AI-companion-product) (Smart 2020). Wallace's profits seem to be sustained by providing technological 'fixes' to the desires and problems it generates – a classic play of capitalism. Wallace also manufactures a technological fix for a devastated environment, seeing even ecological collapse as economic opportunity – revealing how capitalist systems really only want to sustain themselves (Smart 2020). BR2049 shows that capitalism and commerce in the AI age may have a powerful tendency towards inhumanity and manipulation for profit.

Artful Intelligence over Artificial Intelligence

Unlike in the Blade Runner universe, in real-life AI has no humanity for it has no-body senses of its own to empathize with. AI certainly has no ethical sense. Indeed, the *Blade Runner* movies demonstrate that the companies behind AI tools may value commercial gain over gains in well-being. Artful intelligence is the opposite of this. It is built up from embodied sensing and it contains a strong ethical orientation – the long-term good for self and others. The person of artful intelligence perceives the world through their own senses. They are in their bodies. They weigh up sense evidence carefully before doing anything important. They think it through, with well-being as the aim. The person of artful intelligence knows they must make their own mind up. They know the double truth in this. They must think for themselves but they must also build up their own mind by working on it over time. They see the sheen in AI mash ups and they see through it. They don't discard AI altogether for they know there could be good in it, but they are suspicious of GenAI. They know many cynical companies want to plant desires in them, seeing profit in them. The person of artful intelligence works on their own mind, soul and well-being like a sculptor shaping a human form. They make the effort required for deep understanding of what they are sensing, desiring and doing. Artificial intelligence cannot do this. It processes impressively and it can exploit human desires but it cannot (at least not yet) really understand human well-being, for it has no senses to feel well-being.

The Artful Teacher Is an Educator Not a Detective

'Do I need to look into the eyes of my students to know that it is really their knowing on show, their thinking, their creating? Will this face-to-face test be enough to know for sure that a human being is doing the thinking, making or speaking? Or will I need to perform a Voight-Kampff-like test? And what happens when a new version of AI comes along that can cheat that test? How far will the technological innovations go? Will they ever end? Where will the line be drawn? Has it already been rubbed out? It is egregious that AI is forcing me to doubt my students in this way, without the tools to know the human and real from the AI and the fake. No teacher or student deserves this. No-body deserves this. This level of mistrust. We test our students enough already! We should not have to test their humanity too. I am an educator but AI is turning me into a detective. Thrusting a badge in my hands and placing handcuffs on those of my students.' So professes the artful teacher.

Artful Teaching in the Age of AI Efficiency

Efficient 'learning' in the age of AI can be careless with truth – artful teaching takes care to be truthful. Artful teaching is not artful in the sense of cunning and clever, in the sense of the 'Artful Dodger'. If you want to know that sort of artful, study capitalism – always manipulating people into desiring and buying what they often don't need. AI can be full of that sort of artfulness (that is really artlessness). Education and teaching from AI can be artless too, turning humans against themselves, into buyers of products, or sellers, or both. Artful teachers stand opposed to all harmful artificiality in education – they engage students in slow, deep education because they know that real well-being needs real education. Truly *artful teaching* is full of art, art that can help humans be themselves, think for themselves, live their own lives and well. Artful in the sense of skilful human craft and making. Artful in the sense of style and beauty, of graceful movement through the world.

Responses to an Objection and to the Objectionable

I have two responses to any objection that since contract cheating has been implicitly tolerated in higher education for a long time then why not plagiarism via AI too. First, two wrongs don't make a right. Second, GenAI has made cheating much easier – plagiarism is much more ubiquitous. Neither form of plagiarism *should* be indulged though – no one benefits in the long run. Artful teachers persuade students to choose slow study over the fast AI fix. They support students who commit to the journey of real education. They reject popular pedagogical formulas.

The popular formula for education *(the first deception)*

Education = efficient excellence in examination = success (as *capitalism conceives it*)

The popular formula for efficient AI teaching *(the great deception)*

Efficient teaching with AI runs in a straight line *but its ethics run crooked*. It prizes artificiality over reality. It lives on a screen that is bright and flashy – all surface, *no depth*. A screen that spews out mashed up stuff *of unknown authorship – stolen from many, made by no-body. Bending users to the will and shape of the market.*

The response of the artful teacher *(unmasking deceptions)*

Open your own eyes. See. See that there is so much more to real education than artless efficiency.

Ten Ethical Principles That Inform the Practice of the Artful Teacher

1) **(A promise):** The artful teacher says to her students, take your time and I will give you mine. Be yourself and I will be myself too. Stay with your study and I will stay with you. Go with me and I will go with you. Go from me and you will go with my blessing.

2) **(Variety, rhythm and purpose):** Practising, showing, valuable content to share, professing with liveliness, probing questions, letting silence in, listening, attending, responding, reading, stopping, moving, moving outside and revelling in the wonder of it, laughing,

struggling, playing, exploring, conversing, writing, drawing, measuring, errors, errors acknowledged, communicating care, slowing down, building up, letting go. All these things the artful teacher may do. Always so that her students may learn to do these things too.

3) **(The speed and style of learning)**: The artful teacher values slow learning over fast learning, depths over surfaces, doubt over gullibility, honesty over subterfuge, trying over ease, failure over fake.

4) **(Artful teaching and intelligence over the artificial)**: The artful teacher prizes artful intelligence over artificial intelligence, artful teaching over the effective. The artful teacher possesses artful intelligence and they aim (amongst other things) to foster and inspire artful intelligence and practice in students, artful living in students. Students of artful teachers are taught to consider why it is always good to use AI in an epistemically and ethically responsible manner. When a student asks her why she is so against AI the artful teacher replies that I am not against AI per se. I just feel it is turning us against ourselves, generating mistrust of others, making us ill not well, adding to our problems not solving them. If generative AI is unthinkingly embraced in education, does most of our generation for us, we humans will degenerate.

5) **(Debunking deception through the practice of wandering)**: Wandering is a daily practice of the artful teacher. The artful teacher does not worry unduly about outcomes or objectives or tests. She supports her students to prepare for tests in the right way of course but she also helps them see tests for what they are. The artful teacher has a route in mind but she knows the value of the spontaneous diversion. When to go off-trail, when to stay to on course. She talks and walks with her students. She offers no easy answers, only a long hard slog. A circuitous journey with detours of suffering and joy, moments of blindness and sight, a getting lost and a finding out, a working on it, a working it through. She points to a path and they wander on to it together.

A Wandering Interlude of Joy and Pain.

(**Experiencing joy in the interconnectedness of life**): They had walked a while up the hill in the wood when they heard them. One definite snort, then several more. Some pigs waddled into view. All rusty golden hair as thick as fur. One flopped over in front of a student, who gingerly rubbed the belly of the gentle being through the fence. The students and the artful teacher gazed, smiling. A student noticed the roughed-up state of the field the pigs were in and grew concerned. Had the pigs rooted it up? Could anything grow there? A second student said she read that pig rooting can be good for soil in some woodland areas, creating conditions for plant seedlings to grow. She pointed out that little pine seedlings were sticking out of the rooted turf. They laughed with joy at the endeavour of these pigs and the interconnectedness of life.

(**The stun stick and the pig farmer**): A farmer came along with a thick metal stick in his hands. A student asked him what it was for. He pointed to the bolt on the end, 'it's my stun stick. These pigs have been making my farmland go wild so I am going to slaughter them and get cows instead. More money in those.' And stun them he did there and then – one shot square between the eyes for each of them. Each writhing on the floor before going still. After the farmer left one of the students starting crying. The artful teacher stayed a long while with him, the pair united in grief.

6) (**Learning from suffering, learning to love**): The artful teacher falls silent. Let's her students be. It gets dark. They are weary and restless, wondering if the easy way might be better after all. After a while the artful teacher speaks: I see your suffering in not grasping. I care about it. I care about you. Stay with your suffering and I will stay with you. Stay with what you cannot see. Study it slowly, look at it from all angles. Wait for the right light. Stay with the strangeness of this unfathomable thing. Don't give up on it. Learn to love[6] this wondrous thing so that you can come to see it, really see it. Understanding <u>earned</u> in this way is wonderful. Feel how good it feels to learn in this slow, suffering way. All this she says through her daily practice.

7) (**Caring for well-being – learning from ill-being**): The artful teacher cares for the long-term well-being of her students. She cannot promise them well-being but she can point to what she knows of it. She cares about Accuracy and Sincerity[7] – in education and in life. She models these virtues before her students, so that they might come to care about them, practice them too. The artful teacher knows that learning and life involves ill fortune, error and luck. She supports her students through success and failure, gain and loss. She supports them to see that ill-being may sometimes result no matter what one does – and that well-being sometimes needs some ill-being. Some ill-being is just ill but some ill-being can bring good, if it is listened to, if it is learned from.

8) (**Timing the pointing and ripening the self**): The artful teacher draws on music, film, literature, painting, poetry, photography, sculpture, theatre, TV, dance – any artwork that can enliven the senses of her students. Or any arts practice that can work on the souls of her students – work to make them well. But the artful teacher need not

be an arts teacher. The artful teacher knows any subject or object might be capable of supporting a student on their educational journey. If the timing it right. The artful teacher waits for the right moment to point, hoping that the student will study the subject or object, stay with it, suffer in learning to love it, all the while 'ripening in selfhood' and well-being. To support students in their journey to well-being and ripeness in selfhood, teachers need to value this as a worthy goal for themselves too.[8]

9) **(Create yourself out of your cares):** The artful teacher encourages her students to care for what is good (well-being good): She implores them to ask, what do *you* care about? Has caring for your cares been good for you? And what of that and whom you have cared for – has your care been good for them? If you can affirm yes with all honesty then busy yourself. Create yourself out of your cares.[9] Don't let speedy, needy, all too greedy dupers use you, make you or distract you. Flesh out your own form out of what you care about.

10) **(Ethical principles over flat formulas):** The artful teacher resists formulaic pedagogy but they do develop their own ethical principles (that they live by).[10] Their ethical principles evolve, their practice evolving in light of this. They learn from their best teachers (often their students) yet they develop their own pedagogic style. The artful teacher strives to help their students find their own way in learning, their own way of living, their own ethic of well-being.

Epilogue

The artful student says to her teacher: 'you gave me your time and I gave you mine but the rest of my life is waiting. I must go but I want you to know, that your teachings will travel with me'. Sometime later, the artful student stops on the road to talk to a stranger who says. 'I am going through the tunnel to the golden city to take some gold for me.' The artful student studies the man before speaking 'you have gold in you already, more than enough. Besides, all the gold is gone. Just paint now – golden gloss, rotten substance. I have walked there. Most of the people live with screens in their faces and most of their faces are sad. Don't go there, or at least not yet. I know another way. Over the mountain. It is a hard trek – the tunnel is much quicker. But the trail has delightful detours and there are wonderful perspectives at the top. I can show you the path if you like and we can walk and talk as we go?' The stranger replies 'you sound like a teacher' and they set off up the winding mountain together.

Notes

1   For an insightful discussion about this and the virtues of accuracy and sincerity, see Williams (2004).

2   Orwell believed he lived during a grave time that demanded political art and writing, claiming that 'the opinion that art should have nothing to do with politics is also a political attitude' (2021: 229). While it may be objected that artful teaching, ought not be political, it is my argument that the threats posed by AI (to student and teacher well-being) are so grave as to demand a political and not just a pedagogical response.

3   For example, an Apple AI news alert app recently created a story claiming Luke Littler had won the final of the world darts tournament – the only problem was the match had not been played yet!

4   Williamson & Eynon (2020) note how global education businesses like Pearson have been enthusiastically pushing AI education in order to grow market interest in their products.

5   McCraw (2015) similarly suggests that harm can come to people if they are betrayed, misled or otherwise let down by an object that is not epistemically trustworthy.

6   Nietzsche (2001: 334) has informed my thinking here.

7   Williams (2004: 44) uses capital letters for these virtues to denote that they are 'terms of art'.

8   I borrow this notion from Higgins (2003).

9   Nietzsche's (2001: 335) call for human beings to 'create themselves' has influenced my view here.

10   These principles are not intended to be universal pedagogical prescriptions – they merely aim to inspire teachers to find their own principles of artful practice.

References

Blade Runner 2049 (2017), [Film] Dir. D. Villeneuve. USA: Warner Bros.

Blade Runner: The Final Cut (2007), [Film] Dir. R. Scott. USA: Warner Bros.

Bower, M., J. Torrington, J. Lai, P. Petocz and M. Alfano (2024), 'How Should We Change Teaching and Assessment in Response to Increasingly Powerful Generative Artificial Intelligence? Outcomes of the ChatGPT Teacher Survey', *Education and Information Technologies*, 29: 15403–39.

Coldwell, W. (2024), 'I Received a First but It Felt Tainted and Undeserved: Inside the University AI Cheating Crisis', *The Guardian*, 16 December. Available online: https://www.theguardian.com/technology/2024/dec/15/i-received-a-first-but-it-felt-tainted-and-undeserved-inside-the-university-ai-cheating-crisis (accessed 10 January 2025).

Cotton, D., J. Cotton and J. Reuben Shipley (2024), 'Chatting and Cheating: Ensuring Academic Integrity in the Era of ChatGPT', *Innovations in Education and Teaching International*, 61 (2): 228–39.

Dick, P. (1968), *Do Androids Dream of Electric Sheep?*, London: Orion.

Freeman, J. (2025), *Student Generative AI Survey 2025*, Oxford: HEPI.

Higgins, C. (2003), 'Teaching and the Good Life: A Critique of the Ascetic Ideal in Education', *Educational Theory*, 53 (2): 131–54.

Janaway, C. (2014), 'Self and Style: *Life as Literature* Revisited', *The Journal of Nietzsche Studies*, 45 (2): 103–17.

McCraw, B. (2015), 'The Nature of Epistemic Trust', *Social Epistemology*, 29 (4): 413–30.

Mulhall, S. (2002), *On Film*, London: Taylor & Francis.

Mulhall, S. (2020), 'The Alphabet of Us: Miracles, Messianism, and the Baseline Test in *Blade Runner 2049*', in T. Shanahan and P. Smart (eds), *Blade Runner 2049: A Philosophical Exploration*, 27–47, London: Routledge.

Nietzsche, F. (1998), *Beyond Good and Evil*, Oxford: Oxford University Press.

Nietzsche, F. (2001), *The Gay Science*, Cambridge: Cambridge University Press.

Orwell, G. (2021), *George Orwell: Selected Essays*, ed. S. Collini, Oxford: Oxford University Press.

Smart, P. (2020), 'Artificial Economics', in T. Shanahan and P. Smart (eds), *Blade Runner 2049: A Philosophical Exploration*, 185–205, London: Routledge.

University of Edinburgh. (2024), 'Guidance for Working with Generative AI ("GenAI") in Your Studies', University of Edinburgh, 1 November. Available online: https://information-services.ed.ac.uk/computing/comms-and-collab/elm/guidance-for-working-with-generative-ai (accessed 10 January 2025).

Williams, B. (2004), *Truth and Truthfulness: An Essay in Genealogy*, Oxford: Princeton University Press.

Williamson, B. and R. Eynon (2020), 'Historical Threads, Missing Links, and Future Directions in AI in Education', *Learning, Media and Technology*, 45 (3): 223–35.

CHAPTER SIX

Art Is the Mother of Resistance: Must Education Resist Too?

Sonia Sjollema

Introduction

Every day on my way to work, I cycle past the Art Academy of Arnhem in the Netherlands, where the phrase 'Art is the mother of resistance' is displayed prominently. This statement has long intrigued me, and it raises questions: How can we understand the relationship between the arts and society? What does resistance mean in that context, and what should we resist? And, finally, what does the idea of 'motherhood' imply about the possibility of resistance and the nature of that resistance? The statement intrigues because, according to several educational scholars, resistance is an essential part of educational processes. In this book, we explore education as an art form and the artistry of teaching. If we assume there are parallels between art and education, the above questions are also relevant to education and teaching. Furthermore, what role does resistance play in education and teaching? From this perspective, how can we understand the artistry of teaching, and to what extent is resistance to society also relevant to education?

My search for the background of the quote 'Art is the mother of resistance' led me to the work of Theodor Adorno. Although the quote cannot be directly attributed to him, it reflects the essence of his ideas. In this chapter, I discuss how Adorno envisaged the relationship between art and resistance. To understand the role of resistance in education, I draw on Philippe Meirieu's (2008, 2016) concepts of maturity and Gert Biesta's (2015, 2020) ideas of 'grown-up-ness' and 'interruption'. I conclude the chapter by asking how 'motherhood' can be understood in relation to education's resistance to functionality.

Adorno's Critical Position towards Society

Theodor Adorno (1903–69) was born Theodor Ludwig Wiesengrund. He was a German sociologist, philosopher, musicologist, composer and literary critic and a leading member of the Frankfurt School. Before the Second World War, Adorno was a university instructor in philosophy at Frankfurt University and was attached to the *Institut für Sozialforschung* (IfS), where he critically analysed societal developments with renowned German intellectuals, such as Max Horkheimer, Herbert Marcuse and Erich Fromm. In 1933, the university cut ties with the institute, and Adorno and his colleagues were dismissed due to their Jewish background and critical perspective. Adorno fled and eventually ended up in Los Angeles in the early 1940s, where he experienced the rise of the American film industry up close (Bahr 2007; Van den Brink 2013).

Adorno's work was heavily shaped by the period he lived through, marked by Nazi methods of oppression, stereotyping, and exclusion in Germany, which resulted in the persecution of Jews and the Holocaust. The Nazis perfected their methods of purification, depriving target groups, including non-Aryans, Marxists and intellectuals, of their property, citizenship rights and, ultimately, their lives. The arts became special targets; writers, artists and musicians were forced to join the Reich Chamber of Culture, which the Ministry of Propaganda controlled to establish a uniform national culture while purging Jews and politically unreliable individuals from the arts (Bahr 2007).

In their *Dialectics of Enlightenment* (1997), Adorno and Horkheimer searched for the causes of the Holocaust and the barbarism that occurred in Nazi Germany. According to their analysis, the seeds of this dark period had been present in German society long before the rise of fascism and remained present in modern Western society. They concluded the Enlightenment had not brought the liberation it promised. According to Horkheimer and Adorno, science and technology played an important role in provoking functionality in society and human relationships. As science advanced, the concept of reason was replaced by formulas, causes and rules of probability, calculability and utility. In their view, this scientific approach led to a superficial knowledge of cause and effect and the externals of phenomena but ignored deeper layers of knowledge that give meaning to life and coexistence. Science tends to overlook important categories in life, such as substance, quality, activity, suffering and existence, leading to the alienation of human existence. This detachment led to a cold and inhumane society and a loss of quality of life. The Enlightenment did not facilitate the liberation of myths but spread its own myths about what constitutes knowledge and truth, mainly to dominate and exploit both nature and humanity. The authors stated, 'What human beings seek to learn from nature is how to use it to dominate wholly both it and human beings' (Horkheimer and Adorno 1997: 2).

Horkheimer and Adorno identified three dominant myths in their time: the nationalist *Blut und Boden myth* of national socialism, the socialist equality illusion of Stalinism and the capitalist consumer economy of the 'free' West. In the first two, the writers recognized the danger of the individual being forced to conform to the collective of the masses, which equalizes and destroys everything that does not conform. The latter leads to a total privatization of existence, in which desires are materialized in consumer products; all things, including humans, become a resource to be exploited (Van den Brink 2013).

The Need to Resist

The idea of resistance was introduced in *Dialectics of Enlightenment*, but Adorno explained the role of culture in resistance more explicitly in his article 'Culture Industry Revisited' (Adorno and Rabinbach 1975), in which he emphasized the importance of autonomous and critical-thinking subjects in resisting the conformity and domination of the culture industry. According to Adorno, art and culture play a role in resisting the status quo. He wrote of 'the rebellious resistance inherent within culture' (Adorno and Rabinbach 1975: 12). In Adorno's view, culture (high or low) in the true sense, does not simply accommodate reality: '[I]t always simultaneously raised a protest against the petrified relationships under which they [human beings] lived' (Adorno and Rabinbach 1975: 13). Under the influence of the culture industry, the rebellious resistance in culture is changed into a force that duplicates, reinforces and strengthens petrified relationships, presuming them to be 'given and unchangeable' (Adorno and Rabinbach 1975: 12). The culture industry changes human beings into masses, in which they become an 'object of calculation' (Adorno and Rabinbach 1975: 12). Under the disguise of freedom, the consumer becomes a victim of consumption and the satisfaction of needs: 'The consumer is not the king, as the culture industry would have us believe, not its subject but its object' (Adorno and Rabinbach 1975: 12).

What particularly struck Adorno was that pressing questions regarding the social role of the culture industry are often repressed or, at the very least, excluded from public and academic discourse. By excluding normative questions, the culture industry presents 'an idea of the good life as if existing reality were the good life' (Adorno and Rabinbach 1975: 16). In this way, culture loses its rebellious role of resistance and its association with pursuing freedom: 'It proclaims: you shall conform' (Adorno and Rabinbach 1975: 17). Consumerism becomes an ideology that serves to maintain the current reality. Adorno concluded that the total effect of the culture industry is 'anti-enlightenment' (Adorno and Rabinbach 1975: 18), which 'impedes the development of autonomous, independent individuals who judge and decide consciously for themselves' (Adorno and Rabinbach 1975: 19). His cultural critique is, therefore, also a critique of society; by undermining emancipation and the formation of autonomous subjects, the culture industry also affects the conditions for a democratic society, because, as Adorno states, societies need mature, critical-thinking adults ('adults that have come to age') to sustain and develop themselves as democracies (Adorno and Rabinbach 1975: 19). Thus, according to Adorno, culture plays an essential role in resisting domination and transforming petrified relationships (Adorno and Rabinbach 1975: 13). In his perception, there is still a need to resist ideology and dominant myths, even in modern Western societies. The focus of resistance should be on the culture industry, which propagates conformity, infantility and anti-Enlightenment.

Art's Uncertain Role in Resisting Functionality and Domination

Adorno believed art and culture play an important role in resisting domination and petrified societal structures. However, in a time of functionalism, scientism and commodification, this role is under pressure and not straightforward. Adorno's *Aesthetic Theory* (1997), published posthumously in 1970 after he died in 1969, focused on the societal relevance of modern art. The central question he intended to answer in this work was whether art can survive in a late capitalist world and contribute to transforming this world (Pickford and Zuidervaart 2024). In his aesthetic theory, Adorno deviated from an understanding of the arts from the outside. He moved away from objectifying norms and concepts of beauty or sublimity. Essential for Adorno's theory is that he placed the potentiality of aesthetic experience in the work of art itself, in the contradictions and tension within its form, not in the subjective taste of the observer. He avoided a relativistic interpretation of art, stating that the essence of art lies in the truth content. Adorno claimed, 'The spirit of an artwork is not their [rational] meaning and not their intention, but rather their truth content, or in other words, the truth that is revealed through them' (1997: 284).

Art's Complex Relationship with Society: Import and Function

A significant insight derived from Adorno's aesthetic theory is that modern art, if it is to play a relevant role in society, has a dual dialectical nature. Art is socially embedded yet remains a critical distance from society. Art is not solely *for* society, yet it holds significant societal importance. It contains a critical reflection *on* society while being a part *of* it; therefore, art cannot completely transcend its context. On the one hand, art keeps itself 'alive' through its social force of resistance, but nothing in art is immediately social, 'not even when this is its aim' (Adorno 1997: 230).

Adorno highlighted the key tension between the import (*Gehalt*) and function (*Funktion*). These concepts can help in understanding the relationship between the arts and their societal relevance. *Import* refers to the artwork's more profound meaning or essence and *Function* to art's role in society (Pickford and Zuidervaart 2024). The dialectics in *Gehalt* and *Function* can be opposed, unified or contradicted, but always in favour of *Gehalt*: 'Insofar a social function can be predicted for artworks, it is in their functionlessness' (Adorno 1997: 227). According to Adorno, art can only exist autonomously when it resists the idea of serving a functional purpose in society. Adorno emphasized the importance of autonomy over art's social role, arguing that 'art becomes social by its opposition to society, and it occupies this position only as autonomous art' (Adorno 1997: 225). He argued, 'Art keeps itself alive through its social force of resistance; unless it reifies itself, it becomes a commodity' (Adorno 1997: 230). In an age characterized by repressive collectivization, art has the power to challenge domination, and this act of resistance becomes a key measure of both the artwork itself and its social significance. Art is inherently social not simply because it is part of or exists for society but because it reflects the presence of society within it, as demonstrated through its truth content and intrinsic essence (*Gehalt*).

Truth Content and Negative Dialectics

In this notion, the relationship between art and society is understood as the possibility of revealing something beneath the surface that escapes the objectifying rationality of language. An artwork is only understood in its non-identity and its negative dialectics: The contradictions in an artwork can be unified, which, according to Adorno, does not mean the liquidation of the opposites (Jessop 2017). Adorno adhered to this understanding of art's aesthetics in his work. He disrupted a conceptual or rational understanding of aesthetics: The moment you try to pin down a definition of art, it escapes in opposition. At the risk of compromising both his artistic form and his non-conceptual language, I elaborate on some of these dialectics in the following sections.

An artwork is not a fixed 'thing'. Instead, aesthetics can be found in the process of making as well: 'The result of the work is as much the trajectory it traverses to its *imago* as it is the *imago* itself as the goal; it is at once static and dynamic' (Adorno 1997: 86). Adorno explained that a work relates to reality; it possesses the potential to reveal an underlying essence in its truth content. In this sense, artworks 'participate in enlightenment because they do not lie' (Adorno 1997: 5). Art can reveal human needs and suffering, exposing tensions and inconsistencies in prevailing social relationships and norms. According to Adorno, '[T]he unsolved antagonisms of reality return in artworks as immanent problems of form' (Adorno 1997: 6). Each artwork has its own texture and complexity, yet its form is not entirely within the artist's control. The more art is 'created, sought after, or invented', the more uncertain it becomes whether it can truly be made or discovered (Adorno 1997: 26). At the same time, modern art does not imitate reality, as it has a quality of semblance. Adorno argued, 'The reality of artworks testifies to the possibility of the possible' (Adorno 1997: 132). Although works of art need the artist's imagination and subjectivity, the subjective elements are not entirely shaped or created by the individual's unique imagination or expression. This point positions modern art in opposition to the bourgeois 'art religion', which 'confused the imagery of art with its opposite: with the artist's psychological representations' (Adorno 1997: 86). According to Adorno, creating art involves elements of risk and surprise. This process requires a space for experimentation, which encompasses both mastery and unpredictability. Art arises not only from imagination or artistic expression but also from the element of surprise: 'some are desired, others require correction' (Adorno 1997: 38).

In addition, Adorno claimed that true art is not merely affirmative. Autonomous modernist art – such as Schönberg's atonal music and Kafka's literature – resists easy consumption and disrupts expectations. This role challenges the viewer to confront contradictions rather than providing comfort. Adorno stated, 'There is more joy in dissonance than in consonance' (Adorno 1997: 40). Art's criticality lies in its ability to make societal contradictions visible without resolving them. The relationship between art and audience is extremely mediated and not a direct force of influence. The social character of art does not reveal itself directly through rational discourse; rather, it is concealed and can only be understood through interpretation. However, this does not imply that meaning can be 'squeezed out of it' (Adorno 1997: 128). Nevertheless, art communicates a collective language, even if it is dismissed as elitist.

Adorno believed modern art can only exist as art in a non-functional manner, dismissing external objectification and locating its essence in the truth content. Art follows its own intra-aesthetic immanent laws and contrasts with society's utility, efficiency and determinism by simply existing as something that does not conform. Art is part of the Enlightenment project through processes of interpretation and reflection, in which moments of transcendence may appear and deeper truths can be glimpsed. Although art is a kind of illusion (semblance), it carries the promise of something real or true (non-semblance). Artworks may not directly convey truth but point to or gesture towards it through its form and content. Holding on to this truth may seem foolish (folly); however, connecting to something beyond the material, commodified world is still worthwhile, as expressed in Adorno's elaborate style in the following quote.

> Folly is truth in the shape that human beings must accept whenever, amid the untrue, they do not give up truth. Even at the highest peaks, art is semblance; but art receives the semblance ... from nonsemblance [vom Scheinlosen] .... No light falls on people and things in which transcendence would not appear [widerschiene]. Indelible in resistance to the fungible world of exchange, is the resistance of the eye that does not want the world's colours to vanish. In semblance nonsemblance is promised.
>
> (Adorno 1973: 404)

Education as the 'mother of resistance'

If we consider education as an art form, a crucial question arises: Can education also be perceived as 'the mother of resistance'? We can draw upon insights from Adorno's perspective on art, particularly the significance of the formation of a critically thinking, autonomous subject and their resistance to conformity. Moreover, in his aesthetic theory, Adorno questioned whether art can still exist as art if art is confronted with a functionalistic understanding in a world dominated by scientism and commodification. In the same sense, we could ask, how can we understand the role of education in society, and does education need to resist to take care of its own role?

To answer whether education can be considered 'the mother of resistance', it is crucial to recognize that education cannot be understood in one dimension. Biesta (e.g. 2015, 2020, 2024) argued extensively that good education does not focus solely on one purpose but strives for multiple goal domains that should be balanced, including qualification, socialization and subjectification. By qualification, Biesta (2015) referred to acquiring the knowledge, skills and dispositions necessary to participate in the labour market and a complex modern society. In the socialization domain, young people are introduced to traditions, cultures and existing practices of being and acting to prepare them for life as community members. In the subjectification domain, the central aim is the formation of an autonomous and responsible subject (Biesta 2015). The final goal domain of subjectification, or the formation of an autonomous subject, particularly aligns with Adorno's perspective on art and culture, which holds the potential for 'resistance'. Consistent with Adorno's analysis of art and culture, this emancipatory role can be regarded as an essential aim in education. As Adorno asserted, the critical emancipatory role of art in society is to resist domination and 'petrified relationships' (Adorno and

Rabinbach 1975: 13). In this regard, democratic societies require mature and autonomously thinking individuals to sustain and develop themselves as democracies (Adorno and Rabinbach 1975: 19).

Interestingly, and relevant to discussing education's role in society, Adorno highlighted education's vital role in his work, *Education after Auschwitz* (Adorno 1998). He stated, 'The single genuine power standing against the principle of Auschwitz is autonomy,' and he further explained the concept of autonomy with reference to 'the Kantian expression: the power of reflection, of self-determination, of not cooperating' (Adorno 1998: 4). Moreover, Adorno spoke of 'an education for protest and resistance' in a radio broadcast in 1969. The statement *Nicht Mitmachen* (do not join/be out of step) was a favourite slogan of Adorno and his colleagues of the *Institut für Sozialforschung* (Jessop 2017: 419). Adorno's vision of education for maturity entails recognizing how our daily lives are intertwined with larger societal forces and possessing the courage to act ethically, whether that means resisting conformity, voicing dissent, or being 'out of step' when necessary (Ellison and Iqtadar 2023: 504).

Returning to the question: Can education also be perceived as 'the mother of resistance'?, we have to consider the emancipatory role of education, which centres on the autonomous subject and the processes of subjectification. As discussed above, these processes relate to critical reflection, self-determination and not cooperating. From this perspective, education can be understood as the 'mother of resistance'. Therefore, education plays a crucial role *in* society as long as we consider educational aims three-dimensionally. However, the question still remains as to how education and teaching can support processes of subjectification and what artistry is required in this regard.

Understanding the Aesthetics and Artistry of Teaching

Adorno's aesthetic theory defines the aesthetic of art from *within* the artwork, thereby disrupting an objectifying approach from the outside. He argued an artwork should not be defined merely as a 'fixed product', but that aesthetics can also be found in the making process. He focused on the contradictions and puzzles of form and acknowledged the artist's intention while simultaneously emphasizing the uncontrollability of the process. Similarly, we could analyse the teaching processes not solely through the objective measurement of the output but by exploring beyond the black box of cause-and-effect relationships to grasp the complexities of teaching and educational processes. By concentrating on the dynamics at play within these processes and relationships, we can restore our appreciation for educational aesthetics and the artistry of teaching. In this section, I examine Meirieu's work (2016, 2008), which emphasized the importance of education in its emancipatory role and the relevance of emancipatory processes for democracy. However, in the same vein, he demonstrated these processes can only be understood through their contradictions; the processes of maturity require the guidance of an adult but cannot be steered or produced.

Emancipation and Paradoxes in Educational Relationships

Meirieu's work (2016, 2008) is highly relevant for understanding the paradoxes and dialectics in education. According to Meirieu (2016), the paradox between control and freedom is central. A key question concerns how young people can be guided towards freedom under conditions of control and authority. He referred to the radically asymmetrical relationship between the adult (who is already part of society and has acquired the necessary knowledge, norms and values to be so) and the child, who completely depends on the adult and has yet to be introduced to society.

In this asymmetrical relationship, adults need to take their role and responsibility and give young people the attention and guidance they need to introduce them into society and enable them to feel at home in the world and find a place in society. This role requires the effort and responsibility of an adult; without domestication (socialization and qualification), children are left to their own devices. At the same time, this relationship between adults and young people must begin with a child's freedom and autonomy to grow towards independence and responsibility, so a new generation can take its place. For Meirieu, this process is the essence of education and teaching: 'Every time we as teachers or educators meet a child, we must assume our responsibility by creating situations through which they can enter the world and explore their freedom' (my translation, Meirieu 2016: 32).

Meirieu (2016) also presented a democratic argument for the essential emancipatory processes in education. Historically, education has focused solely on guiding the upper class towards successful careers and emancipation was not considered a priority. However, in modern democratic societies, education involves more than merely transmitting existing knowledge, norms, values and social structures. Instead of fostering determinism or merely reproducing social relations, education recognizes individuals as active agents whose paths are not predominantly predetermined by societal influences. Education aims not only to maintain the status quo; it envisions a new generation capable of critical thought and change, enabling them to make their own decisions in their personal lives and as engaged citizens shaping the future of society. As Adorno also emphasized, democratic societies require mature, critical-thinking adults ('adults that have come to age') to sustain and progress as democracies (Adorno and Rabinbach 1975: 19). However, as Meirieu (2016) rightly highlighted, young people do not suddenly leap into adulthood or abruptly take on the role of autonomous citizens; they must explore their freedom to become increasingly independent as they mature.

To enable a child to grow, mature and emancipate, the educator needs to provide room for experimentation. Offering a young person their freedom has, as with the procedure of art, a risk and can lead to surprises ('some are desired, others require correction' (Adorno 1997: 38). Moreover, as in art, education and teaching maintain a relationship with reality while extending beyond the *imago* of what already exists. In teaching and education, the teacher engages with the child as they are and, at the same time, gestures towards the autonomous subject they have yet to become. Meirieu references this openness to the child's future as *Bildsamkeit* (Pols and Verwer 2019), defined as the understanding that education begins from the premise that every child has the potential to 'grow', 'stand up' or 'mature' (*s'élever*) (Pols and Verwer 2019: 280). Education must begin from this premise because, without the idea of the possibility of maturation and change, education would be pointless. However, the potential for change always requires the antidote of the principle of freedom; otherwise, teaching could be mistaken for manipulation, training or production. A fundamental aspect of the artistry and aesthetics of teaching lies in temporarily reconciling these contradictions without resolving them.

Regarding Adorno's aesthetic theory, the aesthetics and artistry of teaching should be sought not so much in the 'result' but in the dynamics of educational processes: 'The result of the work is as much the trajectory it traverses …; it is at once static and dynamic' (Adorno 1997: 86). The artistry is found in navigating the complexities and finding a form of acting in a specific situation considering content, relationships and educational aims. Navigating these complexities is not straightforward; it requires balancing paradoxes and dialectics, much like in art.

The Complex Relationship between School and Society

A second important question Adorno addressed in his work is whether art can still exist as art. Art is part of society and exists *in* society but must consider its import over its function *for* society: it does not exist only and entirely for society (not even when emancipation is its aim). Given the growing tendency to objectify education from the outside, to focus on its outputs, impact and measurable results, this question is also pertinent for teaching. Exploring the concept of resistance in greater depth may lead to a better understanding of school's dual relationship with societal expectations, recognizing its own role without being limited to narrow policy goals and exchange relations. To address this issue, I first address the significance of resistance in educational processes and the concept of interruption. I then discuss the essential quality of school as a place for non-functionality.

Biesta (2015) and Meirieu (2008) argued that resistance plays a prominent role in teaching and education, and they emphasized the non-affirmative quality of 'interruption' (Biesta 2015, 2020). Meirieu (2008) referred to the essential challenge of education and teaching to enable students to live in the world without becoming the centre of the world. This is not an easy challenge, as consumerism tends to encourage the direct fulfilment of desires without considering whether these desires are truly beneficial. Furthermore, with a strong emphasis on consumption, society continually stimulates immediate satisfaction of desires. The term 'whim' represents an infantile stage of childhood and, according to Meirieu, has become the defining characteristic of our era. As discussed earlier in this chapter, Adorno's understanding of maturity involved ethical consideration; the freedom of the autonomous person is not without limits. Becoming an autonomous subject requires an ability to act ethically in one's daily life, recognizing societal forces and the ability to not cooperate and be out of step (Ellison and Iqtadar 2023). In other words, the subject must consider which limits should be applied, which limits are real and which are part of the 'arbitrary (ab)use of power' and need to be resisted (see Biesta 2020).

This understanding of the autonomous subject also has consequences for teaching. When children explore their freedom, they often encounter limits and resistance, as something or someone opposes their plans and intentions. According to Biesta (2020), this situation primarily means they experience the world as real. Resistance can come from physical matter, interpersonal relationships or the absence of the immediate satisfaction of desires. Biesta recognized an important distinction between an 'infantile' and a 'grown-up' way of trying to live one's life. The acting autonomous subject does not pursue their desires merely by doing whatever they want to do; a grown-up way of trying to lead one's life means asking oneself which desires are desirable and 'to come into a relationship with what and who is other, not simply overrule it' (Biesta 2020: 97). This quality of interruption includes, according to Meirieu (2008), moments when children are questioned. In these moments, children have the chance to reflect, to occupy their place but not dominate, and to abandon the impulse to attempt to impose their 'whim' on others who want to live in the world as subjects as well (Meirieu 2008). If we regard emancipation and maturation as significant processes within education and teaching, then understanding the importance of these interruptive processes is crucial for the role of schools in society. To allow for processes of subjectification, a school must not only be a place for effectiveness and efficiency; it should also leave room for experimentation and exploring one's freedom. Instead of excellence and perfection, schools should remain places for imperfection and non-functionality. In contrast to procedures that enhance efficiency and effectiveness, schools need to allow for slowing down, questioning and reflection (Biesta 2015, 2020).

Resistance as New Beginnings

A final consideration in the discussion of education's role in society is how dominant the current discourse of learning for a rapidly changing labour market is and whether there are still opportunities for resistance. To what extent do ideas about emancipation and the formation of an independent subject still resonate in practice? This question also emerged during the interpretation and discussion of my research in a Dutch public library (Sjollema 2025). In the context of non-formal education, libraries are witnessing a trend towards measuring impact and outputs, as they must demonstrate their added value in relation to policy goals. This evidence of impact is vital for securing municipality funding. As libraries expand their roles, the number of educational activities continues to increase, including the introduction of makerspaces. The political discourse surrounding these makerspaces primarily centres on learning to use 3D printers, laser cutters and digital technology, emphasizing developing skills for the labour market: digital literacy, technological knowledge and twenty-first-century skills. Interviews with makerspace coaches have, however, revealed that they do not adhere to narrow aims in the domain of qualification but have broader goals in mind. They exhibit an awareness of the complexity of educational relationships, disrupting a functionalistic approach to education.

I concluded that the librarians resisted the functionalist and one-sided discourse of learning for a rapidly changing labour market. However, this resistance did not target collective action, rebellious revolt or explicit rejection of the policy goals. In contrast, the new educational activities were intentionally developed as secluded spaces, outside the management systems of the public library. Furthermore, library staff were actively encouraged to reflect on educational goals and values within a public context. Can we refer to resistance in this instance? The answer depends on what we understand by the term 'resistance' and the kind of resistance one has in mind. I contend that, in this case, the resistance manifested as critical social awareness and reflection, facilitating a shift in policy interpretation and expanding the scope of various educational aims. The librarians revealed a memory of emancipatory aims in education and found a way to incorporate these ideas into a new activity. This more reflective form of resistance may also raise the question of why the statement 'art is the mother of resistance' uses the metaphor of 'mother' over 'father' or 'source'.

The Metaphor of Motherhood

Does the metaphor of 'mother' suggest a certain kind of resistance? The choice of a maternal figure appears to be more than a mere semantic decision; it possibly reveals something fundamental about the nature of resistance. If we were to associate a maternal figure with the idea of resistance, it should be Penelope, the wife of Odysseus. According to ancient Greek mythology, Penelope awaited Odysseus' return in Ithaca for twenty years since his departure to fight in the Trojan War. After the conclusion of the war, she received no news of him. Her father, Icarius, urged her to remarry; however, Penelope clung on to the hope of Odysseus' return. She promised her father that she would remarry as soon as she completed weaving a tapestry, enabling her to postpone having to make any decision. This work did not progress quickly, as she secretly unravelled her weaving each night to delay completion. In this way, she maintained her freedom and independence.

Adorno himself referred to the myth of Penelope in his *Aesthetic Theory* (1997: 186). In the unravelling of the tapestry, he found the ultimate image of the non-identical nature of a work of art. Moreover, Penelope's act of weaving and unravelling is far removed from the sublimity of art as a finished 'thing'. Instead, her actions draw attention to the process of making rather than the product, preventing the interpretation of art as self-expression or the mastery of materials. I believe the figure of Penelope also aligns with the type of resistance Adorno had in mind. Adorno probably did not envision political revolt but a use of consciousness and critical thinking. His rejection of the student protests in the 1960s is illustrative of this idea: He regarded them as a manifestation of a new form of conformity. For Adorno, resistance need not be collective activism but the ability to think critically and autonomously.

From the perspective outlined in this chapter, Penelope's desire to postpone her remarriage aligns with the importance of interruption and providing students with time for reflection in education processes. Moreover, Penelope's struggle for independence can be considered a reference to the emancipatory aims of education. Her recurring work is not limited solely to the unravelling of her weaving; there is also a new beginning every day. The new beginning could also signify the upbringing of young persons, which takes time, while referring to their attempts to experiment with their freedom with room to try and start over. Finally, and most importantly, the new beginnings could also hint at the possibility for new initiatives to emerge in education, holding a memory of subjectification and emancipatory education. What positions art and, in my opinion, education as the 'mother of resistance' is that teachers and educators keep searching for practices that consider subjectification one of the essential educational aims.

Conclusion

This chapter illustrates that education affects significantly more than the mere qualification of children for the labour market, as revealed by a close examination of teaching and educational processes. The essential role of education, which has a long-standing tradition since the Enlightenment, pertains to the goal of subjectification. This fundamental purpose of education is often overlooked in policy discourse and supplanted by a narrow, one-dimensional focus. However, considering education in a three-dimensional manner and closely analysing the complexity of educational processes and relationships, it becomes evident that what appears effective or efficient in the realm of qualification and 'learning' impacts what is possible in other domains, especially in subjectification. Guiding towards maturity requires artistry in teaching, transcending the mere instrumentality of 'learning', evidence-based interventions and predefined outcomes. This artistry involves navigating paradoxes for which no universally applicable standards exist: conveying without imposing, explaining without standardizing, and guiding without enforcing. The educator must facilitate experimentation to assist a child's maturation. Allowing freedom entails uncertainty and surprises. Much like art, education transcends reality, presuming the autonomous person the child has yet to become. An important term in relation to resistance in education is 'interruption', which disrupts the flow of action and encourages reflection. Similar to the 'dissonance' in music or artwork, the interruption invites interpretation without immediately providing a solution. It is non-affirmative and assumes the possibility of reconsidering one's position towards oneself, others, or the surrounding world, without necessarily imposing change. However, as Adorno argues concerning art, if we abandon the concept of human freedom and the autonomous subject, we betray all that art – and education – can be.

If education is considered 'the mother of resistance', this idea manifests in various ways. First, education and teaching require an understanding of their multiple aims, including the formation of the autonomous subject, who is capable of resisting conformity, voicing dissent, or being 'out of step' when necessary. Second, growth and maturation require reflection on the desirability of various actions. This reflection involves ethical questions, which cannot be addressed in abstract terms but require confrontations with resistance and limitations in reality. Finally, for education to exist with a recognition of its emancipatory and democratic relevance in society, schools and teachers must resist policies and discourses that emphasize narrow educational aims and seek to objectify and measure school effectiveness solely by its outcome. If we wish to overcome the pressure of functionalism in education, we can find inspiration in Adorno's *Aesthetic Theory*. The central point concerns not allowing the essence or import of education to become subordinate to its function; doing so requires an understanding of education that is not objectified or validated from the outside but one that seeks to comprehend it 'from the inside'.

Although Adorno is frequently depicted as pessimistic and his work is undeniably linked to the era in which he lived, his insights remain relevant. With the rise of right-wing populism, both the educational and democratic arguments for maintaining educational integrity aimed at free and autonomous individuals have become increasingly significant. According to Adorno (2020), there are recognizable patterns at play by which non-democratic parties increase their power. Propaganda is a key component, aiming not so much to highlight substantive political plans and intentions but more to play into the general sentiment of crisis, channelling aggression towards those who seem to be the causes. Nationalism cleverly plays on the sense of fear and insecurity and becomes an organ of collective advocacy for groups that feel potentially redundant. A strange contradiction occurs: The rise of nationalist parties creates the perception that there is 'finally something to choose'; however, these parties show little regard for citizens' freedom or democratic participation. Instead, they distance themselves from democratic influence and claim to already understand what 'the people' desire (Adorno 2020).

Therefore, it is unsurprising that government policies, with substantial right-populist influence, target minorities and cut public institutions, the cultural sector, universities and intellectuals – where most critical and independent thought can be expected. Educational agendas often shift towards a 'back-to-basics' approach, focusing on fundamental skills and knowledge transfer. Consequently, subjects and projects that promote reflection on social developments are often neglected, making education 'a province' detached from society (Adorno 1998). Although knowledge and basic skills are crucial aspects of education, I argued in this chapter that an exclusive focus on socialization and qualifications – without nurturing the freedom of the autonomous subject – results in inadequate education. By resisting instrumentalism and emphasizing the intrinsic value of the artistry of teaching, we can prevent education from being reduced to a mere tool for political agendas.

References

Adorno, T. (1973), *Negative Dialectics*, trans. E.B. Ashton, London: Routledge and Kegan Paul.

Adorno, T. (1997), *Aesthetic Theory*, trans. R. Hullot-Kentor, New York: Continuum.

Adorno, T. (1998), *Critical Models: Interventions and Catchwords*, trans. H.W. Pickford, New York: Columbia University Press.

Adorno, T. (2020), *Aspects of the New Right-Wing Extremism*, trans. W. Hoban, Medford, MA: Polity Books.

Adorno, T. and M. Horkheimer (1997), *Dialectic of Enlightenment*, trans. J. Cumming, London: Verso.

Adorno, T.W. and A.G. Rabinbach (1975), 'Culture Industry Reconsidered', *New German Critique*, 6 (Autumn): 12–19.

Bahr, E. (2007), *Weimar on the Pacific: German Exile Culture in Los Angeles and the Crisis of Modernism* (Vol. 41), Oakland, CA: University of California Press.

Biesta, G. (2015), 'The Duty to Resist: Redefining the Basics for Today's Schools', *RoSE – Research on Steiner Education*, 6: 1–11.

Biesta, G. (2017), *Letting Art Teach, Art Education 'After' Joseph Beuys*, Arnheim: ArtEZ Press.

Biesta, G. (2020), 'Risking Ourselves in Education: Qualification, Socialization, and Subjectification Revisited', *Educational Theory*, 70 (1): 89–104.

Biesta, G. (2024), 'Taking Education Seriously: The Ongoing Challenge', *Educational Theory*, 74 (3): 434–48.

Ellison, S. and S. Iqtadar (2023), 'Aporia, Interregnum, & Pedagogy: Education in a Time of Crisis', *Review of Education, Pedagogy, and Cultural Studies*, 45 (5): 481–508.

Jessop, S. (2017), 'Adorno: Cultural Education and Resistance', *Studies in Philosophy and Education*, 36 (4): 409–23.

Meirieu, P. (2008), 'Facing Up to the Modern World by Giving Students Control of their Own Education', https://meirieu.com. Available online: https://www.meirieu.com/ARTICLES/facing_up.pdf (accessed April 4 2025).

Meirieu, P. (2016), *Pedagogiek: De Plicht om Weerstand te Bieden*, trans. S. Verwer, Frankfurt: Phronese.

Pickford, H. and L. Zuidervaart (2024), 'Theodor W. Adorno', in E. Zalta and U. Nodelman (eds), *The Stanford Encyclopedia of Philosophy*, Winter 2024 Edition. Available online: https://plato.stanford.edu/archives/win2024/entries/adorno/ (accessed 14 March 2025).

Pols, W. and S. Verwer (2019), 'De Vraag Naar het Subject: Een Interview Met Philippe Meirieu over de Pedagogiek', *Pedagogiek*, 39 (3): 279–90.

Sjollema, S.C. (2025), 'Can Public Libraries Still Be Public? A Case Study of the Introduction of Maker Education as a New Educational Activity in the Makerspaces of the Amsterdam Public Library', Doctoral thesis, Moray House School of Education and Sport, University of Edinburgh, Edinburgh. http://dx.doi.org/10.7488/era/5896

Van den Brink, B. (2013), 'Goed Leven in een Foute Wereld', *Filosofie Magazine*, 4 June. Available online: https://www.filosofie.nl/theodor-w-adorno-goed-leven-in-een-foute-wereld/ (accessed 14 March 2025).

CHAPTER SEVEN

Challenging Simplistic Storylines: Diversity, Complexity Commonalities and the Artistry of Teaching

Paul McMillan and Mike Jess

Introduction

We align with the overarching premise of this book, which argues that the work of teaching is an art, and teachers' thoughtful judgements are a form of artistry. The first chapter in this book provided an account of art and artistry (see Biesta this volume) and acknowledged this is not a new direction of travel for education. Stenhouse (1988), over thirty-five years ago, set out the art(istry) case to rebuff a growing trend for identifying curriculum and teaching methods that were applicable to all learners. The main thrust of this argument was that such general specifications were not possible. Rather, learners are too diverse, school contexts too unique, learning situations too unpredictable for a formula and, accordingly, teachers need to make skilful adaptations for learners in specific cases and contexts. Our concern, however, is that this previous call did not make a substantive impact. To the contrary, the global climate for tight specifications of curriculum and teaching methods has gained considerable momentum. Allied by progressive government interest in, and control of, education systems the role of teachers and teaching in many countries is presented as a simple and predictable process. It is against this backdrop that art(istry) has resurfaced in contemporary times. We believe it could provide a means of countering the oversimplified narratives that have come to dominate in education. Although, we would argue that the success of this latest attempt hinges on grasping the diversity of individuals within and between educational settings. It tends to be 'grossly underestimated' by stakeholders (Stenhouse 1988: 44), and given that attempts to control teaching have further intensified, understanding diversity in contemporary education is a crucial starting point.

The chapter is split into four main parts. The first part briefly examines the increasing diversity of learner populations. The second part, drawing on four complexity commonalities developed in our previous work (see Jess, Howells and McMillan 2024), presents an overarching framework to re-imagine education in ways that acknowledge learner diversities. The third part explores what teaching as an art and artistry could look like in practice. We share insights on adaptive teaching and outline key features that underpin teacher responsiveness in diverse classrooms and beyond. A final section turns to discuss how school leadership has a pivotal role in enabling artistry to become a reality. Within a political climate that will likely restrict professional autonomy of teachers for the foreseeable future, we argue that insights from complexity leadership can create 'adaptive boundary spaces' in schools. These spaces could harness networks of teachers to explore artistry through collaborative inquiry, which can enhance teacher agency and innovation while supporting schools to become organizations that can better cope with external political pressure.

A Diversity of Diverse Learners?[1]

To avoid the previous pitfalls of underestimating diversity, this section will first acknowledge the diversity of learners, and the ways in which this has potentially further increased in contemporary times. We acknowledge that diversity has long been a part of school life. In other words, we are *not* claiming that schools have only recently had an influx in learner diversity. Rather, it is more likely that diversity has been underestimated previously, while two inter-related developments may have further enhanced diversity since the 1980s. One development is that migration rates have increased exponentially in recent decades. For example, increased levels of migration across Europe have brought together learners with different languages, backgrounds and cultures (Faas, Hajisoterioub and Angelides 2014). Another is that from the 1990s onwards a raft of legally binding agreements has emerged in many countries. These have focused on protecting fundamental rights and ensured that young people, regardless of their physical and mental characteristics, have access to education. A notable, recent example is the UN Convention on the Rights of the Child (UNCRC) (1989). It has, since 2022, become a pivotal, legally binding agreement in many countries. The UNCRC (1989) outlines the fundamental rights of children, regardless of their race, religion, or abilities and includes specific requirements for education.

As learner populations become more diverse, broader conceptions of education are needed to move beyond long-standing exclusionary practices. Diverse learners bring varied cultural backgrounds, languages, abilities and perspectives into school communities. Since the intervention of the UNCRC, schools have been expected to recognize multiple ways of knowing, understanding and being. Consequently, education should not only focus on academic attainment but also promote social integration and personal growth (Biesta 2015). Although this broader conception aligns with contemporary perspectives on diversity and may seem self-evident, education is becoming increasingly restrictive, limiting rather than embracing multiple ways of knowing, understanding and being. For instance, Biesta (2015: 75) highlights how the dominance of a 'language of learning' in policy has positioned a narrow interpretation of learning as the singular purpose of education. While learning is fundamental, this exclusive focus privileges attainment while overlooking broader questions of content, purpose and relationality (Biesta 2015). This shift also affects teachers, reframing them as the primary 'factor' in student achievement (Biesta 2015: 75). Teachers do play a crucial role in the learning process, but learning is influenced by multiple interrelated factors. This overemphasis on learning, therefore, threatens the humanistic dimensions of teaching, which reflect deeper purposes of education, professional judgement and adapting to the needs of learners (Biesta 2015).

Biesta's (2015) three domains of education – qualification, socialization and subjectification – offer a valuable framework for understanding its deeper purposes. Education extends beyond the acquisition of knowledge and skills (qualification); it also introduces individuals to cultural, political and social contexts (socialization) and fosters personal development, critical thinking and autonomy (subjectification). However, these domains are not rigid categories and can be disrupted by external pressures, such as politics and policy-driven emphases on learning and attainment outcomes. To restore a balance, later sections will explore how artistry – through adaptive teaching and supportive school leadership – can address these imbalances.

Recognizing diversity is essential to reviving the case for artistry in education. Fully embracing this diversity requires a comprehensive framework to analyse its implications for teaching practice. To support this, the following section builds on our previous work (Jess, Howells and McMillan 2023; McMillan and Jess 2021) to present an integrative framework grounded in complexity thinking. Drawing on more than a decade of research and practice-based insights, this framework identifies four key commonalities – becoming, lived time, self-organization and boundaries. These elements illustrate that education, along with its stakeholders, is a complex phenomenon capable of rich interconnectivity (Jess, Howells, & McMillan 2024). Placing the term 'rich' ahead of interconnectivity denotes that when elements interact, they can often change one another in unexpected and unpredictable ways. These rich interactions, which can include interaction between humans and with other non-human elements, are possible when some elements have the capability to self-organize and respond to feedback in the system. The next section will explore these commonalities in depth, demonstrating how they coalesce into a coherent theoretical framework.

The Complexity Commonalities Framework

For this chapter's purposes we focus the commonalities framework on learners. This will enable us to explore diversity and, though less so, consider how learners are entangled with other stakeholders and wider layers of the education system. More specifically, then the commonalities are concepts, and we focus them on learners and their interconnected, self-organizing processes of becoming that take place through lived time and within boundaries (see Figure 7.1).

Commonality 1: Becoming

We start with becoming because it is central to engaging with diversity. Put simply, becoming is about *difference* (Deleuze and Guattari 1987). It is a long-term, nonlinear and iterative process that seeks to actively acknowledge difference by uncovering the multiple, diverse possibilities around us. There is

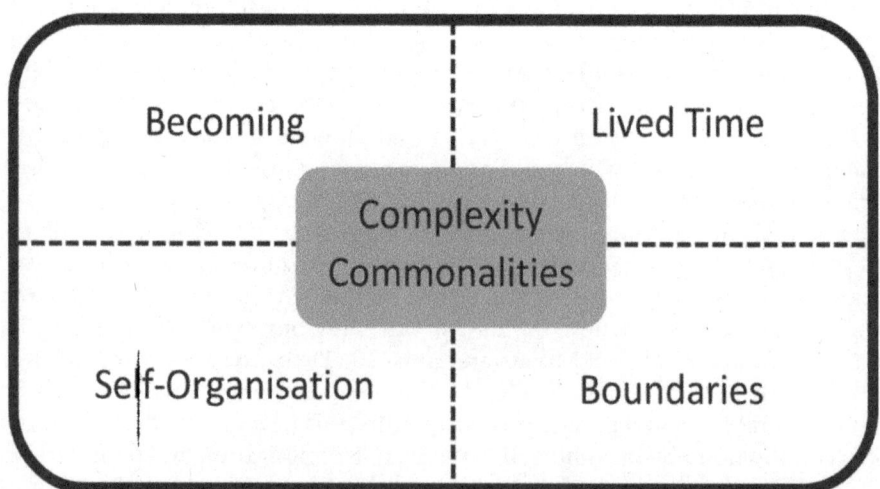

FIGURE 7.1 *Four complexity commonalities (adapted from Jess, Howells and McMillan 2024).*

no order that governs what difference should be, no top-down comparisons for difference to abide by, and no certainty about what ought to become. In other words, becoming is about embracing difference for its *own* sake, rather than difference being subordinated to an understanding outlined by pre-existing norms and expectations. A call for becoming, and the subsequent recognition of difference may sound appealing, but it is not straightforward because modernist ideals have long dominated our thinking. Modernist thinking is based on transcendental, reductionist notions of 'being' (Deleuze 1994: 41); it is characterized by logic, certainty and predictability, bringing a hierarchical sense of order to the world (May 2003). One powerful legacy of modernism is that it has led us to perceive various aspects of the world as 'stable unities' (May 2003: 143), providing tightly defined parameters, reducing the possibility for recognizing difference, and shaping our thinking about how the world ought to be.

Coexistence is at the core of complexity thinking (Davis and Sumara 2006). By recognizing similarities and differences, seemingly opposing phenomena can co-exist through a complexity thinking lens, fostering insights that can transcend polarized perspectives. Therefore, complexity offers a space to not only include elements relating to modernism, such as structure and order, but it can also recognize the capacity for emergence and unpredictability (Davis and Sumara 2006). Acknowledging these integrative ambitions, becoming represents a long-term, nonlinear and iterative process underpinned by the recognition of difference within and between learners. While the focus on difference may imply a search for diversity as part of the becoming process, it also incorporates order and structure. In other words, the prevalence of modernist thinking in how we define the world around us can, on the one hand, help efficiency and the organization of everyday life and, on the other hand, can blind us to all the potential that could have been (Krejsler 2016). Therefore, all becomings, and attempts to think differently, are always situated within the restrictions of communities and contexts.

If we apply this view to learners in schools, it is possible to observe structures that foster predictable behaviours. For instance, as learners progress together, and are involved in ongoing interaction with each other and teachers, some shared patterns of behaviour can be shaped by the rules, routines and expectations of classrooms and school settings. Concurrently, however, significant differences can be seen between the behaviours of learners. For example, these differences could be driven by different abilities, personal interests and previous experiences of learners, which can lead to unpredictable, adaptive, imaginative and, at times, problematic behaviours. Classroom situations are a complex mix of learners making progress at different rates on different topics, working within structures geared towards bringing a degree of order and control while, at the same time, offering the potential for novel, adaptable and imaginative responses. To make sense of these differences, and to start proactively channelling attempts for learners to think differently, we need to challenge taken-for-granted ideas about time. The next section takes up this challenge where the concept of lived time is used to understand how an individual's past, present and possible futures impact classroom life.

Commonality 2: Lived Time

Traditionally, the accepted view of time has been the conception of linear time (Byrne and Callaghan 2014). Linear time involves the quantitative subdivision of specific moments of time into distinct and measurable units (e.g. days, weeks, months). The quantitative features of linear time provide us with consistency, predictability and certainty. Although an alternative conception of time exists, we argue that it should play a greater role in shaping daily life (Jess, Howells and McMillan 2024). This lesser-known conception is that of lived time. Lived time is valuable because it is closely linked to the becoming process and provides the basis for understanding how to think differently. We first discuss lived time and, thereafter, move to consider the significance for learner diversity when lived and linear time coexist.

Lived time is 'complex and multi-dimensional' (Adam 2008: 7). This view of time has qualitative, recursive and nonlinear features, where the past, present and future intertwine as an integrated unity. Within this lived time unity, the past, present and future have distinct roles. That is to say, the present moment is the point in time when the past and future merge together (May 2005). Let us examine two aspects about how lived time operates as an interconnected unity.

1) The present moment always interconnects with the past. This interconnection is possible because an individual's previous life history informs the current context in which they find themselves. In present time, while groups of people may have many similarities, they do not have exactly matching life histories.

2) When future time merges with past and present, it is not clear exactly what will unfold. In other words, what happens in the future is not certain. This uncertainty requires us to accept that present time is not a fixed entity, but rather it is constantly (re)created as a person shifts to a new present.

In relation to becoming, we can start to see the potential (and challenges) created by the conception of lived time. There is, through the life histories of different people, the potential for a vast reserve of possibilities to be deployed in the present moment. However, as Krejsler (2016: 1476) explains, this large swathe of possibilities does not often materialize in future time because: 'our thoughts, minds, and bodies are ... so caught by routine and habit that often, we do not sense the myriad impulses ... that always already surround us'.

This overview has raised the important point that individual learners in classrooms will have distinctly different starting points. This diversity not only emphasizes the limitations of a 'one-size-fits-all' approach to teaching, but it also points up the need to formatively assess learners to help further adapt learning experiences in the future. Additionally, for learners to draw on previous lived time experiences, which may struggle to materialize in the dominant routines of classrooms, then teachers will need to remain alert and make sensitive adjustments to the interaction patterns that take place between learners and the teacher. A later section will introduce the potential of adaptive teaching, whereby micro- and macro-adaptability seem to correlate well with the demands outlined here for teachers' practice.

With these challenges in mind, we turn to our two final commonalities: self-organization and boundaries. The next section presents self-organization and, through rich interconnectivity between learners, provides more insights into how becoming and lived time unfold and can be supported in complex classroom situations.

Commonality 3: Self-Organization

We start by focusing on systems thinking to outline the self-organizing process and, as we shared earlier, why this is an essential ingredient for rich interconnectivity. Generally, a system is 'an interconnected set of elements ... coherently organised in a way that achieves something' (Meadows 2008: 11). The nature of the interactions between different elements of a system can be understood through modernist thinking *and* complexity thinking. Two main types of system are: the mechanical, or complicated, system that aligns with modernist thinking; and the complex, or adaptive, system that has its origins in complexity thinking.

There are key differences between these types of systems. However, complex systems are a hybrid type of system. While some elements interact in a predictable manner, just like mechanical systems, other elements can interact in ways that fundamentally change one another and lead to outcomes that are unpredictable. Self-organization is central for supporting rich interconnectivity and can elicit both predictable and unpredictable outcomes. An important point for our argument for artistry in teaching is that self-organization can recognize the potential for people to be 'dynamic and transformational' (Byrne 1998: 51); thereby offering scope to respond in adaptable and creative ways (Davis and Sumara 2006). The mixture of these self-organizing behaviours – predictability, creativity and adaptability – emerge from the similarities and diversities that coexist in the complex system.

A school classroom is an example of a complex self-organizing system. It will rely on a degree of predictability and similarity due to the school rules, the norms and routines for the class, and the shared experiences of learners as a collective group. Although if all learners were to respond in exactly matching ways to a task, then it would result in too much similarity; it would narrow the creative, imaginative and adaptive possibilities for the task. These similarities are often balanced with the diversities across different learners in the class, with different learners taking different roles, offering different ideas, drawing on different attributes to inform their response to the task. This self-organizing capacity may have a significant influence on the becoming process, but it does not occur in a vacuum. Instead, self-organization is patterned by a plethora of influencing factors. A crucial point for teaching as artistry is to locate these influencing factors, consider how they situate teachers and learners in schools, and offer insights for challenging and negotiating them. To do this, we look at our final commonality: boundaries.

Commonality 4: Boundaries

Boundaries are everywhere and play a major role in shaping the interrelated nature of becoming, lived time and self-organization (Jess, Howells and McMillan 2024). Furthermore, boundaries, while traditionally viewed as negative or divisive, have more recently been viewed in a positive light for recognizing inclusive and transformative possibilities. We find boundaries salient because they can represent boundary lines as both fixed and flexible while offering a holistic perspective that includes physical, social, emotional and cognitive spaces (Khalil and Boulding 1996). Flexible boundary lines can be used to consider individual, contextual and task-related boundary spaces. In other words, malleable boundary lines can enable the deliberate construction of a boundary space that can foster rich interaction between diverse people, phenomena and contexts. To further explore this potential, we examine in this section how *flexible* boundaries can act as key drivers for transformational change and development. A later section will shift focus to adaptive boundary spaces, which we view as sharing many similarities with boundary spaces, considering how school leaders can construct contexts to instigate innovation and change.

The following example from earlier in the chapter seems apposite for flexible boundaries: we acknowledged that a diversity of learners from different backgrounds, cultures and capabilities are increasingly coming together in classrooms. The following two interrelated developments were shared as potentially increasing diversity and can be seen as displaying flexibility in their boundary lines:

1) Citizens in the European Union can now travel freely between countries in the European Union due to changes in physical boundaries/borders.

2) Inclusive legislation continues to evolve in many countries and, consequently, the social boundaries in education are changing to integrate individuals where they were possibly excluded previously.

In these examples, however, fixed and flexible boundaries coexist in the same boundary space. Citizens may travel freely and have a right to be included in schools, but they may be restricted or constrained within the boundaries of the EU and by the availability of resources in schools. This foregrounds the coexistence of boundaries: there is structure and order from fixed boundaries; openness and malleability from flexible boundaries.

Flexible boundaries, and to a lesser extent, fixed boundaries, can alter, often dramatically, in a short period. It follows that disciplinary knowledge on the school curriculum can be framed within fixed and flexible boundaries. Some disciplinary knowledge may remain fixed, in the short term, due to the relevance to high-stakes assessment; while other knowledge may be flexible and open to debate between teachers and learners. Boundary spaces can thus be considered ambiguous in nature. By presenting boundaries as ambiguous, we also imply that different people will engage with boundaries very differently, based on their diverse life histories, their ability to self-organize and adapt *in situ*. For instance, what may be perceived as fixed boundary spaces for some learners will, at the same point in time, be flexible and malleable for others. Therefore, rather than presenting boundaries as rigid barriers, we suggest they offer opportunities for teachers and learners to create 'spaces with potential for learning' (Akkerman and Bakker 2011: 3). As such, boundary spaces are a stimulus for the individual and collective self-organizing efforts of learners while, concurrently, offering scope for teachers to engage with emergent responses from learners in classrooms.

To summarize, this section has presented a complexity commonality framework. The framework exemplified the diversity of learners and their interconnected, self-organizing processes of becoming that take place through lived time and within boundaries (see Figure 7.1). However, this scale of diversity raises the question about how teachers can interweave their practice to harness the opportunities that exist within diverse groups of learners. One response to this conundrum – and a perspective on what artistry in teaching looks like – can be found in the adaptive teaching literature.

Adapting Adaptive Teaching

Our complexity commonalities framework illuminated how learners and learning are entangled with an array of elements inside and outside of education. There was recognition that teachers and teaching would need to be responsive to learners, which is not a new proposal for education. Adaptive teaching has become the most prominent term in the twenty-first century to capture this responsiveness (Parsons et al. 2018). Beyond its popularity, there are several reasons for adopting adaptive teaching in this chapter. One main reason is that we have previously demonstrated its effectiveness in capturing the responsiveness of teachers' practice (see McMillan and Jess 2021; McMillan, Anderson and Jess 2025). Another is that our definition of adaptive teaching, which we introduce shortly (McMillan and Jess 2021), highlights the demands of adaptability and suggests a likely role for artistry. The strength of our definition lies in acknowledging both immediate (micro) and broader (macro) expectations for teachers while emphasizing that responsiveness does not merely involve the teacher being reactive and accommodating to learners. A central feature of adaptive teaching is the ability of teachers to make informed judgements about when and why adaptations are necessary in a given context. These judgements are guided by what we have previously termed 'personal vision' (McMillan and Jess 2021: 276). A teacher's personal vision provides clarity on their educational goals, enabling thoughtful adaptations to teaching methods, lesson content and class relationships (see also Fairbanks et al. 2010).

Preceding paragraphs raise questions about the different kinds of artistry that may be invoked by adaptive teaching. It is important to clarify the links we see between adaptability and artistry. In an attempt to reclaim the art of teaching, Biesta (this volume, Chapter 1), maps out several different kinds of artistry. Our interpretation is that 'practical wisdom' (Biesta this volume, Chapter 1), and what we will call 'ethically sensitive', kinds of artistry appear to align most prominently with the ideas in this chapter.

- Practical wisdom is the application and creation of purposeful teaching in context using professional judgement.

- Ethical sensitivity balances adaptations to practice with a deeper sense of educational purposes/visions.

Therefore, teaching as artistry, and by extension adaptive practice, it not a mechanical process; it requires practical wisdom and ethical sensitivity from the teacher. An ability to make thoughtful, situated judgements that shape meaningful educational experiences by engaging with the unique demands of learners in specific contexts.

While we use adaptive teaching to conceptualize responsiveness in teaching, and have shared links to artistry, we recognize that its conventional usage has become overly narrow. The following section outlines its key features before arguing that existing conceptualizations require expansion. We then propose a broader revision that aligns more closely with the goal of engaging diverse learners.

Micro- and Macro-adaptations

Corno (2008) offers a distinction between micro- and macro-adaptation:

- Micro-adaptations take place in classrooms, they are short term and involve the teacher making immediate adjustments to their practice while working with learners.

- Macro-adaptations involve adapting the curriculum in a school, often to create a programme or intervention to target specific learners. These adaptations may be led by teachers inside schools or by outside stakeholders, and often have a longer-term trajectory for the adjustments needed in classrooms.

One point to note from the above is that there appears to be an interconnection between macro- and micro-adaptations. It can be implied that the adaptability exhibited at the micro level is focused on meeting the immediate needs of learners, but at the same time, longer-term expectations or initiatives at the macro level place demands on teachers to interpret these flexibly at the school and classroom levels. These types of micro- and macro-adaptations are important for connecting to learner diversity and, in the previous section, we highlighted the futility of 'one-size-fits-all' approaches to teaching. However, there appears to be a growing tension, and a major threat to the future existence of adaptive teaching. Hoffman and Duffy (2016: 174) complain that adaptive teaching is becoming increasingly 'rare' due to 'essentialist curriculum, scripted teaching materials, [and] high stakes assessment'. Another point is that micro-adaptive teaching is often defined as occurring in classrooms and being primarily initiated by teachers (Corno 2008). However, some scholars challenge this view, arguing that teachers exert less control in these interactions and must negotiate more with learners (Vagle 2016).

Broadening Adaptive Teaching

We generally align with the work of Corno (2008) and Parsons et al. (2018), but we see a risk in narrowing the scope of adaptive teaching. This narrowing can be seen in the following way: macro-adaptation is less prominent due to the global rise in reductive and top-down policy mandates; micro-adaptation is reduced to a straightforward, teacher-initiated process that is less connected to learners. Our work in other articles (McMillan and Jess 2021; McMillan, Anderson and Jess 2025) has explored these under-researched areas of adaptive teaching. We draw on the following definition to broaden the scope of adaptive teaching by recognizing it as 'a complex process ... [that involves teachers] developing the ability to respond to, and influence, the dynamic and ever-changing environment in which they work' (McMillan and Jess 2021: 276). We see this definition as helpful in two main ways:

1) While responsiveness to learners is implied, it is not purely reactive and accommodating. Instead, it is also shaped by teachers' intentions to actively influence their classroom environment.

2) The teacher is recognized not only as an active influence but also as being influenced by the environment, which includes learners, the classroom and potentially wider layers of the education system.

In emphasizing that teachers can 'respond to, and influence' their environment, this definition compels us to consider the practical realities for micro- and macro-adaptation. To do this, we will now examine the possibilities for broadening current conceptions of macro- and micro-adaptive practice, which will be essential if we are to connect to the levels of diversity we discussed earlier.

In terms of macro-adaptations, we want to consider the prospect of teachers adapting policy to (re)design the curriculum or create a bespoke programme for learners. We would argue that this form of macro-adaptation lies at the heart of adaptive teaching, and while the tension in many countries is noted, it is a significant part of connecting to the diversity of learners. There are similarities between the type of macro-adaption we discuss in this section and what others, such as Priestley et al. (2021), have termed 'curriculum making'. They highlight how current education policy enactment takes place through a complicated process from supra (e.g. policies at international level) through to nano levels (e.g. learner interaction in classes).

Despite Priestley et al. (2021) underlining the dangers of curriculum-making happening in isolation, the arrangement between these supra-to-nano levels is linear and hierarchical. To put it simply, with limited opportunity for these different levels to interact, the possibility for cross fertilization, or what we earlier referred to as 'rich interconnectivity, and the creation of new or unexpected insights for curriculum and policy, is lost. This hierarchical structure, instead, operates by passing information down through the different levels. Rather than broadening opportunities and enhancing learner experiences, policy and initiatives that are dominated by the supra and macro levels can often have unintended consequences at the micro and nano levels. To compound matters, the prospect of teachers engaging in macro-adaptations within this hierarchical system is challenging, particularly when set against the backdrop of global school effectiveness agendas.

Following Priestley et al. (2021), curriculum-making should be a genuine part of the process across different levels of education systems. More specifically, curriculum-making across the system could, at each level (e.g. from supra-nano), involve a cross-section of people from other levels engaging together in the process. We see merit in these ideas. For instance, as presented earlier in the commonalities framework, the process of becoming through lived time reminds us about the marked differences between learner experiences. Therefore, involving teachers in curriculum-making endeavours, particularly at levels of the education system beyond schools, would help fine-tune the process and better prepare curriculum to cope with acute diversity at nano levels. However, for these curriculum-making aspirations to become a reality, school leaders have a significant role to play. This point is discussed in a subsequent section where the role of leadership is examined and, as such, we consider how leaders could foster an increased sense of teacher agency in school contexts and beyond.

Looking at micro-adaptation, our opening point is that making immediate adjustments to practice amidst the flow of classroom events requires a considerable level of skill. The list includes, but is not limited to, deep content knowledge, broad formative assessment techniques, critical reflection, knowledge of pedagogy, personal vision, established relationships and contextual understanding of learners. Over and above these skills and capacities, there is a need to understand how micro-adaptations take place between teachers and learners. To broaden conceptualizations of adaptive teaching, we offer up teaching repertoires and negotiation as central components of the process (McMillan, Anderson & Jess 2025).

Extensive observations in classrooms enabled us to sketch out the broad teaching repertoires and negotiation strategies of accomplished teachers who were skilled in adaptive teaching. The teaching repertoires represented the wide-ranging configurations of power that featured in these classrooms and offered latitude for teachers to exchange responsibility markedly between teacher control and learner control. The participant teachers orchestrated a power dynamic with learners that could generally be viewed as asymmetric, yet cooperative; this fostered in learners an active engagement in lessons and, consequently, the middle-ground of their teaching repertoires often included teacher-guided, teacher-learner-negotiated and learner-initiated practices. These teachers were also skilled at negotiating learning journeys with classes. This was achieved through an array of negotiation strategies; including persuasion, incentives, asserting authority, moral appeals and open negotiation. The negotiation of learning journeys, which involved revising learning tasks and intentions for classes, demonstrates a commitment from these teachers for learners to shape classroom events. Thinking back to the complexity commonalities introduced earlier, we can see how these teachers used teaching repertoires and negotiation to explore the self-organization of learners within the flexible boundary spaces of classrooms. These micro-adaptive exchanges appear to increase the propensity for unpredictable situations to emerge and, in turn, the need to teach adaptively.

We recognize that our ambitions in this section will not be realized without support for teachers at a systemic level and, at the same time, a space for teachers to develop the necessary skills and capacities for micro- and macro-adaptability. Therefore, we now introduce key ideas from complexity leadership to set the scene for how school leaders and teachers can shape the future fortunes of adaptive teaching.

Leadership for Adaptive Education

In this section we discuss how the integration of complexity leadership principles (Uhl-Bien and Arena 2017, 2018) in educational contexts offers a promising framework for navigating and challenging the tensions from external accountability mandates. Established leadership models in education, such as Instructional Leadership (Hallinger 2005) and Distributed Leadership (Spillane 2006),[2] have provided valuable insights for the past two decades. However, as educational institutions become increasingly gripped by external pressures – including prescriptive curricula, scripted teaching materials, high-stakes assessments and competitive league table rankings – there is an urgent need for leaders who can foster adaptability within these constraints. Schools also face internal pressures and tensions, including responses to prescriptive curricula, limited resources and managing learner behaviour. These demands create a need for leaders to develop adaptive responses suited to local circumstances. A key argument in this chapter is that the desire for external predictability – through prescriptive curricula and scripted teaching materials – has created internal tensions, unpredictability and uncertainty regarding how schools and teachers maintain local autonomy.

Complexity leadership can help people in organizations to 'read a system' (Uhl-Bien and Arena 2017: 17). It can create conditions for innovation, collaboration and problem-solving to help people and organizations adapt to instability and uncertainty. The overview below is guided by the work of Uhl-Bien and Arena (2017, 2018). We set out a brief interpretation of complexity leadership before engaging in a closing discussion about the implications for leadership and policy.

Complexity leadership recognizes the following three key roles of leaders:

1) Operational leadership: 'the need to produce'. Most leaders will have a role that includes administration and management. This role tends to link to the smooth operation and longevity of the organization (e.g. target setting, monitoring efficiency, delivering results).

2) Entrepreneurial leadership: 'the need to innovate'. Leaders focus on creativity to support the organization to adapt to external pressures or tensions. This role relies on developing connections and networks between people, providing space to stimulate innovation and novel responses (e.g. alternative ideas, different solutions, new products).

3) Enabling leadership: 'the need to adapt'. The enabling leader plays an intermediary role between operational and entrepreneurial leadership responsibilities. This role can vary over time and include diverse responses (e.g. opening and protecting adaptive spaces, exploring innovative ideas, creating sub-groups to test emerging possibilities, launching the response to the organization).

An important point to emphasize is that these key roles are intertwined with each other, as illustrated in Figure 7.2.

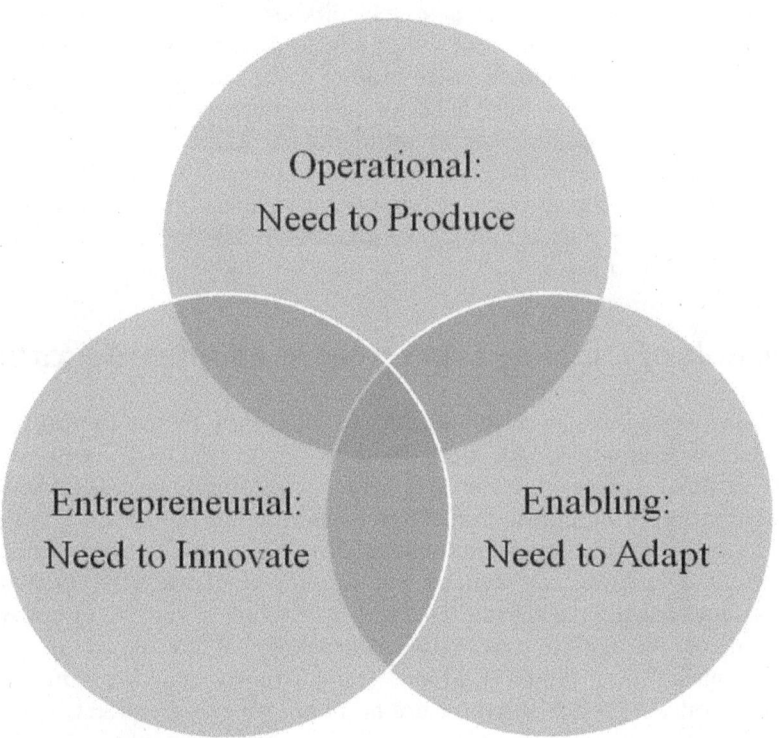

FIGURE 7.2 *The intertwined roles of complexity leadership (adapted from Uhl-Bien and Arena 2017).*

Balancing Operational and Enabling Leadership in Schools

One of the key tensions in educational leadership is the dominance of operational leadership at the expense of entrepreneurial and enabling leadership. The necessity for schools to meet performance targets and comply with external policy mandates often results in an overemphasis on administrative efficiency. While operational leadership is essential for maintaining stability and meeting targets, its unchecked dominance can suppress opportunities for innovation. As discussed earlier, it can create narrow, fixed boundaries that limit – or even delete – the space for adaptive and creative practice. Adaptive leaders seek to navigate these tensions, ensuring that compliance with external mandates does not stifle the dynamic development of the school community.

For school leaders, this means actively constructing adaptive boundary spaces in schools. Building on the earlier discussions about malleable boundary lines, adaptive boundary spaces provide an opportunity for teachers to network and engage in collaborative inquiry, to respond effectively to learner needs and wider educational purposes. These spaces do not emerge spontaneously; they require to be constructed intentionally and protected from the overwhelming pull of bureaucratic demands. With the construction of such spaces, the potential for adaptive teaching, and the broader learning development of the school community, can be enhanced significantly. Notably, the key capacities of leaders also play a role in capitalizing on the possible impact of adaptive boundary spaces, which we address in the next section.

The Role of Enabling Leadership in Adaptive Education

While leadership has received significant attention in the literature, the concept of enabling leadership remains underexplored, even within organizational studies (Uhl-Bien and Arena 2018). Enabling leaders serve as intermediaries, bridging the gap between maintaining institutional stability and fostering a culture of innovation. In educational settings, enabling leadership is particularly crucial for empowering teachers, facilitating professional learning communities, and promoting a culture of collective problem-solving within and between teachers. While there are many key capacities that define enabling leadership in adaptive educational organizations, the following three are pertinent for this chapter:

1) *Managing conflict and tension*: Given the increasing complexity of educational environments, tensions between policy mandates, institutional expectations and classroom practices are inevitable.

Enabling leaders do not seek to eliminate conflict but rather harness it as a catalyst for problem-solving and innovation in teaching.

2) *Encouraging innovation:* By establishing safe spaces for experimentation, enabling leaders can encourage educators to develop and refine novel teaching strategies. These ideas may be tested locally before being scaled across the school or local authority, ensuring that adaptive practices are both contextually relevant and sustainable.

3) *Empowering colleagues:* Enabling leaders foster a sense of agency among teachers by involving them in decision-making, supporting professional collaboration and building networks that extend beyond individual schools. This empowerment can lead to a greater sense of ownership over policy enactment and curriculum development.

These capacities are not a recipe for success. Rather, they offer potential to not only work within external pressures, but also actively use them to challenge the status quo. There are genuine opportunities for school leaders to consider how instability and uncertainty could fuel adaptive boundary spaces and the emergence of new practices that encapsulate the artistry at the heart of this chapter (e.g. practical wisdom and ethical sensitivity).

The relationship described above – where artistry development is shaped by the (un)predictability of external and internal pressures and by the flexible response of enabling leadership – is summarized in Figure 7.3. That is to say, there is a *dynamic* relationship between (un)predictability, artistry and adaptability. It suggests that for artistry in teaching to flourish in schools, it will require acknowledgement and careful negotiation of myriad internal and external pressures. Currently, teaching as artistry is constrained by the uneasy tension between the external desire for standardization, and the need for responsiveness internally to accommodate diverse learner needs. Adaptive teaching has the potential to activate professional judgements,

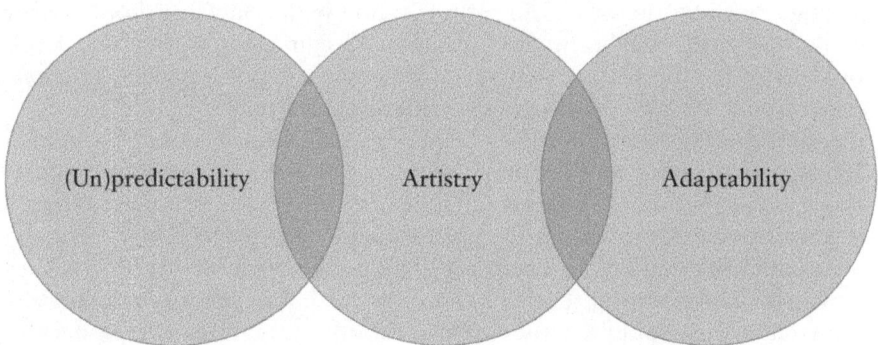

FIGURE 7.3 *The artistry interface – where (un)predictability meets adaptability.*

such as practical wisdom and ethical sensitivity, offering a perspective on what artistry could look like in schools. However, within this dynamic relationship, complexity leadership, particularly enabling leadership, has a crucial role. It provides insights into how schools can evolve into more adaptive organizations. The enabling leader role supports innovation through creating adaptive boundary spaces that cultivate artistry while challenging the rigid structures within and beyond the school. This discussion of leadership, and its role in helping schools navigate (un)predictability, informs broader discussions in our closing section on educational leadership and future policy development.

Implications for Educational Leadership and Policy

The adoption of complexity leadership in education could have significant implications for both leadership practice and future policy development. First, educational leaders have a major stake in the policy arena and should more rigorously advocate for (and defend) flexibility in curriculum enactment and teaching innovation in schools. Current policy trends, characterized by the type of top-down standardization and prescriptive measures discussed throughout this chapter, often limit teachers' ability to engage in micro- and macro-adaptive teaching. By actively seeking to shape policy construction and, subsequently, promoting the importance of adaptive boundary spaces and networking, school leaders can create environments that not only promote, but encourage innovation more widely.

Secondly, complexity leadership can challenge policymakers to reconsider the hierarchical nature of policy enactment. Traditionally, education policies are designed at the supra and macro levels, with implementation occurring at the school and classroom levels. This top-down approach can result in unintended consequences, where policies designed to improve learning instead constrain teacher agency and the possibility of adaptive teaching. By school leaders campaigning for educators to be more widely involved in the policy development process – through participatory decision-making, consultation forums, experimentation with policy in schools before publication and collaborative curriculum design using policy – schools could struggle with (rather than struggling against) policymakers to create more responsive and contextually sensitive expectations for policy.

A final point is that the role of enabling leadership in policy enactment underscores the need for systematic professional development that prepares school leaders to manage adaptive change effectively. Leadership preparation programmes could incorporate complexity leadership principles; a particular focus could be the need to balance different roles and the creation of key capacities that can bring to life enabling leadership in school communities. A related focus could be to explore various modalities for leaders to instigate collaborative professional learning in adaptive boundary spaces with teachers in their schools. We have previously examined the potential of ongoing and long-term collaborative inquiry to progress adaptive teaching in schools (McMillan and Jess 2021). Therefore, a grounding in collaborative inquiry could further equip future leaders with valuable options to innovate within the adaptive boundary spaces they create in schools. This preparation – complexity leadership and collaborative professional learning – can equip future leaders with the skills necessary to balance operational demands with the need for innovation. In sum, professional learning programmes for leaders could focus on cultivating complexity (enabling) leadership capacities, ensuring that school leaders are adept at fostering adaptive boundary spaces and further empowering their staff.

Conclusion

This chapter began by conceding that the case for teaching as an art, and teachers' practice as a form of artistry, could be defeated by underestimating the diversity of learners in schools. In response, we identified factors that have likely contributed to increasing diversity in contemporary education and presented a framework to better understand this diversity. We focused our framework on learners and their interconnected, self-organizing processes of becoming, which unfold through lived time and within boundaries (see Figure 7.1).

We offered a broader conceptualization of adaptive teaching to better engage with the scale of diversity represented in the framework. The distinction between micro- and macro-adaptations was valuable in defining a role for teachers that spanned responsibilities within and beyond the classroom. We acknowledged, however, that the responsibilities associated with adaptive teaching can be a double-edged sword. With an extensive list of skills and capabilities, alongside components such as teaching repertoires and negotiation, we accepted that micro-adaptive teaching could be difficult to master. While the responsibilities inherent in macro-adaptations were considered as problematic, particularly due to the challenge of re-interpreting prescriptive national curriculum policies. We flagged up curriculum making as a possible route to rejuvenate the ailing potential of macro-adaptation, but noted it may remain beyond reach without wider support and radical shifts in hierarchical structures. Thus, in the closing stages of the chapter, we discussed the potential of complexity leadership (see Figure 7.2), suggesting that school leadership and support at systemic levels were required to endow teachers with the space to develop the skills and capacities to perform micro- *and* macro-adaptively.

Our closing message is that there should be cautious optimism that artistry can become a reality. An optimistic outlook, against the strength of political involvement that mitigates against the artistry initiative, may be a leap too far for many readers. However, and crucially, we added an agility in terms of how schools respond: by engaging with complexity leadership and by empowering leaders and teachers to adopt advocacy roles within and beyond schools. Enabling leadership, therefore, has undergirded artistry with the coveted features of adaptability (see Figure 7.3). From this perspective, then, artistry is at the interface between unpredictability and adaptability. Our cautious optimism is warranted because schools, particularly school leaders and teachers, are arguably better positioned to read and then operate within these dynamic and demanding situations.

Notes

1   By 'diversity' we refer to social differences patterned by age, gender, (dis) ability, race, class, ethnicity, religion, together with wider factors such as lifestyle, language and locality.

2   We do not have space in this chapter to provide an extensive overview of different leadership models, or to share a detailed account of Instructional and Distributed leadership. We do recognize a degree of similarity, though, between these two prominent models and what is proposed in this section from organizational leadership literature. As such, the essence of Instructional and Distributed forms of leadership is shared in the bullet points below and, as we set out the key ideas in this section, interested readers are invited to tease out the links.

- Instructional Leadership has teaching and learning as a core objective. In general, the focus of leaders is to improve the quality of instruction and increasing the attainment of learners. Leaders achieve this in myriad ways, including mentoring, feedback and professional development.

- Distributed Leadership has shared responsibility as a core objective. In general, the focus of leaders is to achieve school development goals by sharing responsibilities with staff across the school. Leaders achieve this by promoting opportunities for collaboration, empowering people and utilizing the collective wisdom of staff.

References

Adam, B. (2008), 'The Timescapes Challenge: Engagement with the Invisible', in R. Edwards (ed), *Researching Lives through Time: Time, Generation and Life Stories*, 7–12, Swindon: ESRC.

Akkerman, S. and A. Bakker (2011), 'Learning at the Boundary: An Introduction', *International Journal of Educational Research*, 50 (1): 1–5.

Biesta, G. (2015), 'What Is Education for? On Good Education, Teacher Judgement, and Educational Professionalism', *European Journal of Education*, 50 (1): 75–87.

Byrne, D. (1998), *Complexity Theory and the Social Sciences*, London: Routledge.

Byrne, D. and G. Callaghan (2014), *Complexity Theory and the Social Sciences (2nd edition)*, London: Bloomsbury.

Corno, L. (2008), 'On Teaching Adaptively', *Educational Psychologist*, 43 (3): 161–73.

Davis, B. and D. Sumara (2006), *Complexity and Education: Inquiries into Learning, Teaching, and Research*, Mahwah, NJ: Lawrence Erlbaum Associates.

Deleuze, G. (1994), *Difference and Repetition*, trans. P. Patton, New York: Columbia University Press.

Deleuze, G. and F. Guattari (1987), *A Thousand Plateaus: Capitalism and Schizophrenia*, trans. B. Massumi, Minneapolis, MN: University of Minnesota Press.

Faas, D., C. Hajisoterioub and P. Angelides (2014), 'Intercultural Education in Europe: Policies, Practices and Trends', *British Educational Research Journal*, 31 (2): 139–55.

Fairbanks, C., G. Duffy, B. Faircloth, Y. He, B. Levin, J. Rohr and C. Stein (2010), 'Beyond Knowledge: Exploring Why Some Teachers Are More Thoughtfully Adaptive than Others', *Journal of Teacher Education*, 61 (1–2): 161–71.

Hallinger, P. (2005), 'Instructional Leadership and the School Principal: A Passing Fancy That Refuses to Go Away', *Leadership and Policy in Schools*, 4 (3): 221–39.

Hoffman, J. and G. Duffy (2016), 'Does Thoughtfully Adaptive Teaching Actually Exist? A Challenge to Teacher Educators', *Theory into Practice*, 55 (3): 172–9.

Jess, M., K. Howells and P. McMillan (2024), 'Becoming Physical Education: The Ontological Shift to Complexity', *Sport, Education and Society*, 29 (6): 684–98.

Khalil, E. and K. Boulding, eds. (1996), *Evolution, Order and Complexity*, London: Routledge.

Krejsler, J. (2016), 'Seize the Opportunity to Think Differently! A Deleuzian Approach to Unleashing Becomings in Education', *Educational Philosophy and Theory*, 48 (14): 1475–85.

May, T. (2003), 'When Is a Deleuzian Becoming?', *Continental Philosophy Review*, 36 (2): 139–53.

May, T. (2005), *Gilles Deleuze: An Introduction*, Cambridge: Cambridge University Press.

McMillan, P. and M. Jess (2021), 'Embracing Complex Adaptive Practice: The Potential of Lesson Study', *Professional Development in Education*, 47 (2–3): 273–88.

McMillan, P., C. Anderson and M. Jess (2025), 'Adaptive Teaching and the Interactional Order of Classrooms', *Scottish Educational Review*, 57 (1): 117–144.

Meadows, D. (2008), *Thinking in Systems: A Primer*, White River Junction, VT: Chelsea Green Publishing.

Parsons, S., M. Vaughn, R. Scales, M. Gallagher, A. Parsons, S. Davis, M. Pierczynski and M. Allen (2018), 'Teachers' Instructional Adaptations: A Research Synthesis', *Review of Educational Research*, 88 (2): 205–42.

Priestley, M., D. Alvunger, S. Philippou and T. Soini, eds. (2021), *Curriculum Making in Europe: Policy and Practice within and across Diverse Contexts*, Bingley: Emerald.

Spillane, J.P. (2006), *Distributed Leadership*, San Francisco, CA: Jossey-Bass.

Stenhouse, L. (1988), 'Artistry and Teaching: The Teacher as Focus of Research and Development', *Journal of Curriculum and Supervision*, 4 (1): 43–51.

Uhl-Bien, M. and M. Arena (2017), 'Complexity Leadership: Enabling People and Organizations for Adaptability', *Organizational Dynamics*, 46 (1): 9–20.

Uhl-Bien, M. and M. Arena (2018), 'Leadership for Organizational Adaptability: A Theoretical Synthesis and Integrative Framework', *The Leadership Quarterly*, 29 (1): 89–104.

United Nations (1989), *Convention on the Rights of the Child*. Treaty no. 27531, *United Nations Treaty Series*, 1577, 3–178. Available online: https://treaties. un.org/doc/Treaties/1990/09/19900902%2003-14%20AM/Ch_IV_11p.pdf (accessed 3 June 2024).

Vagle, M.D. (2016), 'Making Pedagogical Adaptability Less Obvious', *Theory into Practice*, 55 (3): 207–16.

CHAPTER EIGHT

Artistry of Teaching as a Practice of Curation: Inviting Possibilities for Knowing and Seeing Anew

Laura Colucci-Gray

Introduction

Expressed quite literally in the language of physics, education commonly understood as the *doings* of the teachers, and the *labour* of the students, is also very commonly described through the language of 'work'. Not dissimilar from the mechanical force exerted by a body onto another body, such work is set to move students forward, in a linear trajectory towards a destination. It is an image of progress and advancement, which is hard to argue against, for its appealing view of education as the driver for social mobility and material amelioration. However, if this was the full ambition of school life, then it would be very odd that we felt any need to do anything about it.

Looking closely, the first detail demanding attention lies in the factory-like frame, in which the work of teachers and students is inscribed. Its most apparent manifestation is the reliance on standardized assessments for international, comparative evaluation (Samier 2002), brought into use by an economically driven society demanding calculable procedures for efficiency and predictability (Howes et al. 2009). While such moves are predicated on the 'premise that a uniform accountability system [will] close achievement gaps between students' (Manum 2017: 248), thus improving equality in education, they also result in 'producing an "iron cage of rationality" that makes life routine, meaningless and devoid of ethical and emotional considerations' (Howes et al. 2009: 127). As Simone Weil already observed fifty years ago (Panichas 1977), in the model of society as a factory and by analogy, the school as a mirror of the social system, the workingman that is so indispensable to the productive process, is in fact accounted as practically nothing in it; its duty is to get on with the job, lest being replaced, like any other part in the mechanism. There is no intimacy that binds them to the workplace and objects 'amidst which their lives are used up' (Weil 1965 cited by Panichas 1977: 63).

In the attempt to think of education *otherwise*, I situate my account of artistry as a construct that stands as both a *possibility* and an *alternative* to the technicist model we are used to. Importantly, by using the word 'alternative' I am not seeking to replace something apparently vile, with its (allegedly) virtuous, artistic opposite. As Elliot Eisner (2002a) acutely noted, such replacement would not only entail knowing that something is to be changed, but also what to offer instead. However, in the realm of everyday experiences, where actions tend to be habitual and assumptions taken for granted, we are often dealing with a secondary form of ignorance, that is *not* knowing what we do not know. It is at this point that artistry – defined by Eisner (2002b) – as the *artistic* performance of practice – plays a role. The term 'artistic' is not intended to dress up what's real with something more pleasing or excusably odd, but following Eisner (2002a), we are engaging with a practice seeking to enhance one's consciousness of what has been created, and as Stenhouse (1988) continued, invite the desire and the imagination to improve it.

This is a clear challenge for many educators, teachers and researchers included. Being concerned with consciousness, and the multiple and different ways in which we may encounter the world, artistry resists scientific protocols. Instead, it may have more to do with *aesthetic sensibility*, as the way in which we are capable to perceive, and assemble things in relation (Eisner 2002b: 54). Yet, while aesthetic sensibility may be orientated towards a collective (Humphreys and Hyland 2002), artistry itself may only be subjectively understood (Casham et al. 2024).

By virtue of this challenge, in this chapter, I will refrain from trying to develop a set of principles to define the artistry of teaching. Instead, working with the invitations offered by Eisner (2002b), I will rely on the process of writing to make sense of artistry, drawing on diverse literatures and experiences – including my own – in the speculative and transitory manner of a curated account. Following a double movement, first I will look at the performance of schooling and the overregulation of aesthetic experience. Then I will engage with artistic performances of practice to expand sense-perception, and explore their educational features, drawing also on experiences in my own practice. These examples are not offered to the reader as empirical evidence of mastery, but as opportunities for talking about artistry in light of the performances that were created (Eisner 2002b). From this, I will suggest that the significance of artistry for education today lies with the way in which a community of teachers and students come together to inquire into their educational experiences, and to address the questions that deeply matter to them, to generate the powerful stories that will allow them to carry on.

The Performance of Schooling

There is a familiar iconographic dimension to the work of teachers and teaching; a visual performance that unfolds with the teacher pointing to the text on the board, and students noting down what is deemed important to be learnt. This image is so common to have become almost the 'natural' way to think of any teachers in any schools, its particular aesthetics resulting from the structuring of a multiplicity of relations, into specific patterns of expected behaviours and modes of being in school. As argued by Vlieghe and Zamojski (2017) drawing on the work of Agamben, the school is essentially a system of use and implementation of particular technologies for organizing time and space, deciding what experiences may be doable and desirable, as well as establishing practices and regimes of 'gestural mechanics', linked to the installation of bodily discipline. In this way, school curricula can act as dispositifs – or *mental devices* (Eisner and Vallance 1974) – with the capacity to filter and emphasize particular forms of knowledge; frame the scope for sense experience, and reinforce the normative expectations set out to maintain the status, power and privilege of dominant groups (see Eisner and Vallance 1974: 6–7). Regardless of their being material, linguistic or abstract, dispositifs will activate and transform the nature of the relationships that individuals are able to forge with other social entities (Dodier and Barbot 2016).

Hence, following Butler (1997), understandings of school practices as performances point to the normative powers of formal education on the formation of the subject; how, on the one hand, they may 'circumscribe the domain of a liveable sociality' (Butler 1997: 21) and its imagined futures; while, on the other hand, they may be enhancing the capacity of students and teachers to redirect the quality of their attention, for example, as a form of care (Haraway 2016). So, what do artistry and artists have to do with this? And in what way may artistry contribute to rethinking the ambition and values of education?

From a Singular Performance to Differencing Modes of Experience

Arguably, teaching as the practice that most directly interfaces with the structures of schools is the first and most direct vehicle for the enculturation of students into the ways in which society makes sense of the world (Humphreys and Hyland 2002). To find an exemplification of this, I turn towards my own field of research in science education that since its first inception in the post-war era has contended with the expectations of the growing capitalist economy on curricula and the work of teachers (Ryder 2015). As evidenced by the number of recurrent calls for programmes to improve uptake of science subjects, increasingly referred to with the applied terminology of Science, Technology, Engineering and Mathematics (STEM), attention has focused on reforming curricula and streamlining content, in order to fix a science qualification pipeline supposedly 'leaking' (Colucci-Gray 2022).

More recently, the call for adding the Arts to STEM – under the acronym of STEAM (Science, Technology, Engineering, Mathematics with the addition of Arts) has called for a new contract between the sciences and the arts, through the affiliated concepts of impact and innovation, marketing and design (Pirrie 2019). While, on the one hand, this gathering of disciplines previously unrelated has been welcomed for its openings towards creativity and a different way to organize resources and the work of schools (Olivato and Castro Silva 2023); on the other hand, simply adding artists to the work of teachers, or making teachers a little 'artier' through the affiliated definitions of teachers as agents, designers and makers of curricula (Murphy et al. 2012) may actually contribute to reinforcing neoliberal contestations, such as the anaesthetization of deeply ethical issues affecting the work of teachers and the status of pupils (Pirrie and Manum 2023); or even, the notion that the outcome of an education in the arts may be a good career choice, when such choice and possibility are profoundly unequal and essentially *un-freeing* within the cultural and economic forces currently at play (Gichuru 2024).

So, turning to artistry, and the definition given by Eisner (2002b) as the *artistic* performance of practice, we are invited to look at the arts not as tools to generate particular experiences for particular goals, but to consider them as *modes* of experience (Eisner 2002b: 10), and specifically, *aesthetic* modes, concerned with the ways in which we enter in relation with the world via sense perception. Drawing on the work of Paul Ricoeur, Josephsson et al. (2022) described aesthetic perception as a kind of world's disclosure, as the phenomena of the world are made present to us, and we are present to ourselves, through everyday interactions.

The function of art education according to Eisner (2002b) is thus that of enhancing one's awareness of sense experience. For example, the arts may help us learn to notice the world in a different way, and beyond the canon of what is customarily deemed worthy of noticing; the arts may help make visible what is made invisible in formalized accounts, as well as cultivate a cognitive disposition,

> to tolerate ambiguity, to explore what is uncertain, to exercise judgment free from prescriptive rules and procedures. In the arts, the locus of evaluation is internal, and the so-called subjective side of ourselves has an opportunity to be utilized.
>
> (Eisner 2002b: 10)

Because of this evaluative function, the ability to consciously understand the nature of our own sense experience is important in educational terms well beyond the realm of art education (Lewis 2012). Artistic performances of practice may give insights into the cultural filters that are at work in any given situation (Dodier and Barbot 2016); the aesthetic gesture is of another kind: to make out what can and cannot be seen and what can and cannot be heard, that being in science or other subjects. In other words, following Lewis (2012) drawing on the philosophical analysis of Jacques Rancière, an aesthetic experience is first and foremost 'a certain disconnection from the habitual conditions of sensible experience' (Ranciere 2006 cited by Lewis 2012: 9). When translated to education, artistry as the artistic performance of practice may thus be more precisely concerned with an *aesthetic sensibility* which – in one sense – *it is related* to gaining awareness of how we come to know what we know; and in another sense, with *inquiring* into what might be other ways of knowing, that may be excluded and encouraged in the process, rather than repackaging curricula or emphasizing aesthetic pleasantries in infusing sciences with arts (Colucci-Gray 2022).

Artistic Performances of Practice in Teaching and the Arts

If the intention is to look further into artistry as the capacity to respond and to inquire into a situation with aesthetic sensibility, then education will be re-defined as the possibility for teachers and students to improve on such ability. Taking distance from the belief in the regularity and universality of knowledge, Eisner (2002a: 383) spoke of artistry as the sensitivity for the particularity of things and situations, and of the teacher's own sense of aesthetic experience: 'the moves the teacher makes, by the plans the teacher designs, and by matters of timing, manner, and tone' shape the environment that both students and teachers share.

To date however, the artistry *of* teaching remains an elusive concept. In a recent review, Casham et al. (2024: 10) summed it up as the 'pursuit of doing things differently; a holistic and more rounded view of practice', including disrupting educational certainties and planning routines. Artistry does involve the arts in various ways, from humour and paradox, to idiosyncratic uses of visual, discursive and auditory forms, whose meaning will sit in between the factual and the fictional (Eisner 2003). Interesting cases also include the use of arts-based methodologies in teacher education, such as portraitures and the creation of public performances as fictional devices, to inquire into art teachers' *becoming-pedagogical* (e.g. see Gouzouasis et al. 2013), that is, with a commitment to embodied and aesthetic engagement with the world as a living, and intimate inquiry.

In order to proceed in this exploration into the artistry of teaching is thus useful to first understand the nature of artistic practices in their intention of being pedagogical. An interesting example is offered by the curator Hand Ulich Obrist (2014) reflecting on the role of the curator situated in between the artists' creations and the public. At a time when securing a museum space was unaffordable, Obrist described the curation of an exhibition in his own kitchen, where the refrigerators and the cupboards afforded the space for displaying common objects (giant-size cereal boxes; marble eggs in the refrigerators; candles in the bin under the sink). There was no attempt to make a spectacular impression – instead it preserved the function of the kitchen by subtly adding to it, drawing on the affordances of space to shift perception and generate potential for newly created linguistic and metaphorical expressions. In the words of the curator, what was powerful in the eyes of the onlookers was the sense of playfulness giving the adults an *Alice in the Wonderland* sense about it, producing a sense of wonder by giving an adult a child's perspective, and offering the chance for unexpected conversations and entanglements about the different objects, often incongruous with their sizing and their positioning in space (Ulrich Obrist 2014: 87). All such examples share in common the production of *aesthetic acts* with the power to influence sense-perception (Lewis 2012), and to surface non-conscious dispositions through the use of different materials that may resonate with people's memories, biographies, hopes and fears (Kipnis et al. 2021). The artistry is thus explicitly relying on artistic devices with a view to invite different points of view, or as Obrist (2014: 10) maintained, to enable an encounter, to start a conversation, with the intention to enable artists make possible 'projects that could not be realized under existing conditions'. From a methodological point of view, a curated space such as that of an exhibition, or an improvised performance in the theatre or in a public square, is described as first and foremost a space of researching the interplay of desires, actions and intentions (Eisner 2002b), as in the manner of a conversation between different parties, rather than an arrangement of work or a specialist space to suit and deliver a pre-existing idea.

So, for the purpose of further understanding the educational significance of seeing teaching as an art and associated with aesthetic acts, the question arising is the extent to which an artistic practice may be deemed educational, and in what way. This is important in order to appreciate what teaching and art may have in common, while avoiding the pitfall of confusing the practical actions and context of the teacher with that of the curator, or those of the artist, as these may well be different. If the artistry of the artist develops from creating artwork and bring it into the world as an aesthetic encounter (Kipnis et al. 2021), the artistry of the teacher lies with the capacity to engender personal, aesthetic encounters with the world (Eisner 2002b). In this sense, the artist may operate as a teacher by inviting a particular way of seeing things *in the world*, while the teacher may work as an artist with the ability to shift codified expectations about what is made visible in the educational space, and invite the students to see through the differences (Lewis 2012). To this effect, I would suggest that the teacher may actually share something with the curator, but a curator of a particular kind, because in the formalized space of the classroom what is different *makes a difference*, for it invites a different kind of attention as Biesta (2022) discussed: an attention that interrupts the flow of regular experiences, while at the same time sustain the possibility to look elsewhere.

This point is critical as the underlying assumption of the technicist model of education is that the value of teachers lies with their effectiveness to induce learning (Luyten et al. 2017), in the manner of a teacher-scientist that can manipulate the nature by knowing its inner laws (Colucci-Gray et al. 2013). Conversely, from the point of view of a curator, concerned with the experiences of the participants, attention is given to the body *in* the performance, and how perception is mediated *through* the body – not simply occurring mechanically by means of it. On these bases, if we extend the artistic practice of curation to teaching, the classroom and the curriculum are not simply formalized spaces where certain activities are performed, but they are socially and historically constructed spaces filled with artefacts – posters on the wall, equipment, furniture – where the processes of education as a cultural and social activity are grounded (Obrist 2014: 168).

Illustrative in this regard are metaphorical artefacts that occur and re-occur across domains of experience and find their way into the science curriculum: the verticality of the ladder climbed by the 'more or less adapted' or the 'more or less evolved' has the power to alter perception, literally 'drawing' lines in space as gestures 'in plain sight' (Colucci-Gray 2024). If teacher artistry is connected to aesthetic sensibility, then recognizing that knowledge is not simply factual, calls for an aesthetic inquiry into their embodied status; how they filter students' encounters with the world (Lewis 2012), and how new conversations may be initiated right there where the possibility already exists.

So, having come closer to the idea of artistry as it was originally put forward by Eisner *as a way of doing things differently* (Casham et al. 2024), the question that opens up is what happens when such practices are enacted – either by artists or by teachers themselves; and in what way may practices of curation maintain the process of living inquiry open and ongoing. To continue this exploration, I will turn to two experiences where I was involved respectively as a participant in an artistic performance curated by two artists, and as an observer of the students' work while engaged in a STEAM activity. In both accounts, I will focus on the cognitive power of the arts to invite different forms of attention, and I evaluate the unfolding performances as distinct educational moments of encountering the world.

First Example: Digging in the Soil

The first experience from a recent project, BRIDGES (Building Reflexivity and response-ability Involving Different narratives of knowledGE and Science[1]), involved a collective experiment with a group of doctoral students and colleagues from across the natural sciences and the humanities, under the guidance of two performance artists (Giuffredi et al. 2025). The project focused on soil as a case in point, being not only a solid material but also a horizon of possible and different ways to view the complex and problematic relationship between humans and their environment.

The invitation was to enact the collective performance of a soil dig which, following O'Sullivan (2024), was configured as an aesthetic device, in the manner of 'archaeo-fictioning', a way to gain renovated exposure to sensorial modalities – such as digging – which have been interrupted or gone obsolete in modern times. In common with archaeology, this performance practice involves a communion with the past, eliciting connections with the ancestors, or a witnessing of the dead in ancestral practices. But *being attentive to the past* is a practice that is both ethical and aesthetic, writes Donna Haraway (2016), for it summons other modes of existence from within the present one, conjuring both a past attitude and a responsibility for what is yet to come.

Hence, situated between the factual and the fictional, the performance of the dig started with the selection of tools – shovel, rake, buckets – which are commonly used in gardening and are also common to some of us who carried out field studies in the natural sciences. Yet, far from being a natural act, this initial step already worked as an interruption of common-sense experience (Lewis 2012). As largely urbanized beings, and favouring seated positions in front of a screen, we have become unused to bending our backs and contend with the nature of the ground upon which we stand; that being the complex root systems of a woodland (Figure 8.1) or the soft soil of a garden patch (Figure 8.2), that has been worked and reworked by decades of agricultural practice.

Drawing on the cognitive power of the arts both to notice things and to encapsulate moments in flow that may be otherwise evanescent

FIGURE 8.1 *Digging through tangled roots in the woodland soil (Italy; Project BRIDGES).*

(Eisner 2002b), the dig was thus a performance in which we were both actors and witnesses of our own selves. To guide us in the observation, the artists invited us to pay conscious attention to the way we approached the dig, for example, by distinguishing between the attention of the archaeologist – that notices the changes in the layers of the soil as specific horizons of time in which objects may be situated, and the attention of the collector, focused on classifying, ignoring or discarding presented objects. As a secondary

FIGURE 8.2 *Digging in the vegetable garden patch (Italy; Project BRIDGES).*

modality for attention, the notebooks (Figures 8.3 and 8.4) and the white cloth (Figure 8.5) accommodated fieldnotes, sketches, soil-painting and a set of 'findings' that each group arranged and curated for a final performance, re-telling the particular story of each dig as we had been able to witness it.

From our own collective reflections on the project, it emerged that for many of us involved in the performance it was difficult to attend to the dig without giving in the desire to know *a priori* what we were set out to find out. While the factual modality of scientific research is orientated towards describing something by asking the question 'what is this?', an artistic performance would instead provoke a more speculative response – 'what is this telling me ...'? – orientated towards understanding how we come to know from within (Eisner 2002a). An inevitable tension also permeated the curation of the 'findings' (Figure 8.5) as the stones, parts of plants, fragments of carbon on the white cloth were not fixed in given categories in the manner of a museum exhibition, but could harbour many potentially legitimate stories within *'an indefinite present time'* (Giuffredi et al. 2025). In the manner suggested by Biesta (2022), the performance of the dig worked educationally by engaging the cognitive power of the arts *to interrupt* sedimented views of research and of being a researcher; and in so doing, it opened up to different traditional of research and different ways of seeing which acknowledge what is commonly left out of the process: our own frustrations, expectations and desires which frame the relational encounter with different kinds of practitioners, humans and more than human others (Haraway 2016).

FIGURE 8.3 *Modes of attention: Writing observation notes in the project notebook (Italy; Project BRIDGES).*

FIGURE 8.4 *Modes of attention: Sketching with soil paint in the project notebook (Italy; Project BRIDGES).*

FIGURE 8.5 *Offerings or Findings? Curation and story-telling from the dig (Italy; Project BRIDGES).*

Second Example: Making a House for a Fairy

The second example is an illustration from an ongoing project 'SENSE. STEAM' funded by the European Union Horizon 2020 scheme's 'Building a roadmap to STEAM education across Europe'. In line with the general attention for increasing the number of science graduates for a more competitive and sustainable Europe (see European Commission 2024), the call was to reinvigorate students' interest in science, especially girls, through the integration of STEAM educational approaches. As indicated earlier and in previous writings (see Colucci-Gray 2022), this position is problematic with regards to reinforcing utilitarian purposes of education, putting arts and sciences to the service of the marketization agenda (Pirrie 2019). So, in this project we attempted to make a counter-turn, and engage with a version of STEAM education as a trans-disciplinary practice, aimed at engaging students and teachers with a plurality of different ways of knowing, and to become aware of how these may work as different gestures, influencing perception and awareness of our own position in the world (Colucci-Gray 2024).

With these intentions in mind, the particular experience I describe here involved two groups of students under the guidance of their youth leaders, respectively in Georgia (Eastern Europe) and in Romania. In both contexts participants would be used to a presentational mode of teaching science, with an emphasis on conceptual delivery (Ciascai, Haiduc and Felezeu 2014); the pedagogical framing of STEAM would also be more closely aligned with STEM applications, such as robotics, while experiences of teaching outdoors were generally unfamiliar in both formal and informal educational settings.

Similar to archaeo-fictioning described earlier (O'Sullivan 2024), the activity was simply described as the practical task of building a house for a fairly; however, in this simplicity also lies the ambiguity of child-play, the house being both a concrete project and a fictional endeavour. Drawing on this inherent ambiguity, the activity shared with the sciences the particular modality of model-building, designed to test a theory and to prototype a design under experimental conditions. Whereas in the arts, one such example is working at a scale in the manner of miniature ceramists, commonly female artists, whose manufacts often feature small houses and tiny chairs relating back to furniture and everyday items in their parental homes (Cai 2024). The miniature work is a response to necessity, such as cost or lack of space; but also the opportunity that miniatures afford for precision and risk-taking; the small scale allows for the possibility of 'going wrong' as well as a certain tolerance of 'wrong doing', as in the dramaturgical device of giving voice to the small person speaking the unwanted and the unsaid (Piazzoli 2018); or performing the collective power of a swarm of hand-knitted tiny creatures in the tradition of craftivism (Bratich and Bush 2011). Students were not primed to follow one orientation or the other but were invited to decide for themselves where to build the house and according to which design and dimensions (see Figures 8.6, 8.7 and 8.8).

As shown in Figure 8.6, the group of girls in Georgia focused on interiors, to make a home that was comfortable in every respect and with a solid structure. Materials played a purposeful role, with each part designed with precision and cut to size. In Figures 8.7 and 8.8, Romanian students worked outside, with materials found in the local environment.

The two different interpretations of the task invite a reflection on the dual nature of making and design. In one case, we see a practical focus, with attention to functionality and reproducibility, while in the other case, the creations are more similar to craft pieces, with its typically 'make and mend' and ad hoc approach (Rawshtorn 2022). In both groups, students discussed matters of aesthetics, focusing on the qualities of materials, the effects that these created and how and where they may be sourced. While the first group favoured a realistic approach to making the house, as if they were prototyping, their attention was also placed on the quality of the experience they produced (Eisner 2002b), as a practice of care (Haraway

FIGURE 8.6 *Purposeful design and domestic comforts: A fairy-house with a light (Georgia; Project SENSE.STEAM).*

FIGURE 8.7 *Observing and Feeling natural textures (Romania; Project SENSE.STEAM).*

FIGURE 8.8 *Adaptive Design and responsive making: A house with moss (Romania; Project SENSE. STEAM).*

2016). Similarly, in the second case, scanning the local area for the best conditions to make a house invited a different attention to the environment of the city: not simply as a container of utilities and resources, but as a legitimate interlocutor in the speculative pursuit of a shared life-project with the creatures they carried in their minds. Was this science education? Or was this art education?

In the miniature world an important line is crossed between the arts and the sciences, and between design and craft, the resulting performance combining the apparently public eye of external scrutiny, with the private world of the intimate and the familiar. Asking what is educational about such practices is thus equivalent to questioning what is *skilful*: an increasing number of contemporary projects see designers making their own parts, often drawing on materials they have at hand, or by recycling and taking apart disused objects. But also, what is *meaningful*: designers become makers taking design away from its commercial function, and turn it into an *attitude* of collective experimentation, to respond to the needs and the challenges of people living in post-industrial societies. Translated to STEAM education, symbolic instruments and practices, as in this case the building of a house for a mythical creature, may allow for 'a different relationship to reality as commonly experienced: a different take on our past that gestures towards a different future' (O'Sullivan 2024: 6 5)

Artistry of Teaching as a Practice of Curation: In Education

Considering the examples presented here from the point of view of the work of a classroom teacher may be perplexing; decisions regarding what may be proposed to students depend on curriculum, the nature of the subject matter as well as what may be deemed age or level appropriate. As remarked by Pirrie and Manum (2023: 862), such is the effect of certain modalities of counterfactual thinking in education demanding 'conformity, uniformity and discipline', while artistic performances are confined to the domain of frills, fun details or furniture (Eisner 2002a). However, if we take the power of aesthetic sensibility seriously, then the artistry of the teacher will not be about delivery and transmission, but as something that Biesta (2017: 19–20) expressed as the educational ambition to 'interrupt' as: 'much of the work of the educator is about creating time, space and forms so that students can encounter their desire, examine their desires, select and transform them'. Key to such process, Naughton (2018) continues, is the shift from seeing the world as something to be mined for its potential to fulfil a demand, and seeing it instead as an affective force that will touch students in different ways, and in the manner of an intimate encounter, that will be different for each one of them, and will depend on the realization that occurs at the time. What is produced by an affective sensation is not a thought response, even though cognitive and conceptual elements may contribute to it, but a 'nervous response' where the world is felt: 'a physiological change, that may not be necessarily recognised amongst the community until a later date' (Naughton 2018: 48).

In this sense, the artistry of teaching in its intent of being pedagogical may invite the use of art-forms, not as tools for 'making art' or delivering products, but as *mediums* for students to perceive a situation from multiple vantage points, moving in-between practical and symbolic values of an action, allowing for the 'what' and the possibility of the 'what if' (Varela and Shear 1999). The educational space so curated is one of infinite conversations, where the aim is not to restrict but to: 'attend to the ongoing research, where learning is not mere doing, [but] is about constructing a view of the world' (Stenhouse 1988: 47).

This is a radical change in the way we see education away from the scientific model of the factory (Manum 2017), but it also calls for thinking about artistry beyond a set of specialist knowledge. This point is important to avoid falling into the trap of generalizing artistry as a prized 'best practice', and see it instead as the particular moment in which the aesthetic sensibility of the teacher meets the aesthetic sensibilities of the students. This encounter has elements of uniqueness, that cannot be captured from an external position, but are intrinsic to – and can only be known from within – the teaching itself, for crucial in this process: 'is the desire of the artist to improve his or her art' (Stenhouse 1988: 50).

Looking back to the experiences I described, it was apparent that the question was never about whether the performance *worked* for somebody or something, as in some way it didn't, but about the nature and the form of knowing embedded in the performance; from this position, the educational task was to stand back and to observe how we came to know the world when digging in the garden as compared to the woodland, and to open up to the specific dilemmas this generated. Similarly in the second example, students were invited to find for themselves what might be their particular appeal to the world; there were no curricular outcomes set *a priori* or retrofitted, but it was for participants to recognize that the boundaries drawn around subjects are not for anybody to keep, but for the community of teacher and students to tease out. Artistry in this sense engages with experiences unfolding in a relational space; asking questions about what is made visible but also how the invisibility of particular relations can be brought to light through intersubjectivity (Varela and Shear 1999). This is by no means a simple feat.

As Zahavi (2008) remarked, common situations are taken for granted, their meaning being already assigned through language, habits and culture. Interrupting established practices may bring very different experiences for different students which for a teacher, also means interrupting oneself, and the flow of expectations that may accompany the unfolding of a lesson. This means watching out for the way in which as teachers we may see the students – recipients at the end of a process – as opposed to legitimate subjects at the beginning of an inquiry, each one with their own way to partake in the performance. Reminded by Biesta (2017), artistry in this sense speaks to a process of seeking and finding direction for one's work in a way that both depends on and brings forth our encounters with otherness, such as what is different 'from' us but also so profoundly unknown. This ethical stance necessitates of a new modality of conceiving reason; that is not the logic of control but an openness towards new points of departure; remaining invitational towards new, uncharted stories and allowing them to carry on.

Note

1   https://www.progetto-bridges.it.

Acknowledgements

This research has been supported by funding from Horizon Europe [Project Number: 101058507, 2022-2025] and the Cariplo Foundation Science, Technology and Society Programme, 2021–2023. I wish to thank Adelina Dragomir from the Group of the European Youth for Change (GEYC) and Anna Samwel from Women for a Common Future (WECF) for supporting the implementation of the activities with students in Romania and Georgia.

References

Biesta, G. (2017), *The Rediscovery of Teaching*, London: Routledge.
Biesta, G. (2022), *World-Centred Education. A View from the Present*, London: Routledge.
Bratich, J. and H. Bush (2011), 'Fabricating Activism: Craft Work, Popular Culture, Gender', *Utopian Studies*, 22 (2): 233–60.
Butler, J. (1997), *The Psychic Life of Power: Theories in Subjection*, Stanford, CA: Stanford University Press.
Cai, S. (2024), *Clayfull. The Big World of Tiny Ceramics*, London: Smith Street Books.
Casham, S., L. Sheridan and S. Agostinho (2024), 'Artistry in Teaching: A Systematic Literature Review of the Research Spanning 50 years (1972–2022)', *Teaching and Teacher Education*, 152: 1–14.
Ciascai, L., L. Haiduc and C. Felezeu (2014), 'How Science Is Taught in the Secondary and High School Levels in Romania?', *Hacettepe University Journal of Education*, 29 (1): 74–86.
Colucci-Gray, L. (2022), 'The STEM, STEAM, STEAME Debate: What Does Each Term Mean and What Theoretical Frameworks Underpin Their Development?',

in J. Dillon and M. Watts (eds), *Debates in Science Education (2nd edition)*, 13–26, London: Routledge.

Colucci-Gray, L. (2024), 'Gesturing in Plain Sight: Dialogical Enactments of Sustainable Futures as Being and Doing in the World', *Cultural Studies of Science Education*, 18 (4): 1101–16.

Colucci-Gray, L., S. Das, D. Gray, D. Robson and J. Spratt (2013), 'Evidence-Based Practice and Teacher Action-Research: A Reflection on the Nature and Direction of Change', *British Educational Research Journal*, 39 (1): 126–47.

Dodier, N. and J. Barbot (2016), 'The Force of Dispositifs', *Annales* (English edition), 71 (2): 291–317.

Eisner, E. (2002a), 'From Episteme to Phronesis to Artistry in the Study and Improvement of Teaching', *Teaching and Teacher Education*, 18 (4): 375–85.

Eisner, E. (2002b), *The Arts and the Creation of Mind*, London: Yale University Press.

Eisner, E. (2003), 'On the Differences between Scientific and Artistic Approaches to Qualitative Research', *Visual Arts Research*, 29 (57), Special Issue Commemorating Our 30th Anniversary (2003): 5–11.

Eisner, E. and E. Vallance (1974), *Conflicting Conceptions of Curriculum*, Berkeley, CA: McCutchan.

Directorate-General for Research and Innovation (2024), *Science, Research and Innovation performance of the EU 2024 report*, European Commision. Available online: https://research-and-innovation.ec.europa.eu/knowledge-publications-tools-and-data/publications/all-publications/science-research-and-innovation-performance-eu-2024-report_e.

Gichuru, J. (2024), 'Enhancing STEM Education through Equity, Diversity, Inclusion and Decolonization', in I. Decoito, X. Fazio and J. Gichuru (editors), *Global Perspectives on STEM Education*, Cham: Springer.

Giuffredi, R., C. Colella, L. Colucci-Gray, A. Caretto, R. Spagna and A. L'Astorina (2025), 'Beyond Crisis Talk: Making Time for Re-searching New Narratives of Human Relations with Soil', *Tecnoscienza, Italian Journal of Science and Technology Studies*, 15 (2): 39–59.

Gouzouasis, P., R. Irwin, E. Miles and A. Gordon (2013), 'Commitments to a Community of Artistic Inquiry: Becoming Pedagogical through A/R/Tography in Teacher Education', *International Journal of Education and the Arts*, 14 (1): 1–23.

Haraway, D. (2016), *Staying with the Trouble. Making Kin in the Chtulucene*, Durham, NC: Duke University Press.

Howes, E., L. Graham and J. Friedman (2009), 'Between McDonaldization and Gardening Pedagogy: How Teachers Negotiate Science Education in Action', *Green Theory and Praxis: The Journal of Ecopedagogy*, 5 (1): 126–51.

Humphreys, M. and T. Hyland (2002), 'Theory, Practice and Performance in Teaching: Professionalism, Intuition, and Jazz', *Educational Studies*, 28 (1): 5–15.

Josephsson, S., J. Öhlén, M. Mondaca, M. Guerrero, M. Luborsky and M. Lindström (2022), 'Using Ricoeur's Notions on Narrative Interpretation as a Resource in Supporting Person-Centredness in Health and Social Care', *Nursing Philosophy*, 23 (3): e12398.

Kipnis, M., L. Costa and R. Kaur (2021), 'Art, Affect, and Art Effects', *HAU: Journal of Ethnographic Theory*, 11 (3): 895–900.

Lewis, T.E. (2012), *The Aesthetics of Education*, London: Bloomsbury.

Luyten, H., C. Merrell and P. Tymms (2017), 'The Contribution of Schooling to Learning Gains of Pupils in Years 1 to 6', *School Effectiveness and School Improvement*, 28 (3): 374–405.

Manum, K. (2017), 'Implications of Counterfactual Thinking in a Pedagogical Context', in T. Strand, R. Smith, A. Pirrie, Z. Gregoriou and M. Papastephanou (eds), *Philosophy as Interplay and Dialogue*, 235–64, Münster: LIT Verlag.

Murphy, M., J. Huber and D. Clandinin (2012), 'Narrative Inquiry into Two Worlds of Curriculum Making', *LEARNing Landscapes*, 5 (2): 219–35.

Naughton, C. (2018), 'The Implications of "Percepts, Affects and Concepts" for Arts Educators', in C. Naughton, G. Biesta and D. Cole (eds), *Art, Artists and Pedagogy*, 43–52, London: Routledge.

O'Sullivan, S. (2024), *From Magic and Myth-Work to Care and Repair*, London: Goldsmith Press.

Obrist, H.U. (2014), *Ways of Curating*, London: Penguin.

Olivato, A.J. and J. Castro Silva (2023), 'Interdisciplinary Teaching Practices in STEAM Education in Brazil', *London Review of Education*, 21 (1): 38.

Panichas, G.A. (1977), *Simone Weil Reader*, London: Moyer Bell.

Piazzoli, E. (2018), *Embodying Language in Action: The Artistry of Process Drama in Second Language Education*, Cham: Springer International Publishing.

Pirrie, A. (2019), 'Where Science Ends, Art Begins? Critical Perspectives on the Development of STEAM in the New Climactic Regime', in P. Burnard and L. Colucci-Gray (eds), *Why Science and Art Creativities Matter: (Re-)Configuring STEAM for Future-Making Education*, 19–34, Leiden: Brill Academic Publishers.

Pirrie, A. and K. Manum (2023), 'Educating (for) the Blossomest of Blossoms: Finitude and the Temporal Arc of the Counterfactual', *Educational Philosophy and Theory*, 55 (7): 855–65.

Rawshtorn, A. (2022), *Design as an Attitude*, Geneva: JRP Editions.

Ryder, J. (2015), 'Being Professional: Accountability and Authority in Teachers' Responses to Science Curriculum Reform', *Studies in Science Education*, 51 (1): 87–120.

Samier, E. (2002), 'Weber on Education and Its Administration', *Educational Management and Administration*, 30 (1): 27–45.

Stenhouse, L. (1988), 'Artistry and Teaching: The Teacher as a Focus of Research and Development', *Journal of Curriculum and Supervision*, 4 (1): 43–51.

Varela, F. and J. Shear (1999), 'First-Person Methodologies: What, Why, How?', *Journal of Consciousness Studies*, 6 (2–3): 1–14.

Vlieghe, J. and P. Zamojski (2017), 'The Event, the Messianic and the Affirmation of Life. A Post-Critical Perspective on Education with Agamben and Badiou', *Policy Futures in Education*, 15 (7–8): 849–60.

Zahavi, D. (2008), *Subjectivity and Selfhood. Investigating the First-Person Perspective*, Cambridge, MA: MIT Press.

CHAPTER NINE

Aesthetics Tensions and Situated Judgements in Teaching

Ramsey Affifi

Introduction

Teachers often make judgements in the face of indeterminate, and indeed indeterminable, situations. And yet, rather than acknowledge and deepen this capacity, teaching is increasingly treated as a practice of implementing specifiable interventions for achieving specifiable aims. This is clear, for example, in how policymakers seek reliable and repeatable quality control measures and 'research-informed' or 'evidence-based' practices for achieving particular ends (Biesta 2007). Education is effectively framed through a quasi-computational 'if x then y' procedural logic, which school leaders and local authorities often reproduce. For their part, student teachers entering the profession often expect (and in the context of consumer-based neoliberal institutions, sometimes even demand) clarity of purpose and explicit directions for achieving intended outcomes, such as 'delivering the practical' or 'managing a disruptive student'. This is in part because early teaching experiences can be frightening, especially when under the watchful eye of assessors and when passing the course is at stake. Meanwhile, teacher educators often feel compelled to provide such solutions for their student teachers and operationalize the means for getting there. The simplicity of 'if-then' logic is often seen as easier to teach, perhaps a temporary 'scaffold' vulnerable new teachers need in the face of chaos, and even part of a duty of care for terrified newcomers they are committed to support. Finally, because the value of judgements amidst indeterminacy is underappreciated, a language to understand and articulate what lies behind such decisions is often lacking, even in experienced teachers, with the effect of devaluing teacher judgements further.

This chapter takes steps towards developing a language that reclaims such judgements, the kinds of educational situations they arise in, and thereby the teaching profession. That teaching happens in inherently uncertain situations is not a problem to be solved through attempting to eliminate ambiguity or by reducing education to mechanical operation. Rather, it suggests that good teaching – and good study – depends on opening to, confronting and working the possibilities inherent in indeterminate situations. A different kind of presence and participation is needed than simply looking at what is occurring in terms of 'means' and 'ends'.

For thinking what this might be in the context of teacher education, in this chapter I put my thinking about aesthetics into dialogue with some ideas from Gert Biesta, whose recent work has provided a useful framing for some core issues at stake. In the face of an educational situation, *artistry* is, as Biesta puts it, the ability 'to make situated judgements about what are desirable ways of acting, [and] which always entails judgement about the "how" and the "what for"' (Biesta this volume, Chapter 1). I will attempt to understand the *aesthetics* of such situated judgements, which I view as intrinsic to their indeterminate nature. For example, educational situations have shifting tensions, resolutions, foregrounding and backgrounding, framing and reframings, forms and contexts, and so on. Indeed, it is of the nature of educational situations that how we teach and what we teach interplay (Eisner 1979), rendering the attempt to treat teaching in terms of means and ends as not only educationally problematic but as naïve and incoherent. Educational situations are *aesthetic spaces* where the quality of shifting relations is felt as variously meaningful or significant for those experiencing it – teachers, students and others. It is this dynamic space that a teacher offers and influences, but does not control, and that a student encounters, participates in or rejects. Rather than seeking to eliminate ambiguity, we might give voice to how and why teachers make use of it, create it, minimize it or surrender to it, in the situated judgements they make. By giving language to how a teacher intends, attends and tends to the aesthetics of educational situations, we can both defend and deepen the teaching practice.

I approach this aim by first tracing some aesthetic contours that artists navigate. I do this by interrogating music, to imagine, define and explore the key concepts of aesthetic attention, aesthetic spaces and aesthetic tensions. I also articulate some tensions that artists and their audiences alike encounter in aesthetic experiences. This starts with the tension between the new and the old, which is crucial in itself but also foundational for others I discuss, such as that between content and context; 'going with the flow' and interrupting it; being active and being receptive; and between risk and safety. It is within tensions like these that artists make their situated judgements, and, as we shall also see, judgements as to *whether* one should make such judgements. From this groundwork, I turn to and build a picture of what is particular to the aesthetics of educational situations and the artistry of teaching and teacher education. The 'how' and 'what for' teachers navigate are contextualized by additional educational tensions, such as those between various purposes of education, as well as the tensions our students face when confronted with their own situations inviting judgement. From this, I close with some reflections on how teacher education can help reclaim the artistry of teaching.

Aesthetic Attention

Your thumb brushes across a string connecting a peg to the bridge of a guitar. As you release the pressure, the tension in the vibrating string is experienced as a certain quality in your body. The feeling cannot be pinpointed in space or time. It is itself spread across your changing body, perhaps echoing between your heart and your gut, or shimmering across your skin. But so too, notice that within the experience of this note, there is a tension felt in the difference between its sound and the preceding silence. Indeed, the felt quality of that note is inextricably linked to the silence it broke. When you come to play another note in turn, it too will be experienced in relationship, not only with the note you just played, but also with the tension that prior note established between silence and sound. And so on.

There is always an experienced relationship between 'what arrives' and 'what it is arriving into', between what is new and the context that 'receives' it. This is true even if the new note is a repetition of what was just played, because *this* repetition is itself new. And each time another note arrives, the one just played transforms its quality. It is no longer the difference-maker: instead, it becomes part of the coherence of the very context it once disrupted, and in turn it becomes part of that which receives and is modified by the next newcomer. When a new note is played, it opposes, develops or harmonizes with its situation, or in some sense does all three, but when the next is played, it becomes part of the situation that the next new note in turn opposes, develops or harmonizes. When a series of notes is played, they can be experienced as a whole (like a melody) which has felt quality given texture by which notes are played, for how long and the silence kept between them, but also by whatever happened in the room prior and during playing, and so on. Another way to say this is that content and context are always in interplay. And while you as player are encountering this ongoing interplay, the same is happening for your listener sitting across from you on the couch.

Put slightly more abstractly, when two or more things happen a space between them opens. It is a space that enables the experiencing of those things in relation. The listener does not simply perceive one input followed by another, like a digital code. Instead, in the distance between the note and the silence that preceded it, there is a space of possibility. The note gains significance through succeeding the silence; that silence is felt differently through the note that came in and interrupted it. The change is felt, and that feeling has a quality which may be abrupt or smooth, welcome or off-putting. By quality, I mean the relationship is experienced as a concrete and particular texture felt in one's body in time. For example, I may experience an event as 'tense' if I feel a tightening in my body. What is happening and how my body feels reciprocally inform each other and, in their syncopation, I am given a sense of the situation.

Of course, aesthetic tensions may not always literally be tense. But even when they are not, they still arise through some contrast or difference between what is experienced as in relationship. This may be variation in colour or shape, perspective or feeling, purpose or aim, or even the mere difference of occupying different locations in space or time. For this reason, there is even a tension in the experience of things in harmony, as, for example, we feel in the relation between the first, third and fifth notes of a major chord. We might think of the feeling of 'resolution', for instance, as the transition from high tension to low tension, but not to no tension – which would imply the absence of relationship altogether. Artistry is directly involved in the intending, attending and tending to tensions, created and arising in aesthetic spaces that opens in the interplay between new events and existing contexts. What a teacher makes judgements about never occurs in a neutral plane of logical inference, but in a dynamic felt world of tensions and intentions.

The experience of relation exemplified in this account of playing music illustrates what I describe as aesthetic, rather than analytic attention (Affifi 2023). Analytic attention decomposes relation, aiming to foreground, isolate or extract components. Aesthetic attention, on the other hand, 'catches gestalts'. Aesthetic attention feels relationships, and as I suggested, this happens not only between one note and another, but between a note and a context into which it arrives. With aesthetic attention, we can perceive melody and rhythm, as well as more complex gestalts that arise out of them. Further, the quality of relation perceived, as already suggested, is never solely between things 'in the world'. Implicit in its etymology is the intuition that *attention* is itself already a tension, a felt relationship between the attender and what is being attended. This is indeed what it means for the relationship I perceive to be felt. But how anything feels is also partially analytic as the distinction between the aesthetic and the analytic is along a spectrum. As certain feelings become more strongly felt, I pay attention to them more directly, and whatever else is going on in my body recedes to some degree. In both the world outside me and my body attuning to it, there is always also the tension between those tensions I pay attention to, and those which tacitly surround but still affect my attention. This happens, for example, when I foreground a melody in my attention without the accompanying chords getting entirely silenced from my awareness.[1]

Artistry in Participating: Intentions

While there is always a dynamic and indeterminate relationship between that which arrives and what it arrives into, there is a similar indeterminacy between what is arriving and what *might* arrive next. To illustrate this, I will keep to my discussion of music for a short while longer before turning to the artistry of teaching. Core to the musician's work is the capacity to perceive existing tensions and to create new ones, to imagine possible new tensions arriving out of them, and to be open to unforeseeable ones too, to which the musician might attend. It is obvious that this requires *judgement* in the face of inherent uncertainty. The artist takes seriously the fact that what she offers changes the character of the perceived past *and* the felt future. She has a great responsibility and yet cannot anticipate what to do nor control the outcomes of her art, either for herself or for others.

To illustrate this, suppose a musician was only concerned with the relationship between two notes, the note she is about to play, and the one that just occurred. Even this impoverished scenario would be full of indeterminacy, given the unexpectedness that arises through the difference between what she actually plays and what was intended, by the creaks in the instrument or the echoes of the room, and so on. If the musician is paying attention, these contingencies might be invitations and sometimes even demands, about what, whether and how she plays her next note (however consciously). But a musician does not play just two notes, and therefore holds more than a single note in memory. Her next 'decision' is happening in response to multiple, overlapping contexts, from the immediate past, to the musical phrase it is located in, to the movement or piece, and on to the performance, her audience, to her history as a person and the memories the notes might summon. Not only is there a tension between what arrives and the context it arrives into, but there is also a tension between these different, overlapping contexts which arrive into one another at different time scales. There is no map to capture this and to calculate the best course ahead, and even if there were, the next moment comes and the topography of the entire thing again ripples into some new shape.

Aesthetic spaces therefore arise from the relationship between overlapping events that have occurred, are occurring, and might occur. There are many relationships between things, actual and possible, present and past, and many directions those experiencing the space (whether as creator or as one encountering it) can 'go'. In other words, there is something very definite that has been given (one note followed by another, etc.) but what one pays attention to, offers back, or makes of it, is full of indeterminacy. Artists do not try to remove this space, which would reduce artwork to code. Instead, they are concerned with the interplays made possible through the relationships offered in the aesthetic space, and which they offer to their audience in turn.

Educational Tensions

Whether writers, painters, dancers or teachers, all artists are involved in the work of perceiving and participating, attending and intending shifting tensions within aesthetic spaces in the senses just described. In each case, new relationships arise continuously as 'the work' develops, and artistry involves skill and sensitivity in perceiving these arising tensions, and making judgements when engaging with what is perceived. Like the musician, the teacher as artist may also attend to the shifting sounds, rhythms and pace in her own voice, and in that of the students she works with, catching something equivalent to keys and tempos, and creating dissonance or seeking the right pitch in what to offer next. Indeed, much of the interplay of body language that forms the ongoing texture of educational situations involves just this, and the tact of teaching depends on it (see van Manen 1991). However, while there may be generic features to engaging in aesthetic spaces across different arts, the nature and quality of the relationships a particular artist attends are saturated with the concrete particularities of *their* medium. So, just as the musician might refine her ability to respond to the relationship between sounds in the form of rhythm, melody, timbre, pitch and so on, the teacher will refine her capacity to create and respond to tensions within, and between aesthetic spaces that open in personal, social, political, educational and existential dimensions of educational situations. And it is within this broader nexus that the teacher's concern with the melody or rhythm of her work resides.

In other words, although there is a necessary aesthetic dimension that teacher artistry contends with, a teacher is not engaged in aestheticizing things framed away from their broader context. Note that while ignoring such broader contexts is sometimes called 'aestheticizing' (e.g. in discussions of 'aestheticizing violence' (e.g. Berleant 2019)),[2] what is problematic educationally is actually that such aims are *insufficiently* aesthetic. To use a distinction offered earlier in the chapter, what is disparaged as mere 'aesthetisizing', actually *analytically* foregrounds certain relations and not others to care for, and in doing so suspends attention to – or anaesthetizes – many relevant possible relations. While teacher educators can gain insight from other artists on how to pay attention to tensions and work with them, they cannot give answers to *what* tensions teachers should attend nor what to do with them. The art of teaching is specific to the teacher's medium, which is a complicated space that involves curricula, students, policymakers, and a clatter of emotions, motivations and interpretations hovering around whatever is happening. It is this that the teacher is in the middle of, in the midst of, literally it is their 'medium'. It is within this medium that judgements about 'how' one acts and 'what for' are made.

Immersion and Interruption

In the following sections, I will explore aspects of what constitutes educational tensions, educational aesthetic spaces and the educational medium, vis-à-vis the artistry of teaching. To start this discussion, I return to how I ended the last section, and ask: what is it like to be in the midst of one's medium?

When perceiving and responding to relationships arising in one's work, artists sometimes feel their agency swept away. Artists speak of a 'muse' taking over, and being guided by a process that, in a sense, they do not feel in control of and through which the art is working itself out. Such immersion is sometimes described as feeling like one is following intuitions or even as obeying commands rather than making decisions. Is this not a case where situated judgements are relinquished for automatic procedures, and if so, is this phenomenon problematically related to the concerns that opened this chapter? As impious as it might seem for this present volume, I must ask: is artistry actually in opposition to mechanical operationalism?

To be sure, there is something different in losing oneself in a generic formula (such as the means to some 'learning intention'), and losing oneself to the (perhaps unique) demands that one's art is immediately, and at each moment, making. But what joins both cases is a tacit acceptance that 'what to do' is dictated by processes outside of 'my' will. It is undeniable that self-effacing immersion is sometimes important or significant for artistic process. One reason artists can create fresh new things is precisely because they 'get out of their heads', and are able to integrate their bodies, their selves and their environment into an ongoing, recursive co-constituting process. Some see this as a much-needed corrective to the arrow-like but narrow focus of conscious purpose (see Bateson 1972). As such, the artistic process might even be humbling, as it acknowledges how creativity is not the output of the conscious ego alone.

Nevertheless, accounts claiming that artistic process is fundamentally about losing oneself are one-sided. It is equally true that an artist will sometimes break their immersion, step outside of the flow and ask what they should do next. In vernacular language, we sometimes say an artist 'got too carried away' when we sense this did not happen. Artistry involves both moments of immersion and moments of asking what one's actions are 'for'. We can distance ourselves and make judgements about what to do rather than being continuously immersed.[3] Artistry involves both tending and working out the existing relations in one's aesthetic space *and* stopping, taking stock, and perhaps, then, rejoining the interaction with a new offering that in turn alters the aesthetic space as well as its tensions and relations (see Affifi 2024).

This discussion brings insight to the problematic 'if x then y' proceduralizing logic that opened the chapter. It is not, solely that categorical templates are applied to unique conditions, silencing the possibilities of people and situations. The question is not whether or not to treat every instance as unique or an example of some generality. This is partly because even treating every situation as unique is itself its own kind of 'rule', but also because, as we have seen, artistry involves moments of stepping back from *however* we are approaching a situation. In practice, this means there are moments we surrender into categories, habits or 'old ways', and moments for questioning whether we should be doing so. It also means there are moments of surrendering into sensitive interaction with what one is immersed in, and moments when we also question where that process is leading. All said, however, there is no meta-rule: no answer ahead of time as to whether I should follow patterns, attend to particularities, sustain immersion or interrupt whatever it is I am doing.

Before closing this part of the discussion, I want to point out how deeply interconnected habit, responsive immersion and detachment are in practice. For example, consider the act of listening and trying to offer something appropriate in an unfolding situation with a student. Responsive attention to what is happening, here and now, contrasts with the if-then mechanistic processing described in this chapter's outset. However, while we may imagine that being 'in the flow' somehow transcends all categorical patterning, such attention *cannot* happen without the teacher artist developing a repertoire of riffs, semi-automated patterns that have 'worked' in various contexts. William James (1890) long ago noted that automating practice into habits might actually be a condition for the possibility of becoming attentive and responsive to other, more significant things. Artists and musicians know this well: 'forgetting' the accompanying left hand helps one lean into the melody one is improvising with the right.

So too, while listening to my student, I must hold back from many calls upon my attention. In educational contexts, teachers often make important judgements in contexts held by more or less stable ways of seeing or perceiving. Without any such know-how, the teacher has no idea how to interact, like a child playing a piano with no knowledge or chords or scales, nor the muscle tone to press the keys. Habits enable the possibility of creating new habit-modulating ways of acting, which in turn can become new habits. But while new ways of responding arise out of concrete encounters, they are always at risk of ossifying, drawing the artist out of contact with their work. As this is happening, judgement can descend upon the dynamic at any moment. But it promises no salvation. While judgement might come and assist the developing situation, it also has the potential to destabilize and ruin a good thing going. Nothing is specifiable and risks abound.

Tending Educational Tensions

In any case, the moment of asking what one should do does not necessarily lend itself to working *with* one's context. The artist teacher's moves arise from, but also arrive into and stir the context she works. While aesthetic attention establishes context, the artist is free to follow what the situation seems to be asking for, with sensitivity or not, or to disrupt it entirely. The artist is not solely after harmony, she sometimes aims for discord too. And just as many great works are concerned with the tension between harmony and discord itself, so too is the artist concerned with the tension between losing herself in the flow and breaking this immersion. For example, a teacher may decide to resolve a tension, or deliberately sustain it, and may do so either 'backstage' from a student's awareness, or stage a tension directly as an educational encounter (see Affifi and Hensley 2024). She may create, ignore, amplify, offer nuance to or harmonize a tension, and is on the lookout for how tensions, and their educative possibilities and constraints, change across time. But what is also asked for in artistry is that the making of judgements about what to do next is sometimes *itself* put to scrutiny. Just as a pianist is more likely to fumble when she starts paying attention to her fingers moving across the keys, there are times a teacher artist deliberately sustains focus in the situation rather than shift out of immersion and look upon it.

Aesthetic attention presences to, and participates in, how relationships get torn apart and healed, destroyed and reconciled (Affifi 2023), and so the artist participates in the remaking of the intermingled past, present and future. Suppose a teacher makes an offering to a student, throwing before them something and inviting a response. There is no answer to how much or how convincing the teacher should be about whatever that 'something' is. Consider, as I often do in my work, offering some 'fact' about the ecological crisis. A student resists engaging, and questions arise within me about whether I ought to persist or pause, modify the offering or abandon it, or do something else. One way or another, I risk not respecting my student's agency, either by ignoring their protestations or because I give up too quickly with the assumption they cannot 'take' any more without losing themselves. But there is also the risk I do not respect the invitation that is uniquely mine to offer, abandoning it too soon or not trusting what it might have already opened up and pushing it too hard. Just as with each new musical note, the next moment of our educational encounter arises from, but also arrives into what is happening, recontextualizes what has been, recolouring it. And so, even if I present in ways I later deem overbearing, I am free to destroy my pushiness by coming into the next encounter more gently, and in doing so, to possibly reconcile it. I can call out what I did and offer my concern or apology to the student as a new invitation or provocation. But it also means

I risk revisiting something that already made its claim upon the student, and muddy it through overworking it. In other words, teaching is always an unfinished art, as each new moment reshapes its context, for better or worse, or both.

Situated Judgements within and between Educational Frames

As I just explored, already within a single context (say, my brief discussion of teaching about the ecological crisis), there is the question of whether to work with what is happening, or to disrupt it. However, because teachers engage with aesthetic relationships within many contexts – and indeed also in the aesthetics *between* those contexts – educational aesthetic spaces and tensions can be very complex and contingent. Our situated judgements about whether to go along with, develop, resist or elaborate whatever it is we are doing within one medium intersect with situated judgements about whether to change focus. The educational medium is a multimedium, even a multi-multimedium.

Many examples demonstrate this point. For example, a teacher will need to make decisions about whether to continue supporting a student emotionally or to 'go back' to the topic, or how much time to invest preparing next week's lesson as opposed to negotiating with school leaders on altering some school policy she considers problematic. Even within student relations, one-to-one interactions with any two students may open and sustain very different aesthetic spaces. On the curricular side, there are not only questions about the aesthetics of a given topic, but of how subsequent topics relate to one another. Some foci may seem more 'foundational' than others, however, since what is possible in one frames and informs the others, a teacher's artistry eventually engages them all. The question shifts to which to focus on, and how or when to move between them. Underneath all these varied concerns, there are also tensions between different purposes of education itself. For example, it is possible to engage with continuities, elaborations, interruptions and interplays between many different relating and arising events – with all the aesthetic attention described so far – and yet to be solely focused on education aimed at providing skills, understanding, knowledge or attitudes deemed to equip the student for their future. All would fall squarely in what Biesta calls the domain of qualification (2020). However, it is also possible to encounter and participate in the aesthetics of educational situations in ways concerned with confronting students with their freedom (i.e. subjectification, more below). How and when to engage in one domain or the other, or how they themselves interplay in the life of the classroom, is itself an aesthetic space.

Recall our earlier exploration of how one note arrives into a context and alters it in turn, and how this led to the realization that the note's significance is not captured when we engage it analytically in isolation. Its significance arises in relation to its context just as its context changes through its arrival. This same pattern arose again when considering immersion and interruption, in which both 'going along with' or disrupting what one has been doing are both forms where the new we offer interacts with its context. However, in the case of the multimedia nature of the educational medium, we see the same dynamic again, where now one medium or domain or situation serves as an overall context into which another one arrives. While we are no longer considering individual and momentary notes, but situations that may endure for some time, the mutual inflection between past, present and future in what we offer to the situation is invariably at play.

The aesthetics of Teaching and of Being Taught in Teacher Education

Although I made brief mention of students' freedom a couple of paragraphs back, readers will note my central focus so far has been on articulating the freedom of the artist teacher when engaging their educational (multi) medium. This is because the discussion has explored how aesthetic spaces open up possibilities, give suggestions and make demands that the artist teacher is free to follow, work with or reject. Those familiar with Biesta's work will note an inversion of the more usual attention on students through my considering how the *artist teacher*'s subjectification is at stake. In all such cases, however, judgements about the 'how' and 'what for' of teaching arise when 'what to do' is not taken for granted and the teacher's choice in the face of indeterminacy is an ongoing issue. Concern with our students' freedom is however intrinsic to such judgements.

One important difference between teaching and most other arts is the extent to which the artist's possibility of freedom and that of their 'audience', in this case their students, are intertwined. The aesthetic space teachers attend to in educational situations is not just sounds following one another, nor lessons interplaying in their sequence; it involves people who are encountering each other in a shared space.[4] While all good art opens and offers an aesthetic space for an audience to explore, rather than giving rigidly prescribed things to see or feel, a different kind of urgency comes when teaching is explicitly concerned with offering students encounters that may redirect them back to questions about what they should do. Similarly, the aesthetic space students experience also includes the fact that there is a teacher there, who is, in different ways, concerned with them. This situation has many implications for the artistry of teaching, but for the moment I will reflect on the mutual relationship between a teacher's and a student's possibilities for facing their freedom. Consider, for example, how when I pay attention to the unanticipated and unasked for that arises in my teaching, my own plans can be interrupted and I may come to ask what I should do. But how I attend to such situations, and inadvertently myself as a possible subject, itself becomes part of what my students encounter, and may become an indirect invitation for my students to also attend to their own situations.

Teaching student teachers concerns the possibility of subjectification for the teacher educator herself, her student teachers and their pupils. A student teacher's openness to attending and inviting possibilities of subjectification in *their pupils* is in turn foreclosed if they themselves do not open to making situated judgements that may, say, ask them to temporarily pause some endeavour they were committed to, to open the space. However, if not encountering it in their teacher educator's practice, student teachers lack examples of such thinking mattering in the profession, and may then less readily engage with making such situated judgements themselves.

The situation, however, is two-sided. On the one hand, the artist teacher educator is concerned with creating and attending to aesthetic spaces, and works with an ongoing sensitivity to them, and this sometimes means presenting things to their students, who will respond (or not) to what is offered. On the other hand, however, the student may respond *anyway*, even when the teacher educator has not engaged in the aesthetics of an event purposefully. Because the teacher does not control what arises, events and encounters also do not depend on their intentions. And so too within the relationship between those students and their pupils. There are spaces opened that are intended as invitations, but there are also spaces opened inadvertently that become invitations.

The Fear and Joy in Student Teacher Artistry

Recall from the very first discussion about music that aesthetic experiences respond to relationships, which are felt as particular qualities in one's body. Consider how the gestalt of 'harmony' between things is felt differently from the experience of 'discord'. Opening to aesthetic attention and participation is therefore not always comfortable. One reason people settle on anaesthetizing shortcuts to navigate indeterminate situations is indeed precisely because of a desire to flee such uncomfortable tensions. For instance, teachers, and especially new teachers, feel a lot of fear especially when they confront the uncertainty and complexity of the educational medium and the freedom it affords. Fearing unwanted consequences is inseparable from fearing feeling one's heart sink or blood stop; of fearing fear itself. If a teacher chooses to evade it, fear can thereby reduce aesthetic attention and artistic participation (see Affifi 2023). It is because there is risk in doing something new, fresh and responsive, that new teachers often want (and often pressure) teacher educators to provide 'what works' strategies. Evading fear can mean turning away from the invitation. In this way, broader economic and political factors buttress and are buttressed by psychological dimensions that mechanize how we attend to our interactions with our students, our peers, the world and even with ourselves.

Artistry involves the capacity to stay with what is happening in the aesthetic space, even if it is uncomfortable. It also is concerned with opening and sitting with new kinds of tensions rather than reducing what is happening to old aesthetic schemas one feels safe navigating. And yet, the tension between feeling safe and being able to take risks is also real, and so it may well be that a teacher educator may decide to give some 'what works' strategies precisely so that students are willing to step beyond the algorithms, even if they know that the strategy doesn't necessarily work, nor work for purposes that should be left unchallenged. For example, I may want to play it 'safe' in ways past students have 'liked', even though I am aware that doing so avoids confronting them with some uncomfortable situation they may not want to face. It is equally clear, however, that if a teacher educator consistently fears their students will feel uncomfortable, then that teacher may shy away from attending in ways that shutter their students from possibilities of attention as well. When to be so open is itself an educational tension, another aesthetic space where situated judgements are asked of us.

Here, however, we come back to some core aesthetic qualities and the importance of recurrence and structure to provide a safe place out of which one can explore the new. This tension between safety and risk arises of course, in all arts. Rhythm and key anchor a listener, providing a comfortable space from which they can then follow a piece of music into wilder melodies and modulations. The twelve-tone compositions of early twentieth century may have been an interesting experiment, but humans seem to return again and again to norms, themes, structures and their accompanying variations and violations, as though both are needed and it is their relationship that matters. Similarly for students, too much structure can be claustrophobic, but too little (especially if they do not have it elsewhere in their lives) is also overwhelming. In working with new teachers, artistry lies in inviting students into different kinds of encounters with structure and uncertainty, not 'as such' (an 'aestheticizing' move, in the sense suggested above) but in concrete situations that matter to them educationally and to which they might respond. This does not mean the kind of scaffolding that would restrict or deny students their reception of tensions. It rather involves pointing them to tensions *from the beginning*, but in a manner (pace, topic, etc.) that is particular and responsive.

But why should my student teachers care, especially if it can lead to sleeplessness? Or if a 'perfect' outcome amidst the indeterminacy is not possible anyway? For those who fear caring, care seems like putting oneself in an unnecessarily vulnerable position. It seems like precarious sacrifice. It certainly doesn't seem relaxing. But those who have devoted themselves to caring know the kind of beauty that can arise when participating in the ecology of the heart: that feedback loop between more deeply encountering and responding to otherness, and more deeply encountering and responding to our selves. We grow as people, into new distinctions, nuances, pains and delights, as we grow more receptive and engaged in the needs and possibilities of another. While self-development is not the aim, it is a consequence of artistry and can be shown as such.

'Tensions' are often mentioned in teacher education programmes, but rarely treated explicitly. Nor is their scope nor aesthetic nature often worked out or explored. There are, however, many ways that teacher educators can work with the educational tensions that suffuse their work, offering student teachers a chance to live in such tensions and experience how, while sometimes painful, experiencing tensions is gratifying, and is what calls an artist back to her work.

Artistry in Teacher Education

Starting with intuitions from music, this chapter built up increasingly complex and concrete aesthetic descriptions of educational situations. I have tried to show how the relationship between the new and the context that 'receives' it is indeterminate, experienced aesthetically, and requires artistry to make judgements about, and that it recurs in various forms and dynamics across the educational (multi)medium. In passing, it is noteworthy that concern about the relation between what is new and the context it arrives into *has itself* been understood as a fundamental educational concern. Notably, Hannah Arendt explicitly frames her conception of education as about attending the relationship between the (human) 'newcomer' and the 'world', and her work concerns the challenges of engaging with the tensions, possibilities and dangers arising through the indeterminate relation between them. For Arendt, the educator's 'task [is] to mediate between the old and the new' (1961: 193) which the reader should see is inevitably aesthetic in ways laid out in this chapter.

In that vein, my work as a teacher educator is concerned with how my student teachers come into the teaching world, how they show up into it. They are newcomers on the teaching profession scene, but have a dual role because they are also part of the existing world into which their pupils are themselves newcomers. In both contexts – as *both* students and teachers – student teachers encounter many overlapping educational tensions between what was, is, and might be, and have to make judgements as to what and how to attend to these relationships. My educational medium therefore does not consist merely of the different 'levels' I have to engage and the dynamics between them, but also of how I work with my students in their encounter with their own levels, from my classroom to theirs, from their relationship with school administrators to parents, and so on. And obviously, my students are themselves concerned with their pupils' presence to their own variegated worlds.

An aesthetic education working towards reclaiming teacher artistry can support this work. I close with gathering several suggestions implied in this chapter. First, a language is needed to articulate educational tensions, their aesthetic nature and dynamics, and how decisions are made in response to them. This can help new and existing teachers tend, intend and attend to educational situations and also provide a vocabulary to defend the work of teaching against technocratic and other incursions. Second, working with the arts can help foreground aesthetics and artistry because the arts are often explicitly about the aesthetics of relationship, offering an alternative discourse in teaching against naive proceduralism. Third, there is a need for new teachers to witness teacher artistry in those who attempt it, those who excel at it, and those who fail in it, and to hear from those who can speak about the situated judgements they make. Fourth, new teachers need to experience indeterminacy in diverse contexts, where questions of 'how' and 'what for' are left for them to make, from the beginning. A core question for teacher educators is how to mediate professional challenges so that they are real and yet do not overwhelm the student teacher. Fifth, in all these endeavours, and in much else too, teacher educators need to practice their own teacher artistry, which involves not only creating and responding to educational tensions, but receiving and working with them too. It also includes the work of supporting students who struggle with the anxiety or fear that can come with taking responsibility for making judgements in indeterminate situations.

Notes

1   There is a tension between the narrowness of my aperture and the world, but also a tension in how open my view is to that which is peripheral to it.

2   An example of this would be appreciating the formal beauty of a military strategy even though it was conducted for imperialist aspirations and caused much harm.

3   Residing between what has just happened and what we anticipate, the present moment has a spaciousness. It holds meanings as it puts into play what is and could be, should be and should not be. The terms 'retention' and 'protention' were introduced by Husserl (2001) in his investigations of the structure of consciousness, to describe how the present moment is not instantaneous but holds its immediate past and future possibilities within it. While I interpret these terms more vaguely here, I employ them because etymologically they hold the important point that I want to make about the tensions that the artist engages.

4   As an environmental educator, I am obviously interested in how humans
     and other living beings also encounter each other (e.g. Affifi 2017). For this
     chapter's focus, I bracket such considerations. The reader is invited to consider
     the relevance of aesthetics and artistry in such contexts.

References

Affifi, R. (2017), 'The Metabolic Core of Environmental Education', *Studies in
     Philosophy and Education*, 36 (3): 315–32.
Affifi, R. (2023), 'Aesthetic Knowing and Ecology: Cultivating Perception and
     Participation during the Ecological Crisis', *Environmental Education Research*,
     30 (7): 1041–60.
Affifi, R. (2024), 'The Ecology of Sublimity: Educational Tensions between
     Existence and the Ungraspable', *Environmental Education Research*, 1–20,
     DOI: 10.1080/13504622.2024.2445233.
Affifi, R. and G. Biesta (this volume), 'Reclaiming Teacher Artistry: The Art
     of Saying "No"', in G. Biesta and R. Affifi (eds), *Reclaiming the Artistry
     of Teaching*, 203–14, London: Bloomsbury.
Affifi, R. and J. Bertoldo (2026), 'The Return of Beauty on a Dying Planet', in J.
     MacAllister, A. Pirrie and R. Affifi (eds), *Artful Education and the Downward
     Journey: Facing Finitude and Death*, London: Bloomsbury.
Affifi, R. and N. Hensley (2024), 'Trickster Teaching and the Anthropocene:
     Disrupting the *Explicitification* of Pedagogy, People and Planet', *Environmental
     Education Research*, 1–18, DOI: 10.1080/13504622.2024.2434608.
Arendt, H. (1961), *Between Past and Future: Six Exercises in Political Thought*,
     New York: Viking Press.
Bateson, G. (1972), *Steps to an Ecology of Mind*, Chicago, IL: University of
     Chicago Press.
Berleant, A. (2019), 'Reflections on the Aesthetics of Violence', *Contemporary
     Aesthetics*, 7: 1–13.
Biesta, G. (2007), 'Why "What Works" Won't Work: Evidence-Based Practice and
     the Democratic Deficit in Educational Research', *Educational Theory*, 57 (1):
     1–22.
Biesta, G. (2020), 'Risking Ourselves in Education: Qualification, Socialization, and
     Subjectification Revisited', *Educational Theory*, 70 (1): 89–104.
Eisner, E. (1979), *The Educational Imagination*, Basingstoke: Macmillan.
Husserl, E. (2001), *Analyses Concerning Passive and Active Synthesis*, trans. A.
     Steinbock, New York: Springer.
James, W. (1890), *Principles of Psychology* (Vol 1), New York: Henry Holt.
van Manen, M. (1991), *The Tact of Teaching: The Meaning of Pedagogical
     Thoughtfulness*, Albany, NY: State University of New York Press.

CHAPTER TEN

Confucius as a Teacher: On His Artistry of Teaching

Chang Liu

Introduction

In this chapter, I will discuss a unique case from the East – Confucius (551 BCE–479 BCE), who is known as 'the Supreme Sage and Paragon Teacher for All Ages' (万世师表. 至圣先师) for his profound influence as an educator and philosopher throughout history. I am interested in exploring what kind of teacher he is, how he teaches and what this reveals about his artistry of teaching. I will base my exploration on *the Analects*, regarded as one of the most important Confucian classics, as it provides the most authentic representation of the daily teaching and learning between Confucius and his disciples.

Confucius is well-known for teaching that is centred on the lifelong striving for *Ren* (仁) (see Li 2003; Tu 1979). This is a difficult word to translate, and its meaning will be explored in different ways in this chapter, but for now I approximate it as a 'humane way of living'. I will particularly focus on Confucius' teaching for *Ren* and demonstrate his artistry by exploring his teaching forms in *the Analects*. Secondly, I will explain why Confucius teaches indirectly through such forms. Thirdly, I will present why I think there is artistry in Confucius' attention to form in teaching. I will conclude that the case of Confucius from *The Analects* provides us with a concrete understanding of what the artistry of teaching entails and reclaims the artistry of teaching that already exists in past wisdom.

How Does Confucius Teach? The Importance of Form

In this section, I will present and discuss different 'forms' of Confucius' teaching that can be found in *The Analects*. These include the use of short aphorisms, dialogue, metaphor and poetics, stories and commentary, and through expression of emotion. In my view, these different forms provide important insights into how Confucius teaches and achieves educational purposes that could not be attained otherwise.

Short Aphorisms

The Analects consists primarily of short aphorisms rather than the lengthy arguments we might expect in a contemporary philosophical work. The words and sentence structure are simple and concise. It is characterized by a few words conveying profound meaning that can even guide people at different stages throughout life (Wu 2011). Consider:

> *The Master said, 'The Junzi* [君子 a person who lives in a *Ren*-like way] *is not a vessel.' (The Analects 2.12)*

> *The Master said, 'A person without concern for what is far away is sure to encounter worries close at hand.' (The Analects 15.12)*

The dialogue does not provide any further explanation, justification or theoretical analysis. Yet, it is interesting to notice that, however brief, it has generated countless interpretations for thousands of years, and which continues to this day (see Hui 2019). For example, one could interpret the first sentence as suggesting that a vessel is designed for a specific use and purpose. A *Junzi*, from this view, should not be a vessel and instrumentally confine themselves in this way. Instead, they are encouraged to cultivate broad knowledge and open-mindedness rather than becoming narrowly skilled specialists or unable to adapt to different situations. In a second interpretation, some scholars (see Qian 2011) suggest that the vessel is a metaphor for 'banking knowledge' and that a *Junzi* should not be trained to be a container or a machine. It implies that there must be a living person behind all knowledge and learning.

One could interpret the second sentence as emphasizing the importance of thinking ahead to prevent potential troubles before they arise. One could also interpret it as emphasizing the importance of thinking about one's ultimate purpose and values in life. One might simply go from goal to goal, reactively concerned with whatever is close at hand as needs shift, situation changes or time passes (Sun 2008) if one does not think about the lifelong purpose and value of living.

It can be argued that the form of teaching through short aphorisms was chosen deliberately. It works very differently than through logical arguments. While such arguments require precision and clarity, short aphorisms are multidimensional and require the participation of the reader to 'realize' their meaning. Lengthy arguments direct readers to consider whether the arguments are strong enough, what might be the counterarguments, and if they follow the logic and can reach the right conclusion. All the work happens mentally. By contrast, the short aphorisms in *The Analects* direct readers to reflect on their own lives and realize their significance through living itself. In other words, this form allows readers to interpret meaning and relate it to their lives individually, instead of doing the thinking for the readers.

Dialogue

Dialogue is another important form of writing in *The Analects*. Confucius never presents a clear and complete definition of his central ideas, such as *Ren* and *Junzi*, which, I have suggested can roughly be translated in English as a humane way of living, and the person who lives such a way, respectively. Instead, he deliberately keeps his central ideas ambiguous and flexible through conversation with his disciples. This is evident in how he offers varying answers to different students in different situations. Consider the following:

Fan Chi asked about Ren. The Master said, 'It is to love men.' (The Analects 12.22)

Zhonggong asked about Ren. The Master said, 'When in public, comfort yourself as if you were receiving an important guest, and in your management of the common people, behave as if you were overseeing a great sacrifice. Do not impose upon others what you yourself do not desire. In this way, you will encounter no resentment in your public or private life'. Zhonggong replied, 'Although I am not quick to understand, I ask permission to devote myself to this teaching'. (The Analects 12.2)

Zigong said, 'if there is someone who can extensively confer benefits on the people and bring succour to the multitudes, what would you say of him? Could such a person be called Ren?' The Master said, 'Why speak only of Ren in connection with him? Such a person should surely be called a sage! Even Yao and Shun found it difficult to accomplish what you've just described. A Ren person (仁者 a humane person) wishes to establish himself, and so he helps others to establish themselves. Wishing to realize himself, he helps others to realize themselves. The ability to make an analogy from what is close at hand is the method and the way of realizing Ren'. (The Analects 6.30)

Yan Yuan asked about Ren. The Master said, 'Restrain the self and return to the Li [礼, the outward expression or practice of Ren, see below]. This is the way to be Ren. If, for one day, you are able to restrain yourself and return to the Li, this means that your capacity to be Ren will open up to the world. Ren rests with the self. How could it come from others?' Yan Yuan [Yan Hui] asked, 'May I ask about the specific steps to go about this?'

The Master replied, 'Do not look at anything contrary to Li. Do not listen to anything contrary to Li. Do not speak in ways that are contrary to Li. Do not act in ways that are contrary to Li'. Yan Yuan said, 'Even though I am not that smart, I will do my best to put into practice what you have said.' (The Analects 12.1)

Such flexibility in engagement does not indicate that Confucian is a relativist whose idea of *Ren* can be interpreted arbitrarily. His *Ren* does have a certain meaning. Instead, the form of variation in dialogue shows Confucius' making situated judgements on how to respond to different students and cases. This is important for his artistry of teaching, which I will explore shortly. For example, Fan-Chi is a bit slow-witted, so Confucius' answer to him is simple and direct: 'to love man'. Zhong Gong serves a government position, so Confucius' answer is governing-related. Zi Gong is overly ambitious, so Confucius points to starting with matters at hand. Yan Hui is the most gifted disciple, so Confucius answers him with a difficult phrase involving both inner constraint and outwardly appropriate behaviour.

His response to Yan Hui also points to a key dimension of how the relationship between form and content is important not only for Confucian pedagogy, but for his approach to *Ren* itself (and which is partly why teaching for *Ren* requires such a pedagogy). Having intentions towards *Ren* alone is insufficient; it also needs to be expressed in appropriate social norms. *Li* refers to such norms and is variously translated as ritual, propriety, manners or appropriate behaviours. It is the outward and cultural expression of the inner *Ren*. However, *Li* is not about rigidly following traditions but is adaptable, just like Confucius' varied responses to his students. The true adherence to *Li* comes from understanding its spirit. Crucially, *practising Li can develop inner Ren, but in turn, Li is empty without Ren.*

This variation in the continuing conversation between Confucius and his disciples reflects his attention to and educational concern for each student. The following quotes from Confucius explain clearly such a concern:

Zilu asked, 'When I hear something [that needs to be addressed], should I take action right away?'

The Master said, 'When your father and elder brother are still alive, how can you take action as soon as you hear something?'

Ran-You asked, 'When I hear something [that needs to be addressed], should I take action right away?'

The Master said, 'Upon hearing such a thing, you should take action right away.'

Gongxi Hua said, 'When Zilu asked you whether he should take action as soon as he heard something [that needed to be addressed], you said, as long as his father and elder are still alive [he should not]. But when Ran-You asked you the same question, you said he should take action right away. Now I am confused. May I beseech you for an explanation?'

The Master said, 'Ran-You tends to hold back, and so I like to urge him on. Zilu has the fire of two, and so I like to restrain him.' (The Analects 11.22)

Confucius' answer varies for each student. His concern is not to help students attain universal, objective knowledge external to their lives, but to guide each student towards personal improvement and the embodiment of wisdom in their unique and concrete circumstances. In other words, if teaching does not care about how students interpret *Ren* and enact *Ren* in their unique lives, then *Ren* would only remain outside of them and has nothing to do with their lives. *Ren* only exists in concrete persons and their lives. Because people are always different in their life experiences, personalities, situations and even at different life stages, the teaching form of *Ren* as a way of living needs to maintain a degree of flexibility and variation in conversation. In such form, *Ren* remains open and alive, requiring students to 'pay attention to the hermeneutical situations' (Chen 2013: 46) of their encounters and to create new meaning by practically realizing the wisdom in the classics.

Metaphor, Poetics and Association

Confucius often uses indirect language, such as metaphors and poetic language, in his teaching. These literary expressions are always suggestive rather than explicit (cf. Feng 1948). They help students to make analogies and associations in their own lives. They enlighten students to learn one thing and understand many, while also prompting them to reflect on their conduct.

Standing on the bank of a river, the Master said, 'Look at how it flows on like this, never stopping day or night!' (The Analects 9.17)

The Master said, 'Only after Winter comes, do we know that the pine and cypress are the last to fade.' (The Analects 9.28)

Passages like these are not simply descriptions of nature's phenomena but rather have significant suggestiveness for one's life. The first sentence refers to the life spirit of a *Junzi*, and can be interpreted as a constantly self-striving. However, it can also be understood as a lament about the passage of time and an encouragement to diligently practice the *Ren*. The second sentence might suggest that a *Junzi* is known for resilience and perseverance in the face of difficulties. All can serve as inspiration and guidance for how one could live one's life. Metaphors have multiple meaning and different people may have various interpretations and connect them to their life situations in different ways. Therefore, like the aphorisms and the dialogues about *Ren* above, the use of metaphor leaves the work of forming relevant connections to the students.

The associative rousing *Xing* (兴) function of metaphors activates the mind, and can be cultivated by learning poems (Yang 2013). Both metaphorical and other poetic forms provide inspiration to imply something that has not been said.

Zigong said, 'Poor without being obsequious, rich without being arrogant – what would you say about someone like that?'

The Master answered, 'That is acceptable, but it is still not as good as being poor and yet joyful, rich and yet loving ritual'.

Zigong said, 'An ode says, "As if cut, as if polished; As if carved, as if ground." Is this not what you have in mind?'

The Master said, 'Zigong, you are precisely the kind of person with whom one can begin to discuss the Odes. Informed as to what has gone before, you know what is to come'. (The Analects 1.15)

Zixia asked, '[An ode says,]

"Her artful smile, with its alluring dimples, her beautiful eyes, so clear, the unadorned upon which to paint." What does this mean?'

The Master said, 'The application of colors comes only after a suitable unadorned background is present'.

Zixia said, 'So it is the rites that come after?'

The Master said, 'It is you, Zixia, who has awakened me to the meaning of these lines! It is only with someone like you that I can begin to discuss the Odes.' (The Analects 3.8)

As shown in the above quotes, students' interpretation of the poems differs from even what Confucius saw in them. Yet Confucius appreciates what such interpretations offer. In the first sentence, disciple Zigong associates admirable qualities of a person to precious jade, and notices it is only through the process of polishing and continuous refinement that jade becomes perfect artwork. To refine admirable qualities towards perfect virtues also then requires such care and effort. The second poem is originally a love poem appreciating a beautiful lady. Disciple Zixia associates it with good character needing perfecting through the learning of *Li* (礼, introduced above). As mentioned above, *Ren* is the fundamental spirit of *Li* and *Li* is the outward and social refinement of one's good character. In this sense, for Zixia, *Li* is to good characters what makeup is to natural beauty. In such a way, he associates the wisdom in the poems with the cultivation of virtues. What Confucius praises is the disciples' ability to think about and associate the unspoken meaning of poems and get inspiration for living their lives.

Some scholars (see Zhang 2006) argue that Confucius' teaching begins with students asking how to achieve *Ren* and ends with him answering concrete actions in various situations. However, Confucius' teaching does not end with his detailed action guides. Rather, his teaching cultivates the ability to form rousing associations, or *Xing*. Through teaching in the forms of poetry and metaphor, he enlightens students to learn one thing and understand others, and grasp the *Dao* (道 way, path, principles) behind everything. In particular, Confucius encourages students to move beyond concrete actions and grasp the overarching ideas behind those actions – to comprehend one thing and understand others. Such an ability can help them realize more and find inspiration and implications in their daily lives by themselves. This ability is always emphasized in Confucian thoughts:

> *The Master said to Zigong, 'Who is better, you or Yan Hui?'*

> *Zigong answered, 'How dare I even think of comparing myself to Hui? Hui learns one thing and thereby understands ten. I learn one thing and thereby understand two.'*

> *The Master said, 'No, you are not as good as Hui. Neither of us is as good as Hui.' (The Analects 5.9)*

> *The Master said, 'Master Zeng! All that I teach can be strung together on a single thread.' (The Analects 4.15.1)*

This enlightenment for students' own thinking, associations and its application is evident in Confucius' statement on his pedagogy:

The Master said, 'I will not open the door for a mind that is not already striving to understand, nor will I provide words to a tongue that is not already struggling to speak. If I hold up one corner of a problem and the student cannot come back to me with the other three, I will not attempt to instruct him again.' (The Analects 7.8)

Metaphorical and suggestive language also frequently appeared in Confucius' interactions with disciples (also see examples in 5.4, 5.10, 5.22, 9.3, 9.8, 9.21, 15.40, 16.1, 17.4, etc.):

The Master remarked to Yan Hui, 'It is said, 'When he is employed, he moves forward; when he is removed from office, he holds himself in reserve.' Surely this applies only to you and me?'

Zilu interposed, 'If you, Master, were to lead the three armies into battle, who would you want by your side?'

The Master replied, 'I would not want by my side the kind of person who would attack a tiger barehanded or attempt to swim the Yellow River, because he was willing to die without regret. Surely, I would want someone who approached such undertakings with a proper sense of trepidation and who came to a decision only after having thoroughly considered the matter.' (The Analects 7.11)

Confucius does not point out directly that Zilu may lack the virtue of *Shi* (时 timely, timeliness), which is the ability to be flexible, cautious and appropriate when confronting a situation (see Slingerland 2003: 67), Confucius indirectly (and maybe on purpose) praises Yan Hui in front of Zilu for such virtue and asks if this virtue only applies to him and Yan Hui. Zilu presumably gets jealous and tries to win Confucius' approval by reminding Confucius of his brave and fearless character (see Slingerland 2003: 67). However, it is precisely Zilu's reckless courage that Confucius wants to remind him of, as already shown in the first statement of teaching (see Slingerland 2003: 67). Rather than directly telling Zilu he should be less bold, Confucius uses indirect metaphors to imply why such boldness is problematic. As Zilu already misses the point in the first statement of teaching, Confucius follows with a more explicit explanation. However, even this explanation still does not directly tell what Zilu should do or not do, but is instead simply declares what kind of people Confucius would like to work with.

The Master said, 'Why do I hear Zilu playing the zither inside my door?' The disciples began to treat Zilu with disrespect.

The Master said, 'Zilu may not have entered the inner room, but he has ascended the hall.' (The Analects 11.15)

Zilu plays the zither, a vigorous and aggressive instrument (see Slingerland 2003). Confucius teaches a more gentle and refined style of music, which he believes is a more appropriate way to cultivate virtues and lifestyle in his students. However, Confucius does not directly blame Zilu for playing such music, or tell him that playing such music is not effective for correcting Zilu's tough and unbending character, but indirectly asks why he hears Zilu playing such music. However, when other disciples take it as a total disapproval of Zilu, Confucius adjusts himself and offers a metaphor implying Zilu has already achieved a certain stage of education but has not yet reached a final stage. This is also an indirect reminder to his disciples that it is unnecessary to disrespect Zilu for a single mistake.

As shown from previous quotes, Confucius displayed indirect teaching (see Saeverot 2022) by using metaphors to comment on the good and bad conduct of his students. This form of teaching does not directly judge students' behaviour or tell them what to do. By using metaphors, it arouses students' thinking and leaves space for their reflections and choices. It allows both freedom and guidance in their conduct.

Stories and Comments

There are many stories and comments about people in *The Analects*. It is calculated that 155 different people appear in *The Analects*, of which Confucius comments on 120, including himself (see Bian 2009). One might ask why so many are packed into such a brief text, which as a whole is only about 15,000 words. The answer again comes back to Confucius' approach to teaching, and the importance of attending to different people and life stories in different situations for insight into how to live.

As discussed in the previous section, Confucius' teachings on *Ren* are not conveyed through abstract conceptual arguments but rather through dialogues with different individuals. His teachings emphasize conduct, as seen in aphorisms such as 'to love others', 'do not impose on others what you do not desire for yourself', 'establish oneself and help others establish themselves' and 'restrain oneself and return to the rites'. His teachings on *Ren* are also embodied in concrete people and life stories. This can occur in situations as trivial as people's everyday interactions, but equally, in those that involve big life decisions:

Confucius illustrates *Ren* through specific examples, such as his commentary on Yan Pingzhong:

The Master said, Yan Pingzhong is good at interacting with others – even after long acquaintance, he continues to treat them with respect.' (The Analects 5.17)

Here, Confucius highlights *Ren* by observing a concrete individual's behaviour rather than providing an abstract definition. Similarly, he describes the demeanour of his disciples:

When Min Ziqian attended the Master, he appeared upright; Zilu looked tough and unbending; Ran Qiu and Zigong appeared affable. The Master was pleased. He said, 'A man like Zilu will not die a natural death.' (The Analects 11.13)

This illustrates that *Ren* can be discerned through an individual's outward demeanour, which reflects their inner spiritual state. His teaching of *Ren* is not through understanding a cognitive concept but is demonstrated through one's disposition and conduct.

At times, *Ren* is demonstrated through profound life decisions, even involving personal sacrifice. Confucius praises three historical figures who made different choices in response to tyranny:

The Viscount of Wei left him. The Viscount of Ji became his slave. Bi Gan remonstrated with him and, because of it, was put to death. The Shang had these three humane men. (The Analects 18.1)

In this passage, 'him' refers to the tyrannical King Zhou, the last ruler of the Shang dynasty (Chin 2014). The Viscount Wei, King Zhou's brother, chose to leave, rejecting his ruling. The Viscount Ji, King Zhou's elder uncle, an important official, feigned madness to avoid persecution while preserving his potential usefulness (Slingerland 2003). Bi Gan, King Zhou's younger uncle, unburdened by familial or official constraints, upheld his integrity by strongly remonstrating with King Zhou, leading to his brutal execution (see Slingerland 2003). While their approaches varied, all three acted for the well-being of the people, exemplifying *Ren* through their deep concern and commitment.

The Master said, 'A person of high purpose and profound Ren does not seek to preserve life at the expense of Ren. There are moments when one must sacrifice one's life to fulfill Ren.' (The Analects 15.9)

However, *Ren* is not solely about life and death (Qian 2011). The *Ren* of these three men was not determined by whether they lived or died but by their efforts to restore harmony and protect the people. Confucius emphasizes that understanding how to live inherently informs how one faces death (Qian 2011). At times, survival should not be pursued at all costs, and in other moments, self-sacrifice is necessary to uphold *Ren*. The significance of Bi Gan's execution was not in the act of dying itself but in his upright stand against tyranny. Likewise, the viscount of Wei's choice to leave or Viscount of Ji's choice to feign madness was not a mere avoidance of death but a strategic means of preserving their ability to act in the future. Each decision realized the value of *Ren* in its own way.

Confucius' teachings on *Ren* are conveyed through real-life examples rather than abstract theorization. He demonstrates *Ren* by commenting on historical and contemporary figures, demonstrating their actions and choices. His teachings on *Ren* are also shown in his own living. *The Analects* records numerous encounters where Confucius actively engages with the world, showing initiative, withdrawal, refusal, prolonged commitment, or swift departure based on his principles of *Ren*.

For example, Confucius, while serving in the government of Lu, witnessed the state's decline when the state of Qi presented a gift of female entertainers:

> *The people of Qi sent a gift of female entertainers. Ji Huanzi accepted them [on behalf of the Duke of Lu], and the court was not held for several days. Confucius thereupon left the state of Lu. (The Analects 18.4)*

As the highest-ranking official in charge of judiciary, criminal law and social order, Confucius seeks to govern through *Ren*. However, the rulers of Lu indulged in pleasure and neglected state affairs. Recognizing that his ideals would not be realized under such governance, he resigns and begins his fourteen-year exile, travelling to different states to advocate his philosophy. His actions align with his own teachings:

> 'When the state possesses the Way, he serves it; when the state lacks the Way, he withdraws'. (The Analects 15.7)

During his exile, Confucius encounters many hermits who withdrew from political life to avoid turmoil. They mock him, believing that he could hardly protect himself, let alone bring *Ren* to the world (see *The Analects* 18.5, 18.6, 18.7). Confucius refuses to live in seclusion. Even in hardship – such as being stranded in the state of Chen and Cai for seven days without food – Confucius remains resolute, refusing to abandon his principle (*The Analects* 15.2). His unwavering commitment to his ideals teaches *Ren* in its truest form – not as an abstract concept but as a way of living, embodied through concrete actions and choices.

The teaching form is not theoretical and analytical but primarily practical. It teaches about how one conducts one's life, what kind of life one lives and what kind of person one has become. Such a form is in line with Confucius' thoughts: the true realization of *Ren* shows in people's embodiment of wisdom, the way they live and the way they act when facing situations. It is in the concrete people and life stories that show *Ren*.

Through discussing examples, learning life stories, examining life choices and the influence of role models, students can experience the meaning of *Ren* in concrete situations. *Ren* is not taught by a direct explanation of what it is but indirectly by the meaning one takes from others' life stories and Confucius as a living example.

Emotionally Expressive Forms

The Analects enlighten readers with thoughts and touch readers with emotions. It displays emotionally expressive or 'lyric' forms. It not only expounds philosophical principles but also reveals genuine and sincere feelings. It expresses emotions rather than merely stating reasons.

For example, in *The Analects*, we can see Confucius' deep sadness by the passing of his beloved disciple. The teacher–student relationship is heartfelt and profoundly touching, as if their close connection transcends time through the writing of *The Analects*:

> When Yan Hui passed away, the Master lamented, 'Oh! Heaven has bereft me! Heaven has bereft me!' (The Analects 11.9)

> When Yan Hui died, the Master wept with uncontrollable emotion. His followers said, 'Master, you have gone too far.' The Master said, 'Have I? If not for this man, for whom should I show so much sorrow?' (The Analects 11.10)

This is the best way of teaching *Ren*: to live with compassion and humanity in all aspects of life. It is a very different teaching form than stating that '*Ren* and caring for others is very important, and it is at the moment of life and death that one's *Ren* is most profoundly revealed. Here are some reasons … ' It touches readers rather than persuades them through arguments.

The Analects picture Confucius's emotions as both a teacher and a human being. It records his peaceful mood in everyday life, his joy in seeing his students practice the *Dao* (道 Way), his anger at the minister usurping etiquette, his lament over the unfulfilled *Dao* and the passage of time, as well as his happiness in his learning and achieving mastery of the *Dao*. His profound affection for the world and his deep desire to save the world leap vividly from the texts.

> In his leisure moments, the Master was composed and yet fully at ease. (The Analects 7.4)

> Confucius said of the head of the Ji family, who had eight rows of pantomimes in his area, 'If he can bear to do this, what may he not bear to do?' (The Analects 3.1)

The Master said, 'Extreme is my decay. For a long time, I have not dreamed, as I was wont to do, that I saw the Duke of Zhou.' (The Analects 7.5)

The Master said, 'Admirable indeed was the virtue of Hui! With a single bamboo dish of rice, a single gourd dish of drink, and living in his mean narrow lane, while others could not have endured the distress, he did not allow his joy to be affected by it. Admirable indeed was the virtue of Hui!' (The Analects 6.11)

The Governor of She asked Zilu about Confucius, and Zilu gave no answer. The Master later said to Zilu, 'Why didn't you simply say that he is the sort of person who forgets to eat when pursuing a question, who forgets to worry when suffused with joy, and who does not note that old age is coming?' (The Analects 7.19)

The Analects show a vivid and multi-dimensional portrayal of Confucius as a teacher and a practitioner of the *Dao* and presents how he embodies and teaches *Ren* throughout his life. The text employs the most simple and sincere description that deeply moves the readers. It is quite different from a form that strives to minimize personal emotions, relying solely on logic and argumentation. Instead, it speaks to the readers, evoking emotions and touching their hearts rather than imposing his way of living. Anyone touched by this book, and by Confucius' lifelong pursuit and practice, may also grow a heart that yearns for such a way of living. It views students not merely as cognitive entities that need to acquire knowledge, but as affective, holistic subjects who live their lives and grow through their life experiences.

Why Does Confucius Teach as He Does?

The forms of teaching serve Confucius's specific educational purposes – *Ren*, which can generally be understood as a lifelong striving toward a significant way of living, 'to become the most genuine, sincere, and humane person he or she can become' (Li 2003: 146). It is not academic, nor is it skill-based or market-oriented, but about how to live. *Ren* is the sincere kindness and warmth among people (Qian 2011). It is rooted in a naturally close feeling parents have for their babies. To practice *Ren* and live in a *Ren* way, one needs to bring this warmth to the wider social circle, to live in harmony (和 he) with oneself, others and the world (Sun 2008). It requires one to be dutiful (忠 zhong), respectful (敬 jing), forgiving (恕 shu), trustworthy (信 xin), and to practice the perfect virtue of courage (勇 yong), wisdom (智 zhi), benevolence (仁 ren) (see Chan 1955; Tu 1981); and to insist on righteousness (义 yi) and express it in proper manner (礼 li). To live with an unceasing spirit towards the improvement of oneself is to become a *Junzi*. In essence, Confucius' educational concern is not academic or cognitive but the spiritual growth and practice of wisdom of his disciples. His fundamental educational concern is not for the transmission of objective knowledge, but a care and concern for students as wholes, as subjects who live their own lives. It requires forms of teaching that pay attention to those specific characteristics of *Ren* as their educational aim.

Ren is primarily practical rather than conceptual. It is a way to live, a way to treat people, a way to conduct rather than an abstract concept. It is a practice in interpersonal relationships (see Ames 2020) that needs to be educated through everyday conduct and interactions rather than abstract moral doctrine. It is always connected with concrete actions.

Although *Ren* strives for a kind of humane life, endeavouring to attain it is also a matter of what Biesta calls 'subjectification' (e.g. see Biesta 2017). This term refers to how one can exist as a subject of one's own life rather than a mere object (Biesta 2017). *Ren* involves realizing and becoming the subject of one's conduct rather than passively accepting knowledge, values, beliefs and so on. *Ren* is not about following external rules but about conscious self-striving as an attitude that permeates daily life. Without direct concern with how 'I' practice *Ren* in my own life, *Ren* has nothing to do with me.

Ren is situational rather than involving fixed moral standards and rules. It occurs in interactions among people rather than in isolated contemplation. It always involves different people and situations. *Ren* is not a dogma but a practice that varies according to people, time and situations. It needs to be realized in varied context and interactions and so is flexible and based on wise judgements.

All those characteristics require *indirect* modes of teaching. Because no one can live *my life* for *me*. No one else can practice on my behalf. No one else can face *my* concrete situation for *me*. Without the *I* to *live my own life* and to practice *Ren* in *my own life*, there is no way to realize *Ren* in *my life. As a subject of my own life, I* need to practice *Ren* in my concrete and situated life. This implies that education cannot give the objective truth of *Ren* to students while the students remain outside of it, existing as objects to receive such knowledge. In other words, education should not give students the objective truth but engage it indirectly and appeal to students to live in a *Ren* way by their own choice.

The five forms displayed in *The Analects* are all indirect forms of teaching as they never tell students what to do or to think. Instead, they appeal to students to act and live as the subject of their own lives. The short aphorism leaves students space to think and interpret. The metaphorical and poetic language enlightens students and makes the association to their lives. The emotional language touches the hearts of the readers. The form of dialogue pays attention to the concrete, hermeneutic situations of different students. Both the stories and comments point to how *Ren* is a practical question embodied in concrete lives and stories approached through considering examples that indirectly ask the students to then consider themselves. Through such teaching forms, Confucius appealed to his disciples to become the *Junzi* and live in a *Ren* way rather than telling them directly what they should do with their lives.

Artistry in Confucius' Teaching: Inventiveness and Aesthetics

In previous sections, I showed Confucius' teaching forms and why Confucius teaches in these ways. In this section, I will further articulate the artistry in Confucius' teaching forms. I argue for two aspects of artistry: inventiveness and aesthetics.

Teaching is an art and not a science because teaching is in the practice of human interaction instead of theoretical life (Biesta this volume, Chapter 1). Teaching is located in the domain of variable, in other words, the domain of change rather than certainty, where similar actions may not lead to the very consequences in different situations. This is because we work with other human beings who can think and act on their own (Biesta this volume, Chapter 1). The scientific logic of finding the unchanging universal law that can apply to every teaching situation is impossible because teaching is a highly situated practice that always involves differences, uniqueness and unpredictability. Therefore, teaching is not about effectively delivering a system to produce pre-defined learning outcomes but is art that always needs to be sensitive to and tailored to the concrete situation – these students, here and now, and so on. This means that teachers cannot simply follow protocols but have to be 'inventive' and creative. To make situated judgements about 'what are desirable ways of acting', to create 'how to teach' and pay attention to the relation between the way to teach and 'what is for' in an always new situation.

The forms presented in *The Analects* show how Confucius always provided different answers to different students or even the same students to his central ideas, such as *Ren* and *Junzi*. This involves the art of judgement. His teaching forms are also variation in different cases. Sometimes the words are concise and thought-provoking, and sometimes they are eloquent and inspire discussion. He uses many different rhetorical techniques, such as those I have articulated in this chapter in his teaching. The form of teaching is flexible and creative. He also likes to use everyday things to enlighten his students: the vessels, the corner, the room, the trees, the river, the star. This process is not to follow procedures but indeed an art of creation and inventiveness that is flexible and creative in new situations. It also shows an artistic relationship between communication and interpretation of meaning rather than intervention.

The way education works is aesthetic (see Chapters 9 by Affifi and 11 by Biesta in this volume). Just like good artwork, it evokes the audience's response, which the artist cares about but does not control. A good artwork evokes the audience to think about 'what this (artwork) asks me' and calls the 'I' into presence. Bad art tries to control the audience's response or allows the audience to interpret it in any way. In teaching, what we pursue is not obedience or indoctrination but students' thoughtful engagement with what is taught. It calls the 'I' into existence, to summon self-action. It works, just like good art, aesthetically. Because the education issue can never be just about whether a certain behaviour is good or bad, right or wrong, but how students become the subject of their behaviour, rather than always need judgement from somewhere else. If the world is not entered aesthetically, students will be dormant and numb, and the 'I' cannot play a role.

The forms of Confucius's teaching also embody aesthetics. Confucius, through all kinds of forms, such as metaphor, poetic, stories and emotional language, tries to 'touch' his students, prompt them, encourage them, perhaps even confuse and irritate them – but in all these ways he tries to leave space for students to come to their own judgements and conclusions and actions. Rather than telling students what they should do with their lives, his teaching forms evoke students' thoughtful engagement, to choose and act on their own. This aesthetic quality of the forms of Confucius' teaching has educational quality as it is interested in the freedom of the student – it does not want to take this freedom away. Through different forms, Confucius appeals to students' subject-ness and meets their freedom there.

Concluding Comments

In this chapter, I have explored Confucius' different teaching forms as presented in *The Analects*. I argue that those different forms are all indirect forms that enlighten students to live significant lives, a life of *Ren*, rather than telling them what they should do with their lives. The flexible application of different teaching forms and variations in encountering his disciples shows Confucius' inventiveness and creativity in his teaching artistry. His care for the freedom of students and restraint aimed at indirectly summoning his disciple's action to live a life of *Ren*, and shows the aesthetics of his teaching. This demonstrates how interesting the case of Confucius from *The Analects* is for getting a better and more concrete understanding of what the artistry of teaching entails.

References

Ames, R.T. (2020), *Human Becomings: Theorizing Persons for Confucian Role Ethics*, Albany, NY: State University of New York Press.

Bian, C.N. (2009), 《论语》人物评传 (*Lunyu renwu pingzhuan*) [Biographical Evaluations of Figures in the Analects], Beijing: Zhonghua Book.

Biesta, G. (2017), *The Rediscovery of Teaching*, New York: Routledge.

Chan, W.T. (1955), 'The Evolution of the Confucian Concept Jen', *Philosophy East and West*, 5 (4): 295–319.

Chen, L. (2013), '"学而时习之"——儒家经典诠释传统的重要原则 ["Xue Er Shi Xi Zhi": The Important Principle of Interpreting Confucian Classics]', 河南社会科学, 21 (8): 44–6.

Chin, A.P. (2014), *Confucius: The Analects (with an Introduction and Commentary by Annping Chin)*, trans. A.P. Chin, New York: Penguin Classics.

Feng, Y. (1948), *A Short History of Chinese Philosophy*, New York: Simon and Schuster.

Hui, A. (2019), *A Theory of the Aphorism: From Confucius to Twitter*, Princeton, NJ: Princeton University Press.

Li, J. (2003), 'The Core of Confucian Learning', *American Psychologist*, 58 (1): 46–7.

Qian, M. (2011), 论语新解 *Lun Yu Xin Jie*, 北京: 生活·读书·新知三联书店.

Saeverot, H. (2022), *Indirect Education: Exploring Indirectness in Teaching and Research*, Abingdon: Taylor & Francis.

Slingerland, E. (2003), *Confucius Analects: With Selections from Traditional Commentaries*, trans. E. Slingerland, Indianapolis, IN: Hackett Publishing.

Sun, Q. (2008), 'Confucian Educational Philosophy and Its Implication for Lifelong Learning and Lifelong Education', *International Journal of Lifelong Education*, 27 (5): 559–78.

Tu, W.M. (1979), *Humanity and Self-Cultivation: Essays in Confucian Thought*, Berkeley, CA: Asian Humanities Press.

Tu, W.M. (1981), 'Jen as a Living Metaphor in the Confucian Analects', *Philosophy East and West*, 31 (1): 45–54.

Wu, Z.J. (2011), 'Interpretation, Autonomy, and Transformation: Chinese Pedagogic Discourse in a Cross-Cultural Perspective', *Journal of Curriculum Studies*, 43 (5): 569–90.

Yang, Y.W. (2013), '从"兴于《诗》"谈孔子教学法 [On the Teaching Methods of Confucius: A Discussion Based on "Xing Yu Shi"]', 孔子研究, 5: 31–41.

Zhang, C.S. (2006), '孔子与苏格拉底对话教学法: 比较文化视角 [The Question and Answer Methods of Teaching of Confucius and Socrates from a Comparative Cultural Perspective]', 教师教育研究, 6: 62–6.

CHAPTER ELEVEN

The Aesthetics of Teaching: How Education Really Works

Gert Biesta

Beauty is in the I of the beholder.

Making Education Work?

In many countries there is enthusiasm amongst politicians, policymakers, teachers and researchers for the suggestion that education can be significantly improved if it is informed by solid research evidence about 'what works'. There are many questions that need to be asked about this suggestion, and also about the enthusiasm for it, not just with regard to notions such as 'evidence' and 'research', but also with regard to the question whose voices count when the question of educational improvement is on the table (see Biesta 2007, 2017a).

One question that is often overlooked in the discussions is a rather simple and fundamental one: How does education actually work? After all, if, in teaching, we want to do things *that* work, we should at the very least have an idea of *how* education works, so that we can make it work better on whatever criterion we want to bring into play. In this chapter I explore the interesting idea that education works *aesthetically*. I will try to make clear what this idea entails and what it means for teachers and their artistry. My approach will be indirect, as a kind of collage, exactly in the way in which teaching itself is essentially indirect (see Saeverot 2013, 2022).

'A Sudden Glimpse to Deeper Things'

The film *A Sudden Glimpse to Deeper Things*, directed by Mark Cousins, documents the life and work of Wilhelmina Barnes-Graham (1912–2004).[1] The website of the Barnes-Graham Trust describes her as 'one of Britain's most significant 20th century modern artists. Scottish born and a prominent member of the post-war St Ives group, she was a sublime painter, draughtswoman, printmaker and a brilliant colourist. Dividing her time between studios in St Ives and St Andrews she followed a consistent artistic vision throughout her sixty-five-year career'.[2] In a rather sober way, the film shows a life devoted to the visual arts. It is interesting that this devotion was not so much a matter of deliberate choice and more a case of 'being found' (for this phrase see Biesta 2024c). As Barnes-Graham put it later in her career, 'painting chose me, not I it' (see Green 2001: 12).

The 'sudden glimpse' in the title of the film refers to an experience Barnes-Graham had when visiting Grindelwald Glacier in Switzerland in 1949. The visit turned out to be a 'pivotal moment in her career' (Button 2020: 67), resulting, among other things, in a series of paintings known as the Glacier Paintings in which Barnes-Graham tried to bring in 'all the angles at once'.[3] What is impressive about Barnes-Graham's career is that materials that have been around for a long time and have been known for a long time – paint, brushes, ink, canvas, pencils, paper – are able to sustain a whole life. And 'whole' here is not just about duration, but even more so about wholeness and fulfilment, or perhaps actually about the *lack* of wholeness, the *lack* of fulfilment, the *lack* of ever reaching an endpoint or final destination. More a matter of a lifelong quest, then.

Much of Barnes-Graham's work can be characterized as 'abstract'. Yet the designator 'abstract' is not to be understood as referring to some kind of inability to be concrete or an inability to accurately represent reality. 'Abstract' is perhaps more a fascination with and devotion to the materials *themselves*, that is to what is *possible* with paint, ink and pencil, which also involves what paint, ink and pencil *allow* the artist to do and prevent the artist from doing, and what, in this way, they *ask* from the artist (see also Dijkman 2019).

And then, 'through' all this, perhaps even in spite of this, but definitely *not* because of insufficient devotion and discipline, there is this 'sudden glimpse to deeper things'. The glimpse is sudden: unexpected and fleeting. It is a glimpse to deeper things; things that are not immediately apparent. And in what, for me as a non-native speaker of English, looks special: it is not a glimpse *of* deeper things but a glimpse *to* deeper things. It is as if, when walking through a corridor, a door opens for a brief moment, a small beam of light shines through, and some voices can be heard. But as soon as the glimpse arrives, it is gone already – at most leaving a trace in our memory. The Glacier Paintings, then, are perhaps a way of trying not to forget.

That is what paintings can do.

'If I Could Say It in Words There Would Be No Reason to Paint.'

This sentence, attributed to Edward Hopper, makes an important point about art. It is not just a statement about the need for taking art seriously. It is first and foremost a statement about the *necessity of the artwork*. The point here is that the artwork – be it a painting, be it a sculpture, a piece of music, a dance, a theatre play, or a poem – is not simply a vehicle for the communication of the artist's idea or intention. It is not that the idea is already fully formed and that the artwork is just a medium for expressing the idea. After all, if that were the case, then artists could save themselves and their audience a lot of time and effort by just saying what they wanted to say, rather than through the onerous detour of the artwork.[4]

The artwork matters, the existence of the artwork matters, and even the *objectivity* of the artwork matters, by which I mean the fact that it exists independent of the artist's intentions, and continues to exist long after the artist has left the room. As such, the artwork stands *in between* artists and their prospective audience, at a distance from both the artists and the audience. In the case of the visual arts this standing can be taken quite literally. In the case of performing arts, the objectivity of the artwork requires re-enactment. The composition needs to be played, the theatre play needs to be performed, the choreography needs to be danced. But when this is done, then there *is* music, then there *is* a play, then there *is* dance.

The suggestion that the existence of the artwork matters, that it's objectivity matters, is not to suggest that artists would be indifferent about their work. I think it is safe to assume that the existence of the artwork matters for the artist and that in some way they hope or expect that the artwork will 'affect' the audience in some way, similar, perhaps, to the way in which at some point their 'own' artwork affected them. They care, therefore, in some way about the response the artwork may evoke.

But whereas sentimental art – or perhaps we can just say: bad art – wants to be in control of the audience's response, wants to produce a pre-determined effect, non-sentimental art – or good art – wants to leave room for the audience.[5] And leaving room means taking the audience seriously. This is the difference between wanting to evoke a response and wanting to determine what the response should be. Artists are not interested in just getting back what they already expected or anticipated or even predicted should be coming back. In that case, after all, there probably would be no reason to paint (it) either.

'The I of the Beholder'

It is here that the idea of the 'eye of the beholder' matters, but I would like to make this sound differently, as the 'I of the beholder'. The image of the eye of the beholder suggests a surveying attitude, one in which the audience, as a spectator, surveys the artwork with their gaze in order then to come to (an) interpretation, (an) opinion or (a) judgement. Such a 'hermeneutic' (Biesta 2016) account of the relationship between artwork and audience is rather problematic, I think. This is not just because it puts the audience, as spectator, in a 'sovereign' position vis-à-vis the artwork, which at the very least raises the question how such a position can be justified and how the spectator has ended up there in the first place.[6] The relationship is also problematic because it reduces the artwork to an object for the spectator's interpretation or a trigger for the spectator's opinion, and, in doing so, leaves little room for the artwork to play a role or have a voice in this.

There is, however, an alternative 'configuration' possible (Biesta 2025). This, to make the point here rather quickly, is a configuration in which it is the 'I' of the spectator that the artwork is after. Let me repeat and slightly rephrase this: it is the artwork that is after the 'I' of the spectator (whether the spectator wants it or not). Here, the guiding question for the spectator is not 'What do I make of this (artwork)?' but 'What is this (artwork) asking of me?', 'What is this (artwork) trying to say to me?'. And perhaps also: 'What the hell should I do with that?' and 'Why me?'.

If one lets oneself be guided by these questions – perhaps: if one lets oneself be affected by these questions – then the artwork may show up very differently from as a stimulus for interpretation. If one let oneself be guided by these questions, then the artwork may also show up as appeal, as call, as imperative even (Lingis 1998), as being-in-search-of me, rather than as object-for-me-and-my-interpretation. And it is precisely this appeal that pulls *me* into the situation, makes me complicit, rather than that, as surveyor, I just observe the situation from a safe distance – which could well be the view from nowhere.

'Das Hauptgeschäft der Erziehung'

The phrase 'Das Hauptgeschäft der Erziehung' – the main task or 'core business' of education – comes from the title of an essay written by the Johann Friedrich Herbart (1776–1841), who is one of the founding figures of education as an independent scholarly field in the German-speaking world.[7] The full title of Herbart's essay is 'Über die ästhetische Darstellung der Welt als das Hauptgeschäft der Erziehung', which translates as 'On the aesthetic representation of the world as the main task of education' (Herbart 1804). I will mainly take inspiration from the title of the essay, as the detail of Herbart's argument goes beyond what I seek to discuss in this chapter.[8]

It is significant, however, that Herbart opens the essay – which is one of the first texts he ever published – with the strong statement that the sole and entire task of education (Herbart uses the word 'Erziehung'[9]) can be captured with the notion of morality (*Moralität*). In German: ‚Man kann die eine und ganze Aufgabe der Erziehung in den Begriff ‚*Moralität*' fassen'. (Herbart 1804). By identifying 'morality' as the sole and entire task of education, and hence as the central *orientation* for all educational endeavours, Herbart is articulating an interest in children becoming subjects of their 'own' moral action, so we might say, and not objects of moral instruction or of external regulation and moralization.

In order to grasp why, also with this moral orientation in mind, the representations of the world that circulate in the classroom ought to be aesthetic, we might start from the other end, that is, by envisaging what education would look like if the ways in which the world is represented is not aesthetic but rather *an*aesthetic (see Biesta 2022 for this distinction; and see Affifi in this volume for an exploration of the idea that rather than an opposition, aesthetic and anaesthetic may better be understood as a spectrum). In such a situation the world is represented as fact or, in more 'didactical' terms, as a *task* for the student. The task for the student is to memorize the fact and reproduce it later at a test or exam. Or, if we take a slightly more meaningful approach (as just storing and retrieving information in your memory barely counts as a sensible case of education): the task for the student is to understand the fact and show evidence of their understanding in a test or exam.

Aiming for understanding is, in itself, not wrong, of course. But if the world *only* enters the classroom as task, and if the only appeal that is issued to the student is that of performing the task successfully – being a good and obedient student – it is clear that there is no space opened for the student and no appeal issued to the student for pondering what that which is encountered actually *asks* of the student. What, for example, follows from knowing chemistry or understanding history? What kind of burden is it to have such knowledge and understanding? And what to do with that burden? Without room for these questions, the 'I' of the student simply isn't brought 'into play', which is the reason why characterizing this setup as 'anaesthetic' is so appropriate. After all, in such a situation the 'I' of the student is not awakened but rather kept in a state of slumber. Like a sleeping dog.

And that is why Herbart argues, and even insists, that the way in which the world enters the classroom must be aesthetic.

'Aufforderung Zur Selbsttätigkeit'

One could of course ask what education has to do with all this. Why is it the main task of *education* to represent the world aesthetically? Why can't we leave that to the arts, or to politics, and let education do its own thing? An interesting and in my view very relevant answer to this question can be found in Dietrich Benner's book *Allgemeine Pädagogik* (Benner 2015), which is an introduction to the general theory of education.

Early on in the book Benner asks a quite fundamental question, namely whether education matters or, in more general terms, what kind of difference the work of educators makes. He approaches this question in a surprising way, namely by asking what the relative contribution of education is in relation to the influence from 'nature' – young people's talents and potential – and the influence from 'nurture' – the impact of the social environment in which children and young people grow up. Educational optimists would probably put a fairly high percentage on the education-component. Biological, genetic or neurological determinists would, on the other hand, put a very high percentage on the nature-component, while sociologists and socio-cultural theorists would probably put the highest percentage on 'nurture'. Benner's remarkable answer to his own question, however, is that while we can disagree about the relative contribution of each component, nature and nurture together *always amount to 100 per cent* (see Benner 2015: 73).

The first time I read Benner's answer, I was not just surprised but actually quite taken aback. Here I was working my way through a pretty complicated German text in which I was hoping to find new insights about the importance of education, and already in the first section of the book the author seems to brush education aside. Yet the ingenuity of what Benner is doing here is to highlight that whereas nature and nurture together determine how we become who we are, as educators we are interested in an altogether different question, which is also a question of an altogether different 'order'. As educators our question is how out of this 'mix' of nature and nurture, which will work out slightly differently in each individual, an 'I' can be called forward.

From the perspective of the 'I' this has to do with the question what I will do with how I have become, with my talents, my knowledge and understanding, my skills and abilities, but also my blind spots and incompetencies. It is, therefore, not about how each individual develops and learns, but how each of us *exists* – as subject of our own life (see also Biesta 2024a). From the perspective of the teacher this has to do with how we can bring this question 'into play' for our students. How, in other words, we can appeal to the 'I' of the student.

Benner has introduced the helpful phrase 'Aufforderung zur Selbsttätigkeit' to characterize what the educational work entails (see Benner 2015; and also Benner 2003; Langewand 2003). We could translate this as 'summoning to self-action', yet it is important to bear in mind that this not the injunction to be *yourself* (and just be content with that), and also not the injunction to just become active. It rather is the injunction to be *a* self, to not forget yourself, to not walk away from the possibility to exist as subject of your own life. In very simple terms we could say that as educators we knock on the 'door' of our students and ask: 'Is anyone there?'. This gesture is precisely a being-awakened for the possibility of one's own existence. This, as mentioned, is an existential matter, and not a matter of how human organisms become acculturated, grow, develop or learn.

If this is indeed education's 'own' concern – and the beauty of Benner's line of thought is that he is able to distinguish this concern from the legitimate but very different concerns of, say, developmental psychology, socialization theory, or socio-cultural theory – then it not just becomes important to consider *how* this concern can enter the classroom. It also helps to appreciate why Herbart insists that the aesthetical representation of the world matters *educationally* and why, therefore, this is indeed the main task or 'core business' – I actually like this phrase – of *all* education.

'Bildungsinhalt' and 'Bildungsgehalt'

The question how the world is represented in the classroom is first and foremost the question of the curriculum. Against the idea that curriculum is equated with content – a view that keeps haunting curriculum scholarship and even more so curriculum policy – I find the definition of curriculum as 'a course of study' very helpful (on this see Doll 1993). Curriculum, so we might say, is the organization of education over time. It is about designing trajectories that enable and encourage students to go from where they are to somewhere else. Getting students from 'A' to 'B' is a short summary of this, but the danger of putting it in that way, is that it might suggest that the task of curriculum is to design the fastest and smoothest way for the student to get from 'A' to 'B' – like a straight line – which is actually not what sound curriculum thinking ought to be about (also not because we cannot assume that in all cases teachers already know what 'B' is or will look like).

The courses of study we design for our students are first of all indeed courses or trajectories that make it possible for students to study, that is, to pay careful attention to what they may encounter during their journey. While they may encounter content on the way, the content itself is hardly ever the point of the journey, but only one of the elements that goes into it. After all, the trajectory may also involve questions, challenges, tasks, stumbling blocks, detours, interruptions, surprise encounters, unexpected experiences and perhaps even sudden glimpses to deeper things. From an educational point of view, therefore, the question is not just *that* students get from 'A' to 'B' but first of all *how* they do this. What matters, in other words, is the educative quality of the trajectory itself.

The German curriculum scholar Wolfgang Klafki has discussed the issue of the educative quality of curriculum by making a distinction between what, in German, he refers to as 'Bildungsinhalt' and 'Bildungsgehalt'. 'Inhalt' translates literally as 'content' and one could say that this is the subject matter presented to students. For Klafki, however, the point of this presentation of subject matter is not to give the student the task to 'acquire' or 'memorize and reproduce' this subject matter, but rather to ponder what this subject matter means *for the student's own existence*. Hopmann (2007), in discussing Klafki, translates 'Bildungsinhalt' and 'Bildungsgehalt' as 'matter' and 'meaning' respectively, but key in this translation is not the 'objective' meaning of the subject matter, but what we might term the subjective meaning.

This is connected to Klafki's ideas that 'Bildung' should be understood as a 'double disclosure' of both 'world' and 'self' (e.g. see Klafki 2007: 96). 'Bildungsgehalt' thus refers to how the self is disclosed, so to speak, in the encounter with subject matter or, more generally, the (trajectory of the) curriculum. Or, with the metaphor I introduced earlier, 'Bildungsgehalt' has something to do with the degree to which a particular subject matter is able to knock on the 'door' of the student and enact the question whether anyone is there or, more specifically, whether anyone is there *in relation to this particular subject matter*.

In his book *Vergessene Zusammenhänge* (Mollenhauer 1983), translated into English as *Forgotten Connections* (Mollenhauer 2014), Klaus Mollenhauer also discusses the question of how the world can be represented in the classroom. Mollenhauer shows how the question of representation only became an issue when everyday life started to lose its educative power. This was the result of the functional differentiation of modern societies, evident, for example, in work moving from home to factories and offices and therefore no longer a part of the everyday life shared with the new generation.

Mollenhauer particularly focuses on the question how the totality of the world can in some meaningful way be represented in the classroom, and how educational scholars from Comenius to Pestalozzi and beyond have grappled with this question, acknowledging that the world is too 'big' for the classroom, so that selection is inevitable. Rather than only focusing on the question how in what is selected we can make sure that what is represented in the classroom leaves sufficient space for the student – the question of the 'Bildungsgehalt' – Mollenhauer also discusses the opposite possibility, namely of a curriculum that has no 'Bildungsgehalt' at all. Such a curriculum is 'totalitarian' (see Mollenhauer 2014: 53) precisely because it doesn't leave any space for the student, but only sends the message that students should comply and obey. This possibility, which became concrete in the educational institutions of Nazi Germany, did indeed result in 'barbaric forms of schooling' (Mollenhauer 2014: 53).

It could be concluded that this means that if the representation of the world loses its aesthetic quality, something goes seriously wrong educationally. But it is important to bear in mind – and this is the warning I take from Mollenhauer as well – that aesthetics can also be used in totalitarian ways, precisely to ensure that people forget themselves and are just pulled into a 'space' in which everything resonates perfectly *so that* no difficult questions are asked or can emerge.[10] The photos and movies of Leni Riefenstahl are a 'good' example of the latter use – or can we just say abuse? – of aesthetics.

How Education Doesn't Work

Before I draw conclusions about how education (really) works, I wish to look briefly at some of the ways in which education doesn't work or shouldn't be made to work, also in order to highlight one further insight about the aesthetics of education. For this I rely on a chapter from Klaus Prange (in Prange 2012). In his chapter, Prange starts from the insight that education doesn't work in the mechanistic and deterministic way in which clockworks work: where all cogwheels interconnect and where the movement of one cogwheel determines the movement of the next cogwheel, whether that cogwheel likes it or not. This insight is, of course, not new. For centuries educators and educational scholars have acknowledged that teaching is a 'weak technology' which is unable to have control over its 'impact' on the student (see Biesta 2007, 2023; see also Bakker et al. forthcoming).

Prange captures this insight with the interesting term 'Lernresistenz' (which I would translate as the resistance *of* learning), with which he expresses the idea that whether teaching has any impact at all on students depends entirely on what students *do* with the teaching they encounter (see Prange 2012: 152). As Prange puts it: 'Who doesn't want to hear, simply won't hear, or won't hear yet or no longer' (Prange 2012: 152). The degree to which teaching 'works' thus depends on the way in which teaching is 'received by' and 'arrives with' the student. It depends on what Prange describes as the 'poetic agency' of the student (in German: 'poetische Selbständigkeit'). That is why their learning, which is what Prange argues that all teaching aims for and hopes for, is also the very thing that *resists* what teachers offer.

In this fundamental sense, therefore, teaching is powerless (see Prange 2012: 154). After all, what we aim for in teaching is *not* external conditioning, *not* total obedience and compliance or indoctrination, but rather what Prange refers to as 'reflexive learning' (Prange 2012: 154) or, in my own words, thoughtful engagement by students with what is 'on offer'. This is where teaching meets the freedom of the student, a freedom that always entails the possibility that the student will decide against what the teacher seeks to teach. Of course, educators can keep trying to close the 'loop' or 'gap', and research can keep looking for more effective methods for doing so, but Prange nicely observes that if we really want total control over our students, we will eventually have to call in the police (see Prange 2012: 154)!

Is there an educational 'way out' of this predicament? According to Prange there is, but the key word here is 'educational', as there are options in the literature which seem to provide a way out but actually are educationally flawed. One option is to say that the most teaching can achieve is to 'irritate' students (this is the word Prange uses here; see Prange 2012: 154), but then leave it entirely to students to decide whether and how they respond to such an irritation. After Herbart, Prange characterizes this as a form of (un)educational 'fatalism' in which we make the student's poetic freedom absolute and, in doing this, give up on the possibility for teaching to have any significance at all. We hand it all over, so to speak, to the eye of the beholder (see also Biesta 2024b).

The other option Prange rejects is the 'statistical' one in which we satisfy ourselves with the knowledge that *some* students may benefit from our efforts – in the discussion about evidence-based education this is often captured in the so-called 'effect-size' of a particular 'intervention' – without knowing or caring about which *particular* students will benefit and which students won't. In this approach the focus lies on the functioning of the education *system*, Prange argues, but not on a concern for each student. Rather than fatalism, where we just don't care about what our students do with what we offer them, this is a form of educational *cynicism*, where we just don't care about the fact that not all students will benefit from what we offer them.

The third option – the educational one – brings Prange back to Herbart and his idea of the aesthetic 'force' of teaching (the German phrase is 'ästhetische Nötigung' – see Prange 2012: 56).

'That Was Not Very Nice of You!'

Prange starts this discussion with the interesting observation that quite often when we see a child doing something that we think is wrong, we say something like 'That wasn't very nice' or 'That wasn't very nice of you'. Interestingly, the German word translated as 'nice' is 'schön', which is actually closer to the English word 'beauty'. While in English we wouldn't say to someone that their behaviour wasn't very beautiful, there is the opposite notion of calling someone's behaviour as 'ugly'. Prange then asks why we actually use words like 'nice' and 'ugly' in such contexts, as it would seem obvious that we should be using moral terms like 'good' and 'bad' and not aesthetic terms like 'nice' and 'ugly'. Is this a 'category mistake', as philosophers call it, where we conflate two different categories, the aesthetic and the moral one? Does it mean that we should be a bit more precise about the language we use?

That is not how Prange sees it, as for him there is an important educational difference between the moral and the aesthetic 'register'. He explains that when we say to a child that their behaviour is wrong, we subject them to a moral judgement. In doing so, we enact a very particular relationship in which we claim the position of moral authority and put the child in the position of the receiver of our judgement. The German phrase Prange uses is quite telling here, as he refers to this latter position as that of a 'normunterworfenen Befehlsemfänger', which literally translates as 'norm-subjected command-receiver'.

Whereas the judgement we make about the behaviour may well be correct – if the behaviour is morally wrong then it is morally wrong – the way in which the judgement is articulated and presented to the child is actually not very helpful from an educational point of view. This has to do with the fact that the articulation of a moral judgement subjects the child to this judgement, so that the child ends up as an object of someone else's moral judgement, rather than as potential agent of its *own* judgement. This is where the aesthetic observation that the behaviour wasn't very nice works differently.

Prange highlights that in saying that something the child did was not very nice, we speak the language of disappointment about the child's behaviour (see Prange 2012: 158), along the lines of 'I really didn't expect that of you', or 'that isn't really you' (see Prange 2012: 158–9). Yet precisely this observation, so Prange argues, not just confronts the child with our image of them, but also allows the child to consider what image it has of itself, that is, how its behaviour 'fits' with that image or not. It thus positions the child as its own judge of its own behaviour, rather than that this is done 'from the outside'.

And that is another reason why the aesthetic way is the educational way. After all, the educational question can never be just about whether some behaviour is good or bad or right or wrong or, even worse, whether some*one* is good or bad or right or wrong. The educational issue is always about how as educators we can appeal to the child's *own* attitude towards its own behaviour, now and in the future (see Prange 2012: 159). In that way, we encourage the child to be(come) a subject of its own moral action rather than remaining subjected to moral judgements from 'elsewhere'.

'Pädagogische Kausalitat'

I started this chapter with the question how education (really) works, and have pursued the idea that education works aesthetically. The keyword here is *education*, because human interactions can work in all kinds of ways, but in education there is something more precise at stake, namely the existence of the student as a subject of their own life and not an object of external forces, interventions, checks and balances, rewards and punishments, pushes and pulls, and so on. The argument that the unique and distinctive causality of education – for which Prange, after Herbart, uses the phrase 'Pädagogische Kausalitat' – is aesthetic, highlights that if in education we are concerned about the student as subject of their own life, our task is to appeal to them as subject, to appeal to their subject-ness, to open a space they can step into, not in order to behave in ways that we have already defined for them, but in order so that they can step into this space *themselves*, pondering what questions they may encounter there, and what question may try to encounter them.

The main implication for teachers and their artistry, if I can put it in this way, is that they – or I should actually say: we – should be aware of the importance of the aesthetic 'register' in everything we do, which also includes everything we deliberately refrain from doing (as there is aesthetic force in that as well). Bringing the arts into the classroom, utilizing their unique educative potential (see Biesta 2017b), is of course one way of doing this. But it is only *one* of the ways in which aesthetics can enter the classroom or educational situation, and perhaps even one that can be a little too obvious or overwhelming (although the arts also enter education in very uneducational ways, of course). The question of the aesthetic force is also critical for the curriculum and actually for all three 'tools' of the teacher – curriculum, pedagogy and assessment – if, again, we want to utilize them in educational ways and not as technologies of control.

After all, if we're after the latter, we'd better call in the police.

Notes

1   See: *A Sudden Glimpse to Deeper Things* (2024) – IMDb (last accessed 1 November 2024).

2   Wilhelmina Barns-Graham Trust (last accessed 1 November 2024).

3   See for the phrase Art Collection – Wilhelmina Barns-Graham Trust, and for the paintings: Works – Theme: Glacier Series – Collections – Barns-Graham Charitable Trust (last accessed 1 November 2024).

4   This is, as Osborne (2013) has pointed out, where the weakness of conceptual art lies, precisely because it tends to see the artwork as the expression of some underlying concept or idea. It is also why Osborne argues that all art should be(come) *post*-conceptual.

5   To readers who feel nervous about my use of the phrase 'good art' and 'bad art' I would say that the difference is not clear-cut and would actually require an exploration of the ways in which an artwork leaves room for the audience, also bearing in mind the point I will be making in this section, namely that this 'room' is not the 'endless room of interpretation'.

6   On this see also Lingis (2007: 7), where he asks – and tries to answer – the question 'How do *I* come to be here?' (Lingis 2007: 7; emphasis in original).

7   The significance of his work stretches beyond the field of education, particularly into psychology and philosophy (see Kim 2015). Under the name

of 'Herbartianism', it also had a significant impact on educational theory and practice in North America from the later decades of the nineteenth century onwards (see Dunkel 1969a, 1969b).

8　Hjulström and Rytzler (2022) have delved much deeper into this text.

9　I have discussed two notions that play a central role in the German educational discourse, namely 'Bildung' and 'Erziehung' in Biesta (2020).

10　I use the word 'resonates' deliberately, as I think that it is a problematic concept that has garnered too much enthusiasm in educational circles recently. I leave it to the readers to make up their own mind.

References

Bakker, A., E. Angerer, W.R. Penuel and S.F. Akkerman (2024), 'Causal Reasoning about Education: What Is It and What Should It Be?', in P. Illari and F. Russo (eds), *The Routledge Handbook of Causality and Causal Methods*, 671–82, London/New York: Routledge.

Benner, D. (2003), 'Über die Unmöglichkeit Erziehung allein vom Grundbegriff der "Aufforderung zur Selbsttätigkeit" her zu begreifen, *Zeitschrift für Pädagogik*, 49 (2): 290–304.

Benner, D. (2015), *Allgemeine Pädagogik: 8. Auflage*, Weinheim/München: Juventa.

Biesta, G. (2007), 'Why "What Works" Won't Work: Evidence-Based Practice and the Democratic Deficit of Educational Research', *Educational Theory*, 57 (1): 1–22.

Biesta, G. (2016), 'The Rediscovery of Teaching: On Robot Vacuum Cleaners, Non-Egological Education, and the Limits of the Hermeneutical World-View', *Educational Philosophy and Theory*, 48 (3): 374–92.

Biesta, G. (2017a), 'Education, Measurement and the Professions: Reclaiming a Space for Democratic Professionality in Education', *Educational Philosophy and Theory*, 49 (4): 315–30.

Biesta, G. (2017b), *Letting Art Teach: Art Education after Joseph Beuys*, Arnhem: ArtEZ Press.

Biesta, G. (2020), 'Can the Prevailing Description of Educational Reality Be Considered Complete? On the Parks-Eichmann Paradox, Spooky Action at a Distance, and a Missing Dimension in the Theory of Education', *Policy Futures in Education,* 18(8): 1011–25.

Biesta, G. (2022), 'Have We Been Paying Attention? Educational Anaesthetics in a Time of Crises', *Educational Philosophy and Theory*, 54 (3): 221–3.

Biesta, G. (2023), Outline of a Theory of Teaching: What Teaching Is, What It Is For, How It Works, and Why It Requires Artistry', in A.-K. Praetorius and C.Y. Charalambous (eds), *Theorizing Teaching: Current Status and Open Issues*, 253–80, New York: Springer.

Biesta, G. (2024a), 'How to Be a Self, Today', in G. Biesta, T.D. Bøe and L. Skregelid (eds), *Being Human Today. Art, Education and Mental Health in Conversation*, 9–22, Bristol: Intellect.

Biesta, G. (2024b), 'Authority in Teaching: Overcoming Didactophobia through Applied Non-Didactics', in F. Brümmel (ed), *Applied Non-Didactics*, 15–38, Helsinki: Academy of Fine Arts, University of the Arts.

Biesta, G. (2024c), 'From the Point Where I Stand to the Place Where I Can Be Found: The Critique of Perspectival Reason as Philosophy for Education',

Educational Philosophy and Theory, 57 (9): 821–35, https://doi.org/10.1080/00 131857.2024.2435336.

Biesta, G. (2025), 'As if the World Is Just Waiting for Our Opinion: In Search of a (Re)configuration', in C.A. Säfström and G. Loughran (eds), *Being in the World Anew: Events of Art and Education in Post-climate Times*, 28–42, London/New York: Routledge.

Button, V. (2020), *Wilhelmina Barns-Graham*, Bristol: Sansom.

Dijkman, B. (2019), '"What Is This Asking from Me?" An Extended Review of *The Rediscovery of Teaching* by Gert J. J. Biesta', *Transactional Analysis Journal*, 50 (1): 93–100.

Doll, W.E. Jr. (1993), *A Post-Modern Perspective on Curriculum*, New York: Teachers College Press.

Dunkel, H.B. (1969a), 'Herbartianism Comes to America: Part I', *History of Education Quarterly*, 9 (2): 202–33, DOI: 10.2307/367318.

Dunkel, H.B. (1969b), 'Herbartianism Comes to America: Part II', *History of Education Quarterly*, 9 (3): 376–90, DOI10.2307/366916.

Green, L. (2001), *W. Barns-Graham: A Studio Life*, London: Lund Humphries.

Herbart, J.F. (1804), 'Über die ästhetische Darstellung der Welt als das Hauptgeschäft der Erziehung', in E. Blochmann, G. Geißler, H. Nohl and E. Weniger (Hrsg), *Kleine pädagogische Texte, Aus Herbarts Jugendschriften*, Weinheim: Julius Beltz Verlag.

Hjulström, E. and Rytzler, J. (2022), 'Herbart with Rancière on the Educational Significance of the "Third Thing" in Teaching', *Ethics and Education,* 17 (4): 421–36, https://doi.org/10.1080/17449642.2022.2153470

Hopmann, S. (2007), 'Restrained Teaching: The Common Core of Didaktik', *European Educational Research Journal*, 6 (2): 109–24.

Kim, A. (2015), 'Johann Friedrich Herbart', *The Stanford Encyclopedia of Philosophy* (Winter 2015 Edition), Edward N. Zalta (ed.), https://plato.stanford. edu/archives/win2015/entries/johann-herbart/.

Klafki, W. (2007), *Neue Studien zur Bildungstheorie und Didaktik*, Weinheim: Beltz.

Langewand, A. (2003), 'Über die Schwierigkeit Erziehung als Aufforderung zur Selbsttätigkeit zu begreifen', *Zeitschrift für Pädagogik*, 49 (2): 274–89.

Lingis, A. (1998), *The Imperative*, Bloomington, IN: Indiana University Press.

Lingis, A. (2007), *The First Person Singular,* Evanston, IL: *Northwestern University Press.*

Mollenhauer, K. (1983), V*ergessene Zusammenhänge, Über Kultur und Erziehung*, Weinheim, München: Beltz.

Mollenhauer, K. (2014), *Forgotten Connections: On Culture and Upbringing*, London/New York: Routledge.

Osborne, P. (2013). *Anywhere or Not at All: Philosophy of Contemporary Art*. London: Verso.

Prange, K. (2012), *Die Zeigestruktur der Erziehung*: 2. Auglage, *korrigiert und erweitert*, Paderborn: Ferdinand Schöningh.

Saeverot, H. (2013), *Indirect Pedagogy: Some Lessons in Existential Education*, Dordrecht/Boston, MA: Springer.

Saeverot, H. (2022), *Indirect Education: Exploring Indirectness in Teaching and Research*, London/New York: Routledge.

Conclusion

Reclaiming Teacher Artistry: The Art of Saying 'No'

Ramsey Affifi and Gert Biesta

A Future without Teachers?

Several authors in this volume have voiced prophetic warnings about the future of education. At least two ominous futures stand out, should trends underfoot be left unchallenged. In one scenario education continues its descent into factory-like standardization, reducing the teacher to a technician delivering pre-established curricula to students, and pressured to game test scores by leaders who are themselves trying to game international metrics. In a second scenario, an AI-assisted revolution extensively, and perhaps entirely, replaces teachers. Proponents for this future, who may actually see in it salvation from factory-like standardization, view AI as tremendously powerful in its capacity to tailor unique and flexible adaptations for each student, with child–computer interfaces able to achieve a degree of 'differentiation' only dreamt of in overworked and overpopulated classrooms. It is perhaps, the final solution in student-centred learning.

When so framed, the future looks like a choice between whether education will ossify into a nineteenth-century Newtonian machine, or evolve into a twenty-first-century complex, adaptive cybernetic machine. In both such futures, the teacher risks becoming deskilled, unrecognized, deprofessionalized, hollowed out of their essential role from the inside or kicked out of it entirely and made redundant. In either case then, the fate of education, such projections would have it, is to become a machine. In this context, a book on reclaiming the artistry of teaching cannot serve to simply offer idealistic glimpses of what a dying profession could have been if only the world had been different. In the spirit of the work collected in this volume, we write this concluding chapter as an invitation and exemplification of what precisely no machine can do, which is to say *no* to such resignation. In doing so, we explore what it might mean to reclaim the artistry of teaching with teacherly artistry and, therefore, with a genuine educational intent.

Seeing Impossible Possibilities

Reclaiming the artistry of teaching, we suggest, begins with the condition of how things are, with unanticipated potential nascent within what is happening, and commits towards a different vision. But how so when the weight of such ominous futures seems to strangle us? Seeing impossible possibilities in what to others seems but a predictable or mundane unfolding is likely intrinsic to an artist's work. Part of the reclamation involves tending and attending to cracks within which seeds may already be taking root, the hopeful ambiguities that still provide space for manoeuvre and indeed listening to beautiful resistances each of us are called into in each our own way.

Possibilities for intervention bubble out of the *entire* system, from a teacher's relationship with a student all the way up to influencing policymaking and beyond. Such opportunities multiply where we believe they exist and look for their quiet call, but perish when we believe they have died. It is, then, the presumption that the structures we live in are robust machines impervious to reform, not the actual imperviousness of those structures per se, which leads to abandoning our existential freedom, dropping what calls us, and submission to subsistence within the alleged mechanisms. This is a destructive placebo effect, or in this case it may be better thought of as a *nocebo* effect because the belief that people cannot change the system from within reduces the believer's capacity to bring about change. The belief that there is no realistic place for artistry in teaching undercuts artistry's potential and actuality.

Luckily, the mere contemplation of these damning futures does not strangle us in their inevitability if we attend to how they influence us. If we listen, these haunting visions ask back fundamental questions about what the role of the teacher is meant to be, what exactly is missing from these technocratic destinies, and indeed clarify not only their own alternatives but also give us the means to counter their clutch. For this, we should perhaps be grateful. But time is short, so let's move on. We grasp that the teacher is not a machine to produce either standardized products or bespoke outputs. Is the teacher a mechanism, then, for some other 'better' intention? Or someone who has an entirely different relationship to cogs and levers?

What constitutes our craft beyond production? What is in the relationship between teacher, student and world that cannot be replaced with silicone or steel?

The Teacher Is a Person

One obvious difference is that the teacher is a person and that even when she is teaching, she teaches as a person. More precisely, she teaches with her views, joy and suffering, responses, manners, interests, history, hopes, hesitations, depths, and so on, not to mention her ongoing relationships with her students, which are very real in the experience of the student, even if they are real as partially occluded. In other words, whatever she teaches occurs in rich contexts, which she and her students do not separate from the lesson. This means her students are taught in spaces they experience aesthetically, and she teaches in spaces she experiences aesthetically as well too.

By 'aesthetically', we do not mean 'as a work of art' or 'sensorally' or 'in terms of beauty and ugliness,' even if these notions may be at times involved with how we aesthetically experience the world. What we mean is that the world is given and engaged as a place of felt meanings, arising in the space and tensions created through things in relation, and framed and modulated by context (see the chapter by Affifi). Consider Sabeti's careful portraiture of two teachers in her chapter. Part of the concrete texture that teachers experience aesthetically is the fact that they are teaching *these* students, just as part of the experience for the student is that they are being taught by *this* teacher, but crucially, this also involves that feeling that 'I' as this teacher, teach these students, and vice versa.

In the same way that a dash of red on a canvas looks different if adjacent to the colour yellow rather than blue, or if the canvas is sitting on the floor or regally framed, all that happens in the classroom is context set by the perceived nature of the relationship between particular human beings. Any presumably stable relationship between what a teacher intends, delivers and is learned, is at best a special case of what might occasionally happen, but is hardly the rule nor generally desirable when it comes to the relation between a teacher and a student. The aesthetics of human encounter is spacious with possibility and shapeshifting, and it is here, beyond machinic instrumentalities, that teaching has always held its promise.

Within the context of this teacher and this student, many other contexts arise, are set, break apart, evolve and endure. The teacher composes topics, juxtaposes themes, curates social relations and responds. Unintentional events come out of nowhere, invite response and are witnessed as such. And so on. Throughout such contexts, the teacher is concerned with opening, sustaining and altering aesthetic spaces, holding things in tension and relation for herself and her students, and for particular purposes. Note though, that however honed a teacher's artistry, experiences arrive to the students, and the teacher too, as mattering or not, and in many different ways, in ways outside the teacher's control (see Affifi's chapter in this volume, and Biesta's chapter on the aesthetics of teaching).

All painting, no matter how masterful the artist, is a process of discovery because the concrete texture of the work arising is unexpected, and a composition sustains more relations within itself than the artist could conceive. It is an attitude of receiving and working with such unexpectedness that is at issue for both the painter and the teacher. The teacher opens, and opens *to* pedagogical spaces, didactic spaces, curricular spaces and spaces between these spaces. Even if a teacher does not recognize how context shapes what she does and what arises in the classroom, even if she tries to actively resist and keep them separate, the aesthetic interplay persists anyway. Indeed the aesthetic space itself then becomes shaped by the very attempt to maintain the separation. The artistry of teaching involves acknowledging and working with this space instead of ignoring it; creating, curating and responding to the relationship between context and content, or what artists often refer to as the interplay of form and content (see Eisner 2003).

Political Aesthetics

This is a very brief sketch but it provides clues on how we might take forward our work not only as teacher artists, but also as teacher activists approaching the political realm itself with artistry. First, it suggests that in our political work, we might also attend to the interpersonal context between ourselves and those we ally with or resist, and that the manner by which we engage in such work also creates many contexts with aesthetic qualities that can matter. Second, this concern with the aesthetics of our action and the interpersonal dimension provides suggestions about how our concern with subjectification (Biesta 2020) in the classroom is also relevant for how we comport ourselves in the political realm: how our redirecting students back to how they show up in the world may also form the basis of how we might think about how we might engage opponents, colleagues, allies, our own 'selves', and so on, in political work. In other words, it sheds light on the artistry of teacher activism.

Let's briefly return to our earlier discussion on beliefs and placebo effects from the aesthetic positioning we have now developed. Beliefs generate contexts with aesthetic qualities and are generated aesthetically. For example, if we believe we cannot change 'the system', this belief results from and re-enforces a perceived aesthetic coherence between our self and the broader system we live in, but at the same time an incongruence between what we perceive our role to be and what we feel we ought to be doing.

Conversely, if we believe that our actions and our values should be congruent, this belief may stem from and contribute to a sense of coherence between our action and values even if this causes disruption between our actions and the system we find ourselves in (see Affifi 2024). In both cases, the feeling of coherence and incongruence, and also whether one foregrounds one coherence and not the other, is often what we are aesthetically given to respond to. Beliefs foreground the quality of some relationships, and raise questions as to whether it is desirable to accept some aesthetic framing or to disrupt it.

While beliefs inform how we experience and create aesthetic spaces, the recreating of aesthetic spaces also opens possibilities to reform beliefs. Reworking the aesthetics of interpersonal spaces with the intention to invite others into their responsibility is crucial to a teacher's artistry. But this same concern, and the tact that comes along with it, can also inform how the teacher conducts herself in other relations and in particular, how she engages political matters pertaining to education. Whether this concerns relations with colleagues, school leaders, or government and teaching councils, an approach that draws on teacher artistry similarly would not seek to create change in others through coercion.

Activism Reconsidered

This is not, however, a common approach in activism. It turns out that a great deal of current political activity is based on the same dehumanizing conception of causal change that pervades the education system – and is even a core approach taken by many who oppose the dehumanization underway. Consider, for example, how 'call out culture' hopes to induce change in people 'with power' by shaming them, with the presumption that shame can linearly advance a desired outcome. Or consider the view that we need to push for policies 'mandating social justice or sustainability in schools', as though it is obvious or desirable that such directives will bring about intended effects (see Biesta 2022). Much of activism takes inspiration from quasi-mechanical conceptions of history and social change, such as trickled down Marxist ideas about linear progress. These, and many other approaches, treat political concerns as though people were more like billiard balls or clay, who can be impacted in predictable ways, or moulded into desired shapes. But what if political action cared about the possibility of subjectification, and therefore took the aesthetics of experience seriously?

In what follows, we investigate two instances of political action which we think worked with and in aesthetic spaces with artistry rather than succumbing to linear and mechanistic logics. Considering these will help articulate what artistry in teacher activism might look like that takes a 'weak' approach, in the sense that Biesta (2014) employs in the context of education. A weak approach acknowledges that expecting predictable cause and effect interactions in education is naïve, and that desiring such interactions is dangerous.

A weak approach recognizes that aesthetic relationships are forming and reforming, partly under a teacher's guidance but with a crucial, unasked-for surplus. Indeed, how a student takes up what a teacher offers arises in aesthetic spaces one cannot control, and thankfully, because if a teacher could control such spaces, she might suffocate the students' possibility of being seized by their own freedom and responsibility. The question is how teacher activists can similarly curate such spaces, redirecting attention within them or through them, and pointing those they engage to what is happening in the world, and in their relationship with the world.

Gandhi's Weak Political Activism

One example of a 'weak' approach in political activity is the non-violent direct action inspired by Thoreau, Tolstoy, the Sermon on the Mount and the Bhagavad Gita, and employed by Gandhi in his resistance work to oppression in South Africa and India. Gandhi is known for developing an approach grounded in the practice of trying to love one's enemy and putting trust in the possibility of their goodness. We might say he advocated trusting in the possibility of his opponent's subjectness, the possibility of their being seized by the question whether what they are doing is indeed what is desirable.

Gandhi's pedagogical intuitions on this front were explicit. For example, he argued that if a British soldier hits you, and you hit them back, then the soldier is now responding from a place in which they are scared, and where your positioning as their enemy can easily become re-enforced. Similarly, for a bystander looking at the altercation, it just looks like a fight with no clear villain. Gandhi was concerned about the aesthetics of the space he could open: what kind of interplay between context and action might turn the soldier towards what they are doing, and ask the soldier what they should be doing? What kind of space is more likely to ask similar questions to the bystander? His intuition was that violent means cannot accomplish non-violent ends, and that residing more deeply in the interpersonal space between oneself and one's opponent holds the possibility of a different way of approaching means and ends.

For Gandhi, this meant not being violent, not only in physical action, but even in thought and feeling. If a non-violent activist was not able to look the soldier in the eye with tenderness, holding in his heart the felt sense that the soldier too is a human being born into a world as a frightened child, with people he loves and who love him, confused and misled in any number of ways – as we all are; if this kind of presence cannot be sustained, then the activist is not ready for the frontlines. It was equally clear, however, that he did not consider this kind of presence as a magic key to brainwash or co-opt the soldier into his cause. He could only interrupt the existing drama, and create a space sufficiently capacious that the soldier *might* have room amidst the intensity to pay closer attention to what they were doing. Like the call into subjectivity in the classroom context, such an invitation cannot be demanded, only offered, and is its own kind of 'beautiful risk'.

Form, Content and Pedagogy

For an artist, form and content cannot be separated. They are in constant interplay and the aesthetics of artistic creation attends directly to this interplay. If one sees form as merely a vehicle to deliver content, one operates via an instrumental rationality that is anaesthetizing: there is nothing new to feel or attend. Note, however that this is the presumption underwriting the logic of standardization, but also indirectly the logic of AI providing appropriately catered prompts to achieve some end. If form and content interplay, one bringing out, accentuating, challenging, qualifying, contrasting the other, the tension between them creates an aesthetic space of possibility rather than determination.

Assuming form can be a silent vehicle for content, mere code or syntax, is a problematic stance not only in how a teacher encounters their students, but also in how teacher activists approach their political relations. After all, the distinction between means and ends, and form and content, is absolutely connected: when we treat content as separable from form, we treat content as an end and form as a means. Further, when we focus on ends instead of means, we ignore the various concrete effects that arise when we cling steadfast to an idea's semantic pull.

In the case of non-violent action, we can see the pedagogy at work. Gandhi is not telling the soldiers how they should feel, nor what they should think. His calmly receiving whatever the soldiers choose to give invites the soldier to attend to what she is doing. His (non)action redirects the soldier back upon herself, and without demanding it, asks her to consider what she should be doing in that situation. This is an instance in activism of what in pedagogy might be called 'pointing' in the sense that Klaus Prange describes (Prange 2012). For Prange, teaching is the art of redirecting another's attention, so that instead of being passively swept by whatever one is doing, a student might instead face the question of what and how they should attend in the first place. In refusing to coerce, manipulate or indoctrinate, Gandhi's non-violent approaches take a similar position.

The Power of 'Weakness'

This brings us to a second political action that demonstrates the power of 'weakness' as an approach. Gregory Bateson tells the story of the Native American Church for whom the psychoactive cactus *peyote* is considered the central sacrament in religious rituals (see Bateson and Bateson 1988).

When the American government was set to ban the plant's use unless its religious value could be proven, a well-meaning anthropologist named Sol Tax offered to film a ceremony to provide such evidence. In the members' deliberations, the central issue was evident: they could not imagine praying in front of a camera. Knowing they were being filmed would fundamentally alter the experience, defiling its integrity, and to do so even for such an end, seemed an impossible choice.

Tax's offer was eventually declined, and the religious group made the decision to let their practice die. It was a painful but necessary choice. Aesthetically considered, the quality of the relations between the form of the ceremony and the experience of sacrament could not be sustained by such well-meaning instrumentalization. But note the important paradox that so stirred Bateson: the truly religious nature of this plant was indirectly proven by the 'refusal to accept the pragmatic compromise of having their church validated by a method alien to the reverence in which they held it' (Bateson and Bateson 1988: 73).

In response to the common trope that the 'ends justify the means', Gandhi offered the following rebuttal which could equally have come from the mouth of a member of the Native American Church: 'They say, "means are, after all, means". I would say, "means are, after all, everything".' It is in our means that we, and others, undergo and respond to the actual effects of what we do. The means are concretely realized and directly experienced, unlike an end, which is abstract and, in a sense, out of time. Indeed. But the effects of the means are no more in our control that the ends themselves and interconnected with them. This is clear in the two actions recounted, where political interplay between means and ends bears more than a superficial resemblance to the artistic interplay between form and content. The assumed separation between means and ends is itself precisely the imagined, or hoped for, severing of the 'how' from the 'what'. Put differently, the relation between means and ends itself opens an aesthetic space, that can also be worked, or not, with artistry, when one takes one's means seriously.

Teacher Activism as Artistry

In 'many – perhaps even all – situations we encounter in our lives, we always have a possibility to say yes or to say no, to stay or to walk away, to go with the flow or to resist' (Biesta 2020: 93). The extent to which means–end thinking suggests we 'go along with' a system we disagree with is a measure of how much we choose to be accomplices in situations we oppose. From the point of view developed here, it is also an indication as to what extent we have anaesthetized our engagement with the world, treating our self and others as cogs and levers. By contrast, the two political actions just described involve saying no to a loss of integrity at stake for the soldier and the plant, a loss that is only apparent for someone who is attending to the aesthetics of the contexts concerned. In both cases, a respect and concern for the other led the actors to take on a burden, which though not intended, in turn returned the actors into their own integrity.

There are many ways to say no to the educational trends underway, and many ways to work with them and transform them. Nevertheless, the two stories presented pose educational questions back upon our activism, such as: How do I meet the situations I face, wherever I am in my life and career? If it concerns other people, how do I attend such that I direct the other back to their freedom? Obviously, it is not as simple as saying 'Hey, you are free – what will you choose to do here?' Gandhi would not likely have been so successful with such a pedagogy, which although concerned with subjectification, has rather crude aspirations of how causality is to work. In other words, the assumption that we can directly 'get' others to acknowledge their freedom is as problematic as the assumption we can get them to learn the right lesson, which is the reason why if education works at all it has to work aesthetically (see Biesta's chapter on the aesthetics of teaching). There are many ways of redirecting another's attention back upon their own responsibility, and not all redirections are direct.

A second question follows. How is my *own* possibility of freely being called into my own responsibility not extinguished in how I encounter the other? Consider the (Levinasian) idea that 'my self becomes an issue for me – not for anyone or for others but for *me* – when I encounter a responsibility … [and] in this responsibility I encounter my own freedom … [where], it is for me to figure out whether I say "yes" or "no", whether I "take up" this responsibility or walk away from it' (Biesta 2024: 9). Am I listening to those calls upon myself, or am I burying my own subjectness in its own system of cogs and levers? Of the battles I am given, which do I accept? How am I to attend them? And so on. And finally: how are these both interconnected? Can we retain agile presence to another and offer invitations with a modicum of aesthetic tact, if we cannot hear all the deafening questions the situation is asking back, and throwing upon us?

And *when* to begin? If, for instance, we believe we ought to only begin political action – this delicate care of listening and taking account of ourselves and our actions – once we reach some position or place 'in power', say, becoming a full [sic] professor, or headteacher, or holding a place at the policy table, we relinquish the possibility of our subjectification while at one and the same time developing habits that keep what summons at a distance.

We Begin Now

Without a practice of paying attention, it is not surprising few in such allegedly safe positions feel safe enough to put what they have gained at risk. In the same spirit, it may be a disservice to treat newcomers into the profession as too insecure or in too precarious a role to also so listen to what is asked of them. We begin *now*, wherever we are. Whether a new career teacher, a teacher educator or an experienced leader, in a fundamental sense there is no distinction: for each, there are possibilities and constraints, situations we can work with and rework towards currently unforeseen ends, and even situations for which we may be called upon to not comply.

One lesson from both the North American Church and Gandhi's non-violent action is that in our political work we need to pay attention to the interplay between what we are doing and the contexts that we are participating in. Although we cannot, and should not, try to control these aesthetic spaces, we can 'tend' them in ways that invite those involved – ourselves and others – to face what they are doing, and ask whether it is desirable to continue in this way.

This could be in conversation, say with a colleague, with someone in a school leadership role, when collaborating with colleagues or community members to gather momentum behind a position, when striking or shutting something down, in silent self-reflection, or in dialogue with a department of education worker we have reached out to. Or it could be through some other medium, like writing or public speaking. In any case, specific recommendations on how to tend this invitation cannot be provided. It is not an instrumental relation that can be described and shared as a recipe, and educationally the attempt to do so would be its own kind of violence or betrayal akin to filming a ceremony.

One thing that can be said, however, is that such invitations are more likely to have artistry if a full presence is committed to the unfolding, and with a clear intention. Consider the Gandhian intention to love one's enemy or the Native American Church's intention to sustain the sacred. For teacher activists, it is perhaps the intention to hold a good will that trusts in the possibility that one's opponent can be called back into their own attention, and with that, perhaps, their own clear intentions. It is about returning ourselves into a place where we approach the other with affirmation of (the possibility of their) goodness. As Gandhi put it, 'Even if the opponent plays him false twenty times, the [non-violent activist] is ready to trust him for the twenty-first time' (Fischer 1982: 36).

This affirmation places no demands on the other. It does nothing causal other than opening up a space for events and encounters that are already possible, if only we and others remember who and where we are. This is achieved merely through the (aesthetic) contrast set between how the situation might proceed if not reflected upon, and what becomes possible once that process is interrupted. And yet, faith in the possibility of goodness in the other is not accompanied by an expectation that the other will do anything in particular. An invitation is only really an invitation when the inviter is detached from expectations about the consequences. The soldier might strike Gandhi down, the plant might go extinct. But even if this happens, the consequences of what happens as a result of these events are themselves also full of possibility, cracks for potential seeds to set root.

Keep Teaching Alive

Affirming the goodness of one's opponent may strike the reader as suggesting a consistently polyannic vision for our activist work. This is not the case. Affirming the goodness of one's opponent rises as an important intention especially when their goodness (and so, our own) is at risk of erasure in the unfolding situation. However, this is hardly the only political situation within which we find ourselves. What happens when we find ourselves engaged, say, with allies already in agreement on some issue? Here, by contrast, teacher activism may be concerned instead with disturbing the space so that what has been unforeseeably silenced under consensus might surface. This is because in such situations we are capable of getting immersed into and lost in some collective interpretation, and when doing so, render that situation monolithic and indeed, again, mechanical. These two scenarios – seeing the good in one's opponent and kicking up dust in the face of convivial consensus – are two extreme situations that point to a spectrum of possibilities in practice.

The question of whether or not to offer an interruption, and how to do so, is an ongoing and general problem for activism – a problem because there are times one will still deem it necessary to strategically rally behind a cause, even if it (invariably) backgrounds some dimensions or stakes. In other words, there will be times when we must instrumentalize things, and teacher activism cannot be a matter of simply 'walking one's talk' all the time. When we interrupt and when we align – such decisions cannot be decided in advance, or once and for all, but need to be resurfaced privately and publicly as recurring questions. Ongoing care for such situated judgements in the phase of shifting aesthetic terrain is what makes our activist work a matter of artistry as much as our teaching is, and it points the way to how one may be taught through one's lessons for the other.

Between flat out refusals and uncomplicated compliance, there are a range of middle grounds, sublations, unthought possibilities of synergy, which all require being open to, and responsive to, the ongoing aesthetic quality of one's relations with others. That said, there may well be situations where, if we listen, we will see we are being called to refuse to comply, and the question arrives upon us: 'how?' The question comes into focus: what is sacred in education – that which you would sacrifice for its sustenance (where the etymology of the word 'sacrifice' means 'to make sacred')? And how does that intuition compel how you serve it politically? Indeed, there may be times where we can only keep teaching alive by risking getting jettisoned from a role or position we expect or wish.

But, like Bateson's paradox, even in such cases, our response to such appeals may be witnessed by others and pose questions back to them, and rather than dying, the possibility of teaching may restore itself anew in some unanticipated form.

References

Affifi, R. (2024), 'Aesthetic Knowing and Ecology: Cultivating Perception and Participation during the Ecological Crisis', *Environmental Education Research*, 30 (7): 1041–60.

Bateson, G. and M.C. Bateson (1988), *Angel's Fear. Towards an Epistemology of the Sacred*, Toronto/New York: Bantam.

Biesta, G. (2014), *The Beautiful Risk of Education*, Boulder, CO: Paradigm Publishers.

Biesta, G. (2020), 'Risking Ourselves in Education: Qualification, Socialization, and Subjectification Revisited', *Educational Theory*, 70 (1): 89–104.

Biesta, G. (2022), 'Why the Form of Teaching Matters: Defending the Integrity of Education and of the Work of Teachers beyond Agendas and Good Intentions', *Revista de Educación*, 395 (January–March): 13–33.

Biesta, G. (2024), 'From the Point Where I Stand to the Place Where I Can Be Found: The Critique of Perspectival Reason as Philosophy for Education', *Educational Philosophy and Theory*, 57 (9), https://doi.org/10.1080/00131857.2024.2435336.

Eisner, E. (2003), 'Artistry in Education', *Scandinavian Journal of Education Research*, 47 (3): 373–84.

Fischer, L. (1982), *The Life of Mahatma Gandhi*, New York: Mentor.

Prange, K. (2012), *Die Zeigestruktur der Erziehung. 2. Auglage, korrigiert und erweitert*, Paderborn: Ferdinand Schöningh.

INDEX